AF733259

THE NEW ENVIRONMENTAL GOVERNANCE

A bold and profoundly new way of governing environmental problems is palpable around the globe and aims to overcome the limitations of the interventionist state and its market alternative to offer more effective and legitimate solutions to today's most pressing environmental problems. The 'new environmental governance' (NEG) emphasizes a host of novel characteristics including participation, collaboration, deliberation, learning and adaptation and 'new' forms of accountability. While these unique features have generated significant praise from legal and governance scholars, there have been very few systematic evaluations of NEG in practice, and it is still unclear whether NEG will in fact 'work' and, if so, when and how.

This book offers one of the most rigorous research investigations into cutting edge trends in environmental governance to date. Focusing its inquiry around some of the most central, controversial and/or under-researched characteristics of NEG, the book offers fresh insights into the conditions under which we can best achieve successful collaboration, effective learning and adaptation, meaningful participatory and deliberative governance and effective forms of accountability. The book synthesizes its findings to identify eight design principles of 'good' NEG that are central to its success and will provide useful guidance for policymakers and scholars seeking to apply new governance to a wide range of environmental and non-environmental policy contexts. The book also advances our understanding of State governance and will be a valuable reference for scholars, researchers and students working in law and regulation studies – especially in the field of environmental law.

Cameron Holley is a Lecturer in the Centre for Legal Governance at Macquarie Law School, Macquarie University.

Neil Gunningham is Professor in the School of Pacific and Asian Studies and in the Fenner School of Environment and Society at the Australian National University.

Clifford Shearing is Professor and Director of the Criminology Centre at the University of Cape Town, and a Visiting Fellow of the Regulatory Institutions Network. He is also Professor in the Department of Administration and Organizational Theory, University of Bergen, Norway.

THE NEW ENVIRONMENTAL GOVERNANCE

Cameron Holley,
Neil Gunningham and
Clifford Shearing

earthscan
from Routledge

First published 2012
by Earthscan
2 Park Square, Milton Park, Abingdon, Oxon OX14 4RN

Simultaneously published in the USA and Canada
by Earthscan
605 Third Avenue, New York, NY 10017

Earthscan is an imprint of the Taylor & Francis Group, an informa business

© 2012 Cameron Holley, Neil Gunningham and Clifford Shearing

The right of Cameron Holley, Neil Gunningham and Clifford Shearing
to be identified as authors of this work has been asserted by them in accordance
with sections 77 and 78 of the Copyright, Designs and Patents Act 1988.

All rights reserved. No part of this book may be reprinted or
reproduced or utilised in any form or by any electronic, mechanical,
or other means, now known or hereafter invented, including photocopying
and recording, or in any information storage or retrieval system,
without permission in writing from the publishers.

Trademark notice: Product or corporate names may be trademarks
or registered trademarks, and are used only for identification and
explanation without intent to infringe.

British Library Cataloguing in Publication Data
A catalogue record for this book is available from the British Library

Library of Congress Cataloging in Publication Data
A catalog record for this book has been requested

ISBN: 978-1-84971-410-5 (hbk)

Typeset in Bembo and Stone Sans
by Florence Production Ltd, Stoodleigh, Devon

CONTENTS

TABLES AND BOXES

Tables

Boxes

GOVERNMENT STATUTES AND AGREEMENTS

Government Statutes

Australia

- *Corporations Act 2001* (Cth)
- *Environment Protection Act 1970* (Vic)
- *Environment Protection (Liveable Neighbourhoods) Act 2001* (Vic)
- *Natural Heritage Trust of Australia Act 1997* (Cth)

New Zealand

- *Environment Canterbury (Temporary Commissioners and Improved Water Management) Act 2010*
- *Local Government Act 2002*
- *Ngāi Tahu Claims Settlement Act 1998*
- *Resource Management Act 1991*

United States of America

- *Endangered Species Act of 1973*, 16 U.S.C. §§1531–1544 (2007)

Government Agreements

Australia

- *Bilateral Agreement between the Commonwealth of Australia and the State of Queensland for the Implementation of the Intergovernmental Agreement on a National Plan for Salinity and Water Quality*, March 2001

- *Bilateral Agreement between the Commonwealth of Australia and the State of Queensland to Deliver the Natural Heritage Trust*, August 2004
- *Intergovernmental Agreement on a National Action Plan for Salinity and Water Quality* (Intergovernmental Agreement), 2001
- *Interim Financial Agreement to Deliver the Natural Heritage Trust Extension in Queensland* (Commonwealth and Queensland), 27 June 2003

New Zealand

- *A Memorandum of Understanding between Avon-Heathcote Estuary Ihutai Trust, Christchurch City Council and Canterbury Regional Council*, 2003
- *Te Waihora Joint Management Plan*, Te Rūnanga o Ngāi Tahu and Department of Conservation, Christchurch, 2005

ABBREVIATIONS

AL	Accredited Licences
BDT	Burdekin Dry Tropics
BDTNRM	Burdekin Dry Tropics Natural Resource Management
CCM	Collaborative Catchment Management
CMA	Catchment Management Association
COAG	Council of Australian Governments
CWMS	Canterbury Water Management Strategy
ECan	Environment Canterbury
EIP	Environment Improvement Plan
ENGO	environmental non-governmental organization
HCP	Habitat Conservation Plan
JSC	Joint Steering Committee
LGA	*Local Government Act 2002* (NZ)
LSP	Living Streams Programme
NAP	National Action Plan for Salinity and Water Quality
NEG	new environmental governance
NEIP	Neighbourhood Environment Improvement Plan
NGO	non-governmental organization
NHT	Natural Heritage Trust
NRM	natural resource management
NRMMC	Natural Resource Management Ministerial Council
NRMSC	Natural Resource Management Standing Committee
NRMTF	Natural Resource Management Taskforce
OMC	Open Method of Coordination (European Union)
RCG	Regional Coordination Group
RGC	Regional Groups Collective
RMA	*Resource Management Act 1991* (NZ)

RNRM	Regional Natural Resource Management
SMEs	small- and medium-size enterprises
US EPA	United States Environmental Protection Agency
VEPA	Environment Protection Authority Victoria

PREFACE

The aspiration of this book is to complement existing research initiatives in the sphere of collaborative governance and to expand our knowledge of reform in this area by showing how existing experience can best be put to practical use, by drawing lessons from experiments in innovative regulation internationally, by conducting our own novel case studies from Australasia and extrapolating from them, and by drawing lessons from experiments in innovative regulation internationally.

Our intended readership includes environmental and natural resource management policymakers; regulatory and other government officials responsible for policy design and implementation; academics and postgraduate students in environmental management, environmental law and environmental policy; and a more general readership within environmental policy and management studies. It will also be of interest to environmental non-governmental organizations and those in industry, such as environmental and regional natural resource managers, who are considering their role in and use of more innovative environmental and regulatory strategies.

In writing the book we have incurred numerous debts. Unfortunately, farmers, community activists, industry bodies, Indigenous Australians, Māori, scientists, national, state, regional and local government employees, and others interviewed for this study cannot be identified because the customary social science guarantee of anonymity applies. We thank them anyway.

We are particularly indebted to our partner agencies, Environment Protection Authority Victoria and Environment Canterbury. Dr Bryan Jenkins, then Chief Executive of the latter, not only provided his personal support to the project but read and provided invaluable feedback on a number of drafts. Terry A'Hearn, former Acting Chief Executive of Environment Protection Authority Victoria also provided his personal support and facilitated our interaction with numerous staff within that agency.

Our thanks and appreciation go to Bradley Karkkainen, Brian Head, David Farrier, Darren Sinclair, Allan Dale and two anonymous reviewers who read and commented upon individual chapters, or who in other ways deepened our understanding of a number of critical issues relating to the programmes we studied and new trends in environmental governance. Bradley Karkkainen, especially, provided commentary and support well beyond the call of duty. We are also indebted to Ricky Rontsch for providing excellent editing assistance and to the staff of Earthscan, our publishers, more generally.

We also benefitted from the intellectual support provided by our colleagues at the Regulatory Institutions Network, the Climate and Environmental Governance Network and the Fenner School of Environment and Society at The Australian National University (ANU).

And we are grateful to all those who participated in workshops on the themes of the book under the auspices of the Australian Academy of Social Sciences in Canberra in 2010 and the University of Cape Town in 2011.

The project benefitted substantially from a Linkage Grant and a Discovery Grant provided by the Australian Research Council (ARC) initially to Neil Gunningham and Clifford Shearing (and subsequently solely to Gunningham following Shearing taking up a position at the University of Cape Town). In its final stages, the project also benefitted from a Macquarie University CORE grant.

The majority of Cameron Holley's contribution was made while undertaking postdoctoral research at the Regulatory Institutions Network under the above named ARC Discovery grant. Holley is not only the first named author but the lead author in every sense. Many of the themes and design principles that are developed in our book were first explored during his PhD thesis, undertaken at the Fenner School of Environment and Society at the ANU, under Gunningham's supervision with the support of panel members Monique Marks and Shearing. A disproportionate amount of the subsequent fieldwork and drafting of the main chapters was undertaken by Holley, albeit that the wider themes of the project were the subject of on-going discussion between and writing involving all three authors. While the book is very much the product of a collaborative process, it was Holley's unstinting efforts that drove it towards a (we hope) successful conclusion.

Some aspects of Chapter 3 first appeared in Holley, C. (2010) 'Removing the Thorn from New Governance's Side: Examining the Emergence of Collaboration in Practice & the Roles for Law, Nested Institutions & Trust', *Environmental Law Reporter*, vol 40, no 7, pp10,656–10,686. Similarly, some of the material in Chapter 4 was developed from ideas originally appearing in Holley, C. (2010) 'Public Participation, Environmental Law and New Governance: Lessons from Empirical Research for Designing Effective Participation Processes', *Environmental and Planning Law Journal*, vol 27, pp360–391.

Some elements of Chapter 5 initially appeared in Holley, C. (2010) 'Facilitating Monitoring, Subverting Self-Interest and Limiting Discretion: Learning from "New" Forms of Accountability in Practice', *Columbia Journal of Environmental Law*, vol 35, no 1, pp127–211; and Holley, C. and Sinclair, D. 'Collaborative

Governance and Adaptive Management: (Mis)applications to Groundwater, Salinity and Run-off', *Australasian Journal of Natural Resources Law and Policy* (forthcoming, 2011). In addition, some of the material in Chapter 6 was developed from ideas originally appearing in Holley, C. (2009) 'Aging Gracefully? Examining the Conditions for Sustaining Successful Collaboration in Environmental Law and Governance', *Environmental and Planning Law Journal*, vol 26, no 6, pp457–485.

Portions of the work contained in Chapters 1 and 7 first appeared in Holley, C. and Gunningham, N. (2011) 'Natural Resources, New Governance and Legal Regulation: When Does Collaboration Work?' *New Zealand Universities Law Review*, vol 24, pp309–327; Gunningham, N. (2009) 'The New Collaborative Environmental Governance: The Localization of Regulation', *Journal of Law and Society*, vol 36, pp145–166; and Gunningham, N. and Holley, C. (2010) 'Bringing the "R" Word Back: Regulation, Environment Protection and NRM', *Occasional Paper of the Academy of the Social Sciences in Australia*, vol 3/2010, Canberra. Some elements of our case study analysis initially appeared in Holley, C. and Gunningham, N. (2011) 'Natural Resources, New Governance and Legal Regulation: When Does Collaboration Work?', *New Zealand Universities Law Review*, vol 24, pp309–327; Gunningham, N., Holley, C. and Shearing, C. (2007) 'Neighbourhood Environment Improvement Plans: Community Empowerment, Voluntary Collaboration and Legislative Design', *Environmental and Planning Law Journal*, vol 24, no 2, pp125–151; and Holley, C. and Gunningham, N. (2006) 'Environment Improvement Plans: Facilitative Regulation in Practice', *Environmental and Planning Law Journal*, vol 23, pp448–464.

Cameron Holley
Neil Gunningham
Clifford Shearing

Sydney, Canberra and Cape Town
August 2011

1

INTRODUCTION

Thomas Hobbes' classic text first published in 1651 has, as its frontispiece, an image of a benign giant, a Leviathan, made up of the bodies of people (Hobbes, 1651). He stands over a landscape that he rules on behalf of the people who make up his body. In his left hand he carries a crosier that symbolizes his legitimacy as a ruler. In his right is a sword that symbolizes his ability to overcome resistance to his rule. This is a powerful image of governance, and it is one that has inspired people in the West (or what is now increasingly being called the 'Global North') ever since.

For Hobbes, 'good governance' is conceived of as rule by a single sovereign who represents 'the people' – a ruler who has exclusive jurisdiction over a unified territory. Although this image has never constituted an entirely satisfactory empirical account of the realities of governance – either in Europe or elsewhere – it has provided a powerful way of *imagining* good governance. As such it has provided inspiration and a benchmark, setting out what governments should strive to realize.

Such was still the case when, in the 1970s, governments, confronted by increasingly visible ecological degradation, and strident public demands for environmental protection, sought to determine their response. By this time, a modern version of the Leviathan – state power through hierarchy – had become dominant in the Western world (for a recent review of the governance literature see Burris et al, 2005, pp30–58). So it seemed natural to Western governments to address environmental degradation, such as air and water pollution, by establishing environmental protection agencies, applying what has come to be known as 'command and control' regulation.

This approach, with its Hobbesian resonances, was based on the idea that governments would command through law by establishing a variety of environmental targets expressed in prescriptive standards – for example, vehicle and factory emission standards. Government agencies were then authorized to 'control' those whose behaviours were to be modified, by monitoring their compliance and imposing penalties where standards were breached (Gunningham et al, 1998, pp3–7, 343–448).

Command and control, at least in some circumstances, proved to be relatively effective in regulating large industries, and a number of impressive gains were recorded in halting and reducing cases of severe environmental degradation (Cole and Grossman, 1999, pp888 and 893; Durant et al, 2004b, pp644–645). However, as might be expected, command and control approaches have had a number of significant limitations. For example, this adversarial form of governance, characterized by stick-waving government agencies (or in Australia, those with very small twigs), very often encouraged counterproductive resistance from both individuals and businesses. Furthermore, its centralized nature and emphasis on detailed and uniform rules has also been widely criticized as costly, cumbersome and inefficient, because this approach is by definition insensitive to local conditions (Ackerman and Stewart, 1985, pp1335–1336; Stewart, 2001, p61; Lazarus, 2004, pp67–98; Karkkainen, 2006b, p293).

These problems are exacerbated when seeking to manage human activities that have an impact on large-scale and complex environmental systems. These activities typically involve multiple sets of actors who are acting across large scales. Governing these activities requires, it is argued, much more holistic, integrated and at the same time localized ecosystem-level approaches that are inimical to centralized and fragmented command and control mechanisms (Karkkainen, 2002/2003; Freeman and Farber, 2005, pp806–814). As a consequence of these and similar criticisms of command and control approaches, there were increasing calls for alternative governance approaches that are less centralized, more inclusive and less autocratic. In response, environmental governance began to shift away from the state-centred, hierarchical style of traditional regulation toward an array of decentralized approaches.

One of the earliest, and most often touted of these alternatives, was market-based instruments (Freeman and Farber, 2005, pp814–819). From the 1980s onwards, neo-liberal economists, in particular, increasingly entered the public domain, suggesting that Adam Smith's vision of an 'invisible hand' would, if allowed to manifest, lead rational, self-maximizing individuals to promote 'public interests' without the need for heavy-handed government intervention (Smith, 1776). Markets, if properly constituted, it was argued, would overcome the limitations of command and control strategies (Gray, 1998, pp25–26). They would do so by integrating widely dispersed capacities located away from political centres so as to improve governance (and environmental) outcomes.

The standard refrain from those working within this governance paradigm was that environment degradation was occurring as a consequence of a failure of markets to value environmental endowments properly (Cutting and Cahoon, 2005, p55; Roma, 2006, p534). As no price was emerging in markets that would put a value on resource scarcity, markets as they were presently constituted were failing to fulfil a fundamental governance function, namely, providing an appropriate rationing of scarce assets. What was needed was the creation of market signals that would place a value on and charge appositely for the use of scarce resources. For example, under a market-based approach, a government might establish the amount of pollution that a particular environment could assimilate and then allocate rights to those emissions – while allowing 'the market' to determine the price of these rights (Stavins and Whitehead, 1997; Gunningham and Sinclair, 2002).

A variety of government-supported, market-based instruments subsequently emerged, such as 'cap and trade' schemes, along with a variety of subsidies and, to a lesser extent, pollution taxes (Gunningham et al, 1998, pp69–83). Prominent market-based instruments introduced to address point-source pollution included the acid rain, sulphur dioxide trading scheme developed in the USA (Stavins, 1998) and the load-based licensing scheme developed in Australia (New South Wales Environmental Protection Agency, 2001). Economic incentive-based schemes have also been used to address more complex 'second generation' issues, such as urban air pollution (Western Australia Department of Environment and Conservation, 2006). Related subsidy and other market approaches, such as land acquisitions and payments, have also been employed, particularly in Europe (Farrier, 1995, pp399–405; Curnow and Fitzgerald, 2006).

Yet, despite some successes, many market-inspired approaches have proved to be less environmentally effective than command and control approaches (Howes et al, 1997, ch 9; Gunningham et al, 1998, pp69–83; Blackman and Harrington, 2000, p32; Freeman and Farber, 2005, pp815–819). Furthermore, market-based instruments tend to operate at the margins of environmental governance – used only to address environmental issues in a limited number of contexts (Farrier and Whelan, 2004). In part, this is because of the difficulty market approaches can face in identifying tradable units (i.e., fungible commodities) when dealing with complex problems. In addition, efficiency benefits are often undermined by a variety of practical and contextual difficulties faced by governments who seek to develop and rely on market mechanisms. Indeed, despite their claims to knowledge mobilization, many market instruments share with command and control a requirement for centralized planning and knowledge, such as setting the right level for a tax, charge or even for capping levels, which can often be difficult for policymakers in the absence of an existing market reference (Sabel et al, 1999, pp2–3; Freeman and Farber, 2005, pp815–819). In summary, market-based approaches, like command and control regulation, suffer from limitations and provide only partial answers to the range of environmental challenges facing society, particularly those of a complex nature.

Recognizing this, environmental policymakers, during the 1990s, began to search for governance instruments that overcame some of the limitations of earlier approaches and that would be better suited to contemporary challenges. Some have experimented with business-led voluntary approaches (Segerson and Dawson, 2001) or education and informational strategies, such as product labelling and corporate reporting (Weil et al, 2006, p156). While the former has achieved limited success, it is unlikely to make a substantial contribution as a stand-alone approach, given its demonstrated failure to achieve acceptable levels of industry-wide compliance, particularly where the gap between the private interests of business (not least, making a profit) and the public interest in environmental protection is substantial (Gunningham and Sinclair, 2002, pp145–148 and 155; Freeman and Farber, 2005, pp831–832). Information-based strategies, too, have limitations, operating successfully mainly to the extent that they are complements of traditional regulation (which facilitates the collection and dissemination of accurate information) (Stewart, 2001, pp141–143), rather than being of themselves a stand-alone approach (as with the Toxic Release Inventory in the USA) (Fung and O'Rourke, 2000).

More recently, and particularly in the last decade, policymakers and theorists have increasingly focused on a very different form of governance, involving collaboration between stakeholders to an extent that would have been unimaginable some years before. Commonly referred to as the 'new environmental governance' (hereafter NEG) this enterprise involves collaboration between a diversity of private, public and non-government stakeholders who, acting together towards commonly agreed (or mutually negotiated) goals, hope to achieve far more collectively, than individually. It relies heavily upon participatory dialogue and deliberation, devolved and decentralized decision-making, flexibility (rather than uniformity), inclusiveness, knowledge generation and processes of learning, transparency and institutionalized consensus-building practices (see, generally, De Burca and Scott, 2006; Trubek and Trubek, 2006/2007).

We might equally describe this initiative as one of 'polycentric governance' (McGinnis, 1999), with decision-making involving the totality of interactions between public and private actors, and the state no longer necessarily playing the central role in decision-making. For example, a variety of non-state actors may assume administrative, regulatory, managerial and mediating functions previously undertaken by the state. As such, this polycentric vision conceives of many centres of decision-making and action that are formally independent of each other, but that can function either independently, or constitute an interdependent system of relations (Ostrom et al, 1961; Ostrom, 2010, p643).

Certainly, the shift to the NEG has to some extent been shaped by unique, country/political influences (Holzinger et al, 2006, p409; De Burca, 2010, pp227–232), but generally speaking it has come about because of the perceived capacity of NEG to deliver effectiveness and/or legitimacy in circumstances where traditional approaches cannot. For example, prescriptive regulatory standards – and even caps/taxes in some market-based instruments – depend upon a degree of centralized knowledge (e.g., in order to set suitable standards) that is often not available. In contrast, the sort of collaborative, participatory and deliberative approaches contemplated by NEG are said to lead to problem solving that is inclusive of local circumstances and able to capitalize on the unique local and other knowledges and capacities of multiple public and private actors. Direct involvement of these actors in deliberative styles of governance can also foster stakeholder ownership and buy-in and can give greater voice to marginalized interests (as contrasted to an exclusive reliance on science in prescriptive regulation or on price and competition in markets).

Processes, such as learning and adaptation, meanwhile, are thought to ensure that NEG copes better with the dynamism, uncertainty and complexity of environmental problems than either traditional prescriptive regulation (which can easily ossify, freezing standards at a particular point in time) or many market-based approaches (where significant post-hoc programme corrections to pollution levels and permits set from the centre become very difficult without undermining the security of ownership rights on which the market itself depends) (Orts, 1995, p1238; Sabel et al, 1999, p3; Durant et al, 2004a, p4; Lobel, 2004b, p502). Collaborative approaches may also help to leverage government expenditure by mobilizing the resources of others in implementation, monitoring and enforcement roles.

Much of the focus in reshaping governance, particularly in relation to challenges involving global public goods and major free-rider problems, has been on designing and implementing new systems of global governance (Stiglitz, 2002; Castells, 2008; Okereke et al, 2009). In the absence of world government, this necessarily involves developing strategies and governance mechanisms to encourage cooperation between nation states with regard to protecting and sustaining the services that the Earth provides, not least, a stable climate. At international and global levels, this new approach is coming to be termed 'Earth systems governance' (Biermann, 2008).

But there has also been increasing interest in environmental governance initiatives at regional and local scales, and in integrating governance between different scales (for reviews, see Burris et al, 2008, and Hooghe and Marks, 2001). This interest in multi-scale and multi-level environmental governance (Rauschmayer et al, 2009) has directed attention to experimentation that has been taking place in response to a host of threats, which human action has caused primarily at the regional or local rather than the global level: challenges such as biodiversity, natural resource management and the depletion of fisheries. Increasingly, the response to such challenges has been through the pursuit of cooperative and collaborative governance arrangements, directed at mitigating environmental degradation and improving natural resource management at these lower levels and at integrating initiatives at different levels.

It is within this agenda, and with an interest in promoting collaborative and multi-scale environmental governance that this book is situated. Its particular focus is on how to imagine and promote effective collaborative governance mechanisms at various scales, and whether, to what extent, and in what ways to blend polycentric elements with state-centric governance understandings and practices so as to better govern human impacts on the environment.

This last question is an important one. The move to collaborative governance and polycentricity has not resulted in the unicentric vision of the Leviathan being relinquished, but rather in the development of approaches that seek to relate these two ideals of governance in a variety of ways. The mainstream of NEG developments has taken place, not divorced from, but rather within the shadow of state governance (see Galanter, 1981, pp1–47 for an early discussion of hybridity and the shadow of state law), and has emerged as states have sought to find better ways of responding to governance challenges and thus to govern better in terms of efficiency, effectiveness and legitimacy (Loader, 2000). This Hobbesian and Westphalian shadow has given these explorations a particular colour, as those developing governance innovations have sought to reconcile various state-centric ideals, institutional arrangements, and ways of governing, with more polycentric ones (see Osborne and Gaebler, 1993 for an influential discussion on neo-liberal thinking). We return to the implications of hybridity between different forms of governance, and the specific relationship between hierarchy and collaborative governance, in the final chapter.

In the remainder of this chapter we frame our analysis by outlining the context, focus and aims of the study.

Context – What is New Governance?

In this book we understand governance very simply to mean the intentional shaping of the flow of events so as to realize desired public goods (Parker and Braithwaite, 2003, p119). This is distinct from the concept of 'government', which we define as a political authority/state auspice (Bayley and Shearing, 2001). Our particular concern is with an emerging and innovative form of governance being developed under state auspices, which seeks to shape the flow of human events so as to facilitate the more effective and legitimate provision of ecological services (for a general discussion in the context of debates over democracy see Dryzek, 2009; for an even broader philosophical discussion see Latour, 2004). Hence, what in the literature has come to be termed 'the new governance' or 'the new environmental governance' (Karkkainen, 2004a; Cohen, 2008; Head, 2009; Lockwood et al, 2010; NeJaime, 2009, pp330–337; De Burca, 2010). This literature argues that what is 'new' about this governance is a shift in emphasis away from traditional approaches that have typically involved representative democracy, singular authority, centralized and hierarchical commands, rigidity, and uniform regulatory rules. In contrast, the new governance involves a series of innovative experiments intended to develop forms of public governance that are 'less rigid, less prescriptive, less committed to uniform outcomes, and less hierarchical in nature' (De Burca and Scott, 2006, p2; see also Karkkainen, 2004a, p472; Walker, 2006, pp21–22).

These governance experiments are often depicted in terms of the key characteristics that they exhibit: characteristics that are thought of as remedying the perceived pathologies in conventional forms of environmental regulation (Karkkainen, 2004a, pp473–474 and 496; Lobel, 2004a, pp371–404; De Burca and Scott, 2006, p3). Although there is little agreement on a single set of characteristics that offer a definitive 'new governance model', some of the most common characteristics identified by researchers internationally are forms of governance that are open-textured, participatory, collaborative, deliberative, flexible, integrative, multi-level, adaptive (Karkkainen, 2004a, pp473–474 and 485–489; Lobel, 2004b, pp502–503; Walker, 2006, p22; De Burca, 2010, p235; Trubek and Trubek, 2010) and (at least according to some NEG theories) involve 'new' forms and mechanisms of accountability (Freeman, 1997, p30; Holley, 2010).

Commentators on NEG agree that not all of these characteristics need to be present for a particular programme to fall under this sign, and indeed, as a matter of fact, there are very few, if any, examples that do so. However, the more characteristics that are present, the stronger the argument that the programme can be classified as 'new governance' (De Burca and Scott, 2006, p3; Gunningham, 2009, p146).

It is, of course, easy to overstate the novelty of these characteristics identified in NEG. Forms of multiparty collaboration, for example, have had a long history (Head, 1997). Like most claims to 'newness' the existence of NEG is a matter of degree and emphasis (McDonald, 2004, p221). What is clear, however, is that when new governance programmes are compared with established approaches, NEG represents at the very least a 'new' trend in environmental governance (De Burca and Scott, 2006, pp1–2).

For completeness, we should note that while subsequent chapters of this book will interrogate the new governance as it plays out in the environmental arena, the new governance has many dimensions, spans many spheres of social policy and is being applied across a variety of governance domains. Take, for example, the development of collaborative governance with respect to physical (in)security, as with the development, globally, of city improvement districts that are explicitly designed to identify, mobilize and coordinate the activities of a variety of stakeholders – residents, businesses, governments, private security, the police and so on (see for example, Vindevogel, 2005; Morçöl, 2006; Wolf, 2006).

Locating Our Contribution within the NEG Literature

While there have been influential theoretical arguments favouring multi-scale government initiatives of various sorts – for example, the Hayekian argument that the demands of governance required state governments to find ways of better utilizing local knowledges and capacities, particularly through market mechanisms – polycentric governance initiatives have also been promoted on the basis of pragmatic concerns. For example, within the environmental arena the ineffectiveness of government attempts to regulate human impacts on the ecological systems have been attributed to the lack of 'fit' between the boundaries of ecological systems and political ones (Odum, 1953; Karkkainen, 2002/2003). An associated issue has been the need to circumvent the increasingly rigid and cumbersome process of centralized rule-making to better account for and adapt to the dynamic nature of ecological systems (Holling, 1978; Walters, 1986; Lee, 1993; Gunderson and Holling, 2001). There has also been a concern to better involve civil society in environmental decision-making and to ensure that various stakeholders have a voice in wider democratic decision-making (Arnstein, 1969; Putnam et al, 1993; Habermas, 1996; Cohen and Sabel, 1997; Dryzek, 2000). These and similar issues have generated a variety of pragmatically grounded polycentric governance initiatives.

These more bottom-up explorations have been studied by a growing number of scholars. One of the better known is the 2009 Nobel Laureate in Economic

Sciences, Elinor Ostrom. Ostrom demonstrates that polycentric solutions to these pragmatic concerns can be developed through local experiments and that on the basis of these it is possible to develop 'design principles' based on this locally based, pragmatic learning (Ostrom, 1990). It is within this context of bottom-up, pragmatically inspired knowledge about polycentric forms of environmental governance that this book is also located.

Our particular focus within this context is on attempts to develop collaborative, polycentric forms of governance at sub-state levels that are capable of effectively and legitimately governing the impacts of human activities on the environment. Fortunately, this turns out to be a rich terrain that scholars and practitioners have been tilling for some time.

What the now very sizable literature on these developments reveals is that over the last couple of decades a profoundly innovative and very different approach to environmental governance has emerged across the globe. This reorientation in both environmental policymaking processes and the implementation tools that have been employed have seen state governance processes shifted 'downwards' to regions, 'outwards' to a host of non-state actors and, in some cases, 'upwards' to transnational institutions and organizations (Karkkainen, 2004a, p473; Lawrence, 2005, pp145–174).

In Australia and New Zealand, where our own empirical studies were conducted, such trends are clearly evident in a range of collaborative efforts. These include, centrally, three novel and innovative programmes in Australia that form our principal studies:

1. collaboration between local residents, regulators and 'big' industry enterprises to reduce pollution impacts in Victoria (Holley and Gunningham, 2006)
2. attempts to foster partnerships between communities, small- and medium-sized enterprises (SMEs), state agencies, local governments and environmental groups to address diffuse and complex environmental problems in the neighbourhoods of Victoria (Gunningham et al, 2007)
3. broader-based regional initiatives throughout Australia, resulting in the establishment of 56 regional natural resource management bodies (Lane et al, 2009).

This last initiative has involved billions of Australian dollars being invested in wide-reaching 'partnerships' between federal, state, and local governments, regional communities, farmers, and industry bodies in an attempt to address natural resource problems (Lane et al, 2009). So also in New Zealand, the site of our three comparative demonstration studies, where there has been considerable collaborative experimentation brought about by a national government that devolved control and management of natural and physical resources to elected regional councils. These councils, in turn, have developed various voluntary, collaborative and community-based approaches to negotiate and draft water policies, manage specific urban and rural water bodies, and restore small streams (Jenkins, 2007b; McCallum et al, 2007).

Interestingly, very similar endeavours can also be found in a number of other regions. In the European Union there has been increasing multiparty collaboration and participation via environmental assessment and framework directives, the Open Method of Coordination and various forms of voluntary agreements with industries (Holzinger et al, 2006; Scott and Holder, 2006; Baker and Eckerberg, 2008; Newig and Fritsch, 2009). The United States has also been at the forefront of such trends – most notably in the endeavours of multiple agencies and stakeholders to address competing demands on water resources in areas such as the San Francisco Bay Delta and in multiparty, regional landscape-scale habitat conservation planning by landowners, various tiers and agencies of government, conservationists, independent scientists, and other interested citizens (Karkkainen, 2003a; Sabatier et al, 2005a; Wiersema, 2008; see also President of the United States, 2009). These examples represent just a few of the experiments that constitute NEG, and they, and many others, provide evidence of a fundamental global rethinking of how we can and should cope with the pressing environmental problems of our time (Salamon, 2002, p1; Ribot, 2002).

Although the emergence of NEG can now be found taking place in regions across the globe it remains unclear whether it will in fact 'work', and if so, when and how (Koontz and Thomas, 2006, p113; Karkkainen, 2006a, p212). Although NEG has generated significant praise as a way of generating innovative and more democratic solutions to environmental problems, it has also faced a litany of criticisms, including claims that it leads to lowest common denominator solutions, rent seeking, dominance by self-interested economic actors and disenfranchised environmental interests.

Considerable empirical research is required to resolve these arguments about the impacts of NEG (Hornstein, 2005, pp949–951; Karkkainen, 2006b, pp295 and 316–317), as it is the principles and practical conditions that will enable successful NEG experiments to be replicated (Karkkainen, 2002/2003, pp225–243; Collaborative Democracy Network, 2006, p169; Solomon, 2008, pp833–834; Menkel-Meadow, 2008, pp850–851). Similarly, the implications of NEG in practice also require further research, since an understanding of the role of state governance (which is arguably 'decentred' by such initiatives) within NEG also remains uncertain (Karkkainen, 2002/2003, pp237–38; Karkkainen, 2004b, pp75–78; Lobel, 2004b, p502; Gunningham, 2009, p159). NEG scholarship has only just begun to grapple with these concerns, as it has, for the most part, remained focused on 'first principle' debates regarding its merits (Karkkainen, 2006a, pp211–212).

In the chapters that follow we take a hard look at NEG in practice and seek to provide insights into these and related issues (Karkkainen, 2006a, p212; Camacho, 2007, p295) through the vehicle of these several Australian (and, for comparative purposes, New Zealand) 'experiments' in NEG mentioned above. In particular, we interrogate the question: Under what conditions can 'good' NEG be achieved?

Our empirical data is principally drawn from three leading NEG programmes in Australia. Under each of these programmes (by which we mean a planned and orchestrated series of actions designed to achieve particular environmental and social outcomes) there were multiple on-ground, collaborative groups established to make decisions and take actions to improve the environment. Our study draws on over 80 interviews collected from 12 such collaborative groups. As discussed further in the Appendix, these groups are referred to as our 'cases'.

This detailed empirical analysis is complemented by a more modest empirical examination of over 40 interviews, across six case studies that were drawn from three recent NEG programmes in a single region within New Zealand. This combined material is used to test theories, speak to key debates and draw lessons on an array of environmental governance issues.

Examining the New Environmental Governance: Empirical Questions

Although the appearance of NEG has generated a flurry of scholarship heralding its potential to provide an alternative to traditional modes of governance, there has been surprisingly little investigation of *whether, how, or to what extent NEG institutions actually deliver their purported benefits in practice* (Lobel, 2004b, pp499–509; Karkkainen, 2006a, p212). Despite some emerging empirical research (see, for example, Wondolleck and Yaffee, 2000; Koontz et al, 2004; Heikkila and Gerlak, 2005; Sabatier et al, 2005a; Lane et al, 2009; Scott, 2009), a substantial gap in NEG scholarship remains because most studies have been confined to a few institutional examples, or have lacked grounding in NEG scholarship or related theories (Sabatier et al, 2005a, pp3, 11 and 13). As a result, there is little evidence that NEG actually delivers on its normative promises, or that it improves environmental outcomes (leading some to suggest that NEG may be guilty of 'all talk and no action') (Lubell, 2004, pp549–550; Fadeeva, 2005, pp168–169). These deficits in empirical research have given rise to much debate and many disagreements about the impacts and effectiveness of NEG (Fung and Wright, 2003b; Koontz and Thomas, 2006, p113; Orts and Coglianese, 2007; Trubek and Trubek, 2006/2007, p541; Head, 2009; De Burca, 2010, pp236–237).

While we will not canvas the full range of empirical and theoretical disagreements here, some of the most heated debates and most fundamental questions have been raised in relation to five key characteristics of NEG, namely collaboration, participation, deliberation, learning and 'new' forms and mechanism of accountability. It is these characteristics that will be our focus in the chapters to follow.

A fundamental question that haunts the NEG literature is whether, when and how effective *collaboration* can be achieved without succumbing to collective action problems, excessive transaction costs and/or the likelihood of lowest common denominator solutions arising from consensus decision-making processes (Steinzor, 2000; Hornstein, 2005, pp949–951; Margerum, 2007; Orts and Coglianese, 2007, pp297–299; Solomon, 2008, p833). This question also draws attention to a 'knowledge gap' within the NEG literature on the challenges associated with sustaining successful collaborative organizations – including what happens to collaborative efforts when they have substantially achieved their goals (Koontz et al, 2004, p183; Bonnell and Koontz, 2007, p154; Margerum, 2007, p141; Menkel-Meadow, 2008, p847).

Regarding *participation*, a lack of empirical evidence on representation and participation patterns in different and varied NEG institutions has left NEG vulnerable to critics who remain unconvinced that NEG can facilitate 'real participation'. Many questions accordingly remain about what kinds and levels of participation and what group of non-governmental actors are actually being brought together in practice (Karkkainen, 2003a, pp221–223; Tushnet, 2003, p170; Collaborative Democracy Network, 2006, pp168–169; Camacho, 2007, pp308–323; Cohen, 2008, pp515–516; Koehler and Koontz, 2008, p151; Smismans, 2008, p876). A related concern has been questions about the participation of environmental interest groups and their potential to 'countervail' against powerful existing stakeholders (McCloskey, 2000; McCloskey, 2001; Fung and Wright, 2003a; Leach, 2006, p108; Sturm, 2006, p331).

With respect to the issue of the demands of *deliberation* in practice, two related and controversial issues have emerged. Both relate to a concern that decision-making within NEG will be dominated either by (i) better resourced parties, such as the industries that are being regulated, and/or (ii) those well placed to influence regulatory decisions, such as bureaucrats and government agencies (Steinzor, 1998a, p142; Abers, 2003, p200; Fung, 2004, p25; Cohen, 2008).

Regarding *learning*, there has been remarkably little investigation into the existence and operation of mechanisms for learning and adaptation, including approaches such as reflexive law, adaptive management and more systemic styles of pragmatist/experimentalist learning. Questions, accordingly, remain as to when, how and to what extent actors can gather, analyse and act on information about shortcomings in their practice (Karkkainen, 2002/2003, p243; Sturm, 2006, pp327–328; Camacho, 2007, pp323–344; Solomon, 2008, p833; Robinson et al, 2009, p245; Schramm and Fishman, 2010, pp519–520).

The final area that will concern us is the issue of 'new' *forms of accountability*. As with most Western approaches to governance, accountability is a vital safeguard designed to prevent the abuse of public authority – in particular abuse of public resources (May, 2007, p11). Critics of NEG suggest its features, particularly collaboration, and the flexibility associated with learning and adaptation mean that NEG is at substantial risk of being 'captured' or perverted into a rent seeking vehicle (Farber, 2000, pp74–75; Fung and Wright, 2003b, pp21–22 and 36–37; Karkkainen, 2003b, p963; Markell, 2005, pp56–57; Sturm, 2006, pp331–334). A related criticism is that NEG encourages the dismantling of established accountability mechanism by untried alternatives that have yet to prove their value – for example, mechanisms that seek to capitalize on the involvement of new parties in NEG so as to enable 'mutual' accountability between collaborators (Freeman and Farber, 2005, pp906–906 and 908; Harlow and Rawlings, 2007, p545) and 'professional' accountability of industries (Freeman, 2000a, p665; Coglianese and Lazar, 2003, p726; Fiorino, 2004, p415).

As a consequence of these critiques it is now increasingly recognized that more research is needed to support the normative claims made by NEG advocates. Research is needed not only to resolve the above disagreements and provide insights into many unanswered questions, but also to determine what does and does not work at the levels of policy implementation (Koontz and Thomas, 2006, p133; Head, 2009; Trubek and Trubek, 2010, pp719, 725–726).

In what follows we interrogate these questions through an examination of new governance *in practice*. The general normative question that guides our analysis is: under what conditions can 'good' NEG be achieved?

The notion of 'good governance' is widely debated (United Nations Development Programme, 1997; Rhodes, 1997). We employ a concept that arises from the NEG literature we have briefly reviewed. Thus 'good governance' in this context means governance that meets each of the criteria of desirable NEG we have outlined, namely governance that realizes effective collaboration, participation, deliberation, learning, and new, more horizontal forms of accountability. Although controversy remains over the precise characteristics and nature of NEG, this is, nevertheless, a fair test as there is considerable agreement across many NEG advocates that it is precisely these features that define NEG as a more desirable form of environmental governance. Having said this, as will become apparent in the next chapter, just what these standards are is often a matter of debate (Conley and Moote, 2003, pp376 and 382). Accordingly what can be counted as success or failure of an example of NEG, even where the criteria are broadly agreed, is not a simple matter. Given this, we will define and make clear the standards of 'success' used when analysing and drawing conclusions regarding a specific defining feature of 'good' NEG so as to facilitate transparency in research and any subsequent efforts to learn from its insights into NEG (Conley and Moote, 2003).

The remainder of the book is structured as follows. Chapter 2 provides detail and context with regard to our three foundational programmes from Australia, and a brief outline of our three demonstration programmes from New Zealand. In Chapters 3–6 we analyse the Australian programmes in depth. At appropriate points in the text, this analysis is complemented by reference to three demonstration studies (based on additional fieldwork that took place in New Zealand) through a series of boxes inserted at appropriate points in the text. Our New Zealand research was narrower in scope and the breadth of data collection insufficient to give us confidence in making theoretical propositions with regard to that data. Nevertheless, we frequently found it to be of value in reinforcing findings that we had made in similar circumstances in the foundational Australian studies, and this was particularly the case when it came to identifying and illustrating design principles. In our final chapter we set out our conclusions and develop such principles for realizing 'good' NEG. In that chapter we also revisit the theoretical themes and debates in the regulatory literature, which we have briefly reviewed above.

Finally, it is appropriate to say something about what we have *not* done, and what is beyond the scope of this book. Inevitably, as a single empirical-based study, our research was not able to engage with the entire range of complex issues relevant to new governance. For example, we recognize that not all participants in the ongoing debate over new governance will agree on the importance of each of the characteristics we identify as central to 'good' NEG. But at the very least, our focus on these characteristics has ensured that we engage with *some* of the most contentious and important issues and disputes raised in the broader literature.

There is also a risk that our theoretical orientation, which approaches NEG on the basis of broad characteristics and principles, will not sufficiently take account of significant theoretical and practical differences *within* the evolving NEG field (Karkkainen, 2004a, p472; Lobel, 2004b). However, we have been conscious of the risks of generalization, and there are considerable benefits to be gained from grouping different theories and scholarship within a NEG framework. Indeed, consistent with emerging understandings within the NEG literature itself, adopting a generalized rubric of NEG (with apposite attention to differences) facilitates the linking and comparison of theories and enables the testing, development and reformulation of theory. Doing so ensures a better understanding of what is occurring, and offers a constructive approach for developing a normative vision capable of influencing the direction of environmental governance (Lobel, 2004b, pp501–506; Walker, 2006).

From a methodological standpoint, we also recognize that there are limits to our case-study approach and dangers in seeking to generalize from specific cases drawn from particular contexts. But at a relatively early stage in the development of a field, such studies may provide substantial insights and address questions that quantitative studies are ill-equipped to answer – not least because quantitative research cannot probe general responses for concrete details, and because even where correlations can be established, it is not possible to do more than speculate at the causes that lie behind them. In any event, at the present time there are few, if any, *large* studies addressing the questions that are our central concerns. Accordingly, there is considerable virtue in conducting individual case studies. These can provide in-depth qualitative analysis of when new governance actually works and does not work in practice. There is also particular value in studying context and the institutional arrangements of NEG, and the behaviour, attitudes and practices of those *actively engaged* in new governance. By so doing, it may be possible to identify which conditions were important, beneficial and/or detrimental for fostering successful collaboration, meaningful participatory and deliberative processes, and to clarify which frameworks are effective in terms of learning and accountability.

There are of course risks with samples such as ours, which consist largely of active participants in new governance. Indeed, active participants may exhibit a bias toward a more favourable view of the success and value of these efforts than that held by other, possibly equally well-informed persons who elected not to participate, or participated and then left (Coglianese, 2003; Conley and Moote, 2003). However, as discussed in the Appendix, we have been conscious of this potential sample bias, and have sought to mitigate it through triangulating opinions of different and diverse respondents, as well as comparing interview data with documentary evidence. As with most social research, the ethical and confidentiality requirements of the research require us to preserve the anonymity of our specific interviewees, save for a general description of their stakeholder category. Throughout the book, when discussing our data, we accordingly reference interviews in the text only by indicating an identifier number and the general stakeholder category of the interviewee.

Finally, the focus of our study was to identify conditions that promote good NEG *processes*. It was not to assess the extent to which these processes in fact produced desired environmental outcomes. While this question is crucial, and it is an issue that we touch upon in our analysis throughout, considering this issue fully would take us well beyond the scope of our limited enquiry. One of the reasons for this is that the programmes we studied were all relatively new (six years or less). As environmental outcomes typically have long gestation periods it is too early to be able to assess outcomes. Further, such an assessment would require before and after data. With our programmes such data is lacking. Given these constraints, and many others, clearly our research will not be the last word on the evolving subject of new governance (Koontz and Thomas, 2006).

2

THE PROGRAMMES – ASPIRING TO NEW ENVIRONMENTAL GOVERNANCE

Introduction

In this chapter we explore the history of our Australian programmes with a view to understanding the intentions of those who promoted and designed each of these governance initiatives. For each we will identify the feature of these initiatives that constitute them as experiments designed to promote NEG. To do this we focus on the five features of NEG we identified in Chapter 1, namely, collaboration, participation, deliberation, learning and 'new' forms and mechanisms of accountability. As we will see, in each of our programmes these features take different forms and are understood differently. This reflects the fact that innovations of governance are dynamic developments that are constantly evolving as practitioners and policy analysts reflect on what they have sought to do and what they have done, and as they compare this with what others have done and are doing.

Accordingly, while each of the Australian programmes, which constitute our primary focus, shares family resemblances that can be used, as we have done, to identify it as an example of NEG, there are also significant differences between them. In this chapter we seek to identify both these shared features *and* the variation that distinguishes them. Given our concern to identify the conditions that promote 'good' environmental governance, these variations are essential to our analysis – hence our focus on both the similarities that identify these programmes as examples of NEG as well as their differences. For us a distinguishing feature of the evolving terrain of NEG is that while it, by definition, expresses key characteristics, these have been, and are being constantly interpreted and reinterpreted as policy analysts, politicians, practitioners and scholars (to name only some of the players) explore new ways of governing humans as they engage their socio-natural environments.

In identifying the defining features of the NEG found in each of our programmes we will draw upon a variety of materials – parliamentary speeches, legislation, guidelines and interviews with policymakers. A key objective for us in exploring the programmes in this way will be to begin to articulate the evaluative standards against which we will be making judgements about the 'goodness' of our examples. This will prepare the way for our analysis, in subsequent chapters, of the conditions that best promote good NEG. This, in turn, will provide the basis for our normative claims about how best to promote good NEG – our design principles.

Our analysis of the three foundational Australian programmes is complemented by three demonstration programmes intended to throw light on the broader applicability of findings from our principal programmes. For convenience, and to avoid disrupting the narrative involving our foundational programmes, reference is made to the demonstration programmes through a series of boxes inserted at appropriate points in the text in Chapters 3–6. Box 2.1, toward the end of this chapter, briefly introduces these demonstration programmes.

Environment Improvement Plan

During the early 1990s the Environment Protection Authority Victoria (VEPA) pioneered the Environment Improvement Plan (EIP). It was heralded as a mechanism to engage a broader range of stakeholders in the regulatory process and to generate cooperative and innovative approaches to addressing the environmental challenges confronting single industrial enterprises – especially large companies (VEPA, 2002a, p1).

Like many NEG initiatives, the concept of EIP evolved not from elegant theorizing but as a practical response to a concrete and pressing environmental problem, in particular, a stand-off between a local community and a collection of industries that made up the Altona Chemical Complex in Melbourne (the Complex) (Meek, 2004, p2). The Complex, although initially located at some distance from residential areas, came to be located, as a consequence of urban development, very close to several residential areas. These local communities and the Complex became increasingly polarized over the Complex's pollution impacts, such as odour, noise and unsafe chemical discharges that had an impact on the health of people living in the vicinity (Meek, 2004, p2).

Finding the Complex's management unresponsive, residents turned to the VEPA and insisted that it take action to address their concerns. After an investigation the VEPA concluded that there was no easy solution to the conflict – tough action to reduce pollution might threaten the economic viability of chemical complex facilities, and there was little room for compromise. For a period, there was a stand-off. The community, unhappy with the VEPA's slow response (Wills and Fritschy, 2001, p159; Meek, 2004, p3), began to oppose *all* development proposals including, for example, a proposal for a bike shed (Wills and Fritschy, 2001, pp158–159; Meek, 2004, p2)! In 1989, the local Member for Parliament, facing heated demands from both sides, called a number of public meetings between concerned community members, the industries, the VEPA and local government members. One outcome of these discussions was an agreement to form the Altona Complex Neighbourhood Consultative Group, which included all the main stakeholders (Wills and Fritschy, 2001, pp158–159; Meek, 2004, pp1–2).

At this point the VEPA took on a new role (Meek, 2004, p2). It facilitated the consultative group's development and steered it towards the development of a negotiated solution. The solution committed the Complex to improve its airborne emissions, reduce its liquid and solid waste generation and better manage its noise emissions (Robinson, 1999, p7). In return, the local community (or more precisely its leaders in this matter) agreed to stop blocking the Complex's expansion plans. Over time, through continuing dialogue and the consultation process, the industries in the Complex came to enjoy an increasingly productive and less adversarial relationship with the local community and VEPA (Meek, 2004, p3; Robinson, 1999, p7).

The VEPA was so pleased with the Altona initiative's success that it decided to construct a model of what had been done, which could, and should, be rolled out across the state (Meek, 2004, p4; Gunningham and Sinclair, 2002, p159). They did so under the banner of an Environment Improvement Plan (EIP).

As conceptualized by the VEPA, an EIP involves a company making a public commitment to enhance its environmental performance. This involves the development of a plan that outlines areas of a company's operations that are to be improved and is usually negotiated in conjunction with the local community, local government, the VEPA and other relevant government authorities. Where possible, the plan should contain definite timelines for completion of improvements and procedures for ongoing monitoring. Improvements may include such actions as new works or equipment, or changes in operating practices. Monitoring, assessments and audits are undertaken to plan and support these improvements (VEPA, 1993).

While these features are common to most plans developed under the EIP programme, over the decade and a half since the EIP was introduced, several distinct forms of EIPs have emerged. First, in principle the EIP process may abandon direct local stakeholder involvement in favour of a bipartite approach involving just the industry and VEPA; however, these are very uncommon. The present research focuses principally on *voluntary and multi-stakeholder* EIPs. These comprised the majority of the approximately 70 EIP plans that were operational, or being negotiated, when this research was undertaken. These forms of EIP arose from the VEPA's broad enforcement powers, which require that the agency conduct enforcement of environmental requirements with the goal of 'better protecting the environment and its economic and social uses' (*Environment Protection Act 1970* (Vic), s 1K). This broad discretion allowed the VEPA to design a form of EIP that involved the industry enterprise, local stakeholders and VEPA in developing an EIP plan pursuant to voluntary VEPA guidelines (VEPA, 2002a, pp2 and 13; VEPA, 2004a, p2; Gunningham and Sinclair, 2002, pp171–174). These guidelines were designed to encourage both poor and better performing industries to volunteer to participate in the EIP process.

A related type of voluntary EIP emerged in 1994 as a part of VEPA's legislatively backed *accredited licence scheme* (*Environment Protection Act 1970* (Vic), ss 26A–26E; VEPA, 2006). Accredited Licences (AL) were developed with leading environmental performers in mind and were intended to provide them with a less prescriptive alternative to the established works approval and licence (*Environment Protection Act 1970* (Vic), s 26B(2)(c)). To voluntarily obtain an accredited licence, a firm is required to develop, or already have in place, a voluntary EIP (*Environment Protection Act 1970* (Vic), s 26B(2)(c)). Existing research on ALs in Victoria has demonstrated that very few enterprises have gone down this path (Gunningham and Sinclair, 2002, pp171–174). Indeed, based on our research, only 21 ALs had been granted, out of the approximately 1000 licensed industry premises in Victoria (VEPA, 2003a, p2).

Beyond these two types of voluntary EIP, there are two compulsory forms. The first is an EIP under s 31C of the *Environment Protection Act 1970* (Vic) (hereafter referred to as the Act). This section empowers the VEPA to effectively compel industries to develop and implement an EIP. This is achieved through a complex mechanism, which involves 'declaring' a highly polluting industry sector subject to s 31C of the Act, and then offering individual industry enterprises within it the 'option' of entering an EIP as a more palatable alternative to a mandatory environmental audit (see *Environment Protection Act 1970* (Vic), s 31C(6)).

The second compulsory EIP arises from VEPA's legislative powers, which empower it to impose an EIP on any regulated premises as a licence condition, or as a term of a work approval (VEPA, 2002a, p1), notice or other statutory mechanism (VEPA, 1989, cl 17A-17G; VEPA, 2001b, cl 20; VEPA, 2002b, cl 17; see, for instance, *Environment Protection Act 1970* (Vic), s 20(6)(b) and VEPA, 2002a, p1). These powers, as well as s 31C of the Act, are rarely used (Gunningham and Sinclair, 2002, p163). Indeed, the VEPA has only sought to use its powers under s 31C of the Act once, and EPA confirmed that imposing licence condition EIPs was rare in practice. However, as we will see in subsequent chapters, they are far from redundant and can play an important role as an incentive-altering mechanism to tip industry's cost-benefit equation and encourage them to collaborate.

Regardless of the particular form an EIP takes, they all share the same general goal, namely, to accomplish continuous corporate environmental improvement, including extending 'compliance' beyond legal requirements through the use of a collaborative governance mechanism (VEPA, 2002a, p1; *Environment Protection Act 1970* (Vic), ss 26B and 31C).

Initiatives, with similar objectives, have been pursued through international NEG initiatives. The process-based approach of EIP (discussed further below), for example, mirrors a range of environmental management systems championed through what Orts terms 'reflexive environmental law' (1995). Other family members include the Wisconsin Green Tier Initiative and Project XL in the USA, and environmental agreements and covenants in Europe (Orts and Deketelaere, 2001, p5; Trubek and Trubek, 2006/2007, pp540, 541 and 543). Like EIP, these NEG initiatives have focused on encouraging 'good' environmental performers to voluntarily aspire to or go beyond legal compliance. Two factors, however, set the EIP apart from other NEG experiments of this sort. First, the EIP is one of few NEG approaches to focus on improving the environmental performance of both the best and the worst industries. Second, the EIP was introduced a number of years before other 'regulatory flexibility initiatives', such as Project XL, were developed. This makes the EIP a more mature example of NEG (Gunningham and Sinclair, 2002, p158).

Such differences aside, as with all NEG experiments focused on pollution control, the EIP represents a move away from conventional command and control regulation. This is true despite the fact that VEPA's traditional regulatory powers underpin the EIP – nonetheless this, as we will see later, is a context that has important implications for the operation of the EIP.

Thus, as with its counterparts in Europe and the USA, the EIP was (and remains) emblematic as a 'new' way of governing industry pollution (Hirsch, 2001). This 'new' way of governing is evident in the design of the EIP – a design that involves the quintessential features of NEG: (i) *collaboration* between industry, VEPA and non-government stakeholders; (ii) *participation* of local residents and non-government actors and *deliberative* decision-making; (iii) 'reflexive' and 'adaptive management' processes of *learning and adaptation*; and (iv) many *'new' forms of accountability*, including third-party monitoring, process and performance-based accountability regimes. We discuss these defining characteristics in turn below.

At the heart of the EIP is a desire to promote 'effective collaboration' (VEPA, 2002a, pp2 and 10; VEPA, 2004a, p1) between industry, VEPA and non-government stakeholders (VEPA, 2001a, pp2–3). This design feature is reflective of VEPA's overall approach to governance, which assumes there is more to be gained through 'strategic alliances and forming or facilitating partnerships for environment protection with industry, local government and the community' (VEPA, 2002e, pp6 and 41; Government of Victoria, 2002, p22) than by adversarial, government-centred regulation. Indeed, for VEPA, face-to-face negotiation among partners and cooperative action is thought more likely to dissipate conflict, mobilize new resources and provide innovative solutions than the other more conventional tools in their kit (VEPA, 2004a, p1). Achieving such benefits through a collaborative EIP process has been a particularly important feature of VEPA's efforts to respond to situations in which pollution impacts are considerable, but where established governance tools have proven to be ineffective. The collaborative approach that was hoped would emerge under the EIP involved the relevant stakeholders forming a 'Community Liaison Committee', modelled on the tripartite consultation process that proved so successful at the Altona Complex discussed earlier. This committee is flexible in size – the ideal is regarded as being about 12 members coming from the enterprise, government (local and VEPA), interested groups (such as NGOs) and five or six local community representatives (VEPA, 2001a, pp1–3). These members are responsible for defining and assessing the industry's environmental performance, and are expected to tailor the EIP to the specific environmental and industrial conditions (VEPA, 2001b, p3; VEPA, 2002a, p5; Gunningham and Sinclair, 2002, p157).

The Committee develops, agrees to monitor, evaluate and adjust a plan that governs improvements to industry's environmental performance for an agreed period (usually between one and three years). The EIP is not, however, intended to be a 'once off' collaborative problem-solving endeavour (VEPA, 2002a, p9). While the guidelines do not offer any specific time line as to the length of time committees are expected to continue, the EIP is designed specifically to be a long-term collaborative endeavour (VEPA, 2001a, p3). Indeed, when an industry has completed implementation of a given plan, the committee is encouraged to draft, and agree to, a new plan in a manner that is consistent with the EIP's goal of continuous environmental improvement and adaptive management (see below).

In addition to collaboration, the EIP has identifiable participatory and deliberative aspirations (Fung and Wright, 2003b). Indeed, the EIP is one of the key environmental governance instruments in the State of Victoria intended to deepen the ways in which non-governmental actors participate in and influence decisions about environmental problems and policies that affect their lives.

In Victoria, as elsewhere, political appeals for a 'third way' (Giddens, 2000) and for non-government participation in governance have grown considerably over the last three decades (Wiseman, 2006, p96) – culminating in the *Growing Victoria Together* plan (Government of Victoria, 2002). Like other 'third way' reforms in Australia (Reddel, 2004), this plan embraces 'building cohesive communities', 'partnerships' and 'community participation and engagement' (Government of Victoria, 2002, p22). These goals have been translated into the VEPA's corporate objective (VEPA, 2003b, p7) to 'engage with and enable communities in ways that are meaningful to people' (VEPA, 2002e, pp1, 6 and 41).

The EIP has a particularly significant role to play here, as it was developed specifically to give voice to those who so often bear the brunt of society's industrial lifestyle. It is encouraged and/or required to involve the 'affected community', to ensure 'as much resident participation as possible' and to include 'different community interests and perspectives' (*Environment Protection Act 1970* (Vic), ss 26B(2)(c) and 31C; VEPA, 2001a, pp1–3, 4 and 6; VEPA, 2002a, p10; VEPA, 2004a, pp3–4). Decision-making is recommended to occur through 'negotiation', and industry is to 'communicate clearly and without the use of jargon and industry specific language' and should treat non-government actors fairly and as equals (VEPA, 2001a, pp4–5; VEPA, 2004a, pp1–4). The committee is given the task of arriving at joint decisions about objectives, targets and actions designed to improve industries' environmental performance. The intent is that over time, using this participatory and broadly deliberative approach, residents' comments and suggestions will lead to effective solutions to their long-standing problems (VEPA, 2004a, pp1 and 4).

The third NEG feature embraced by EIP is processes of learning and adaptation. This is evident in EIP guidelines, which suggest that the collaborative group should set measurable objectives; identify critical aspects of each objective and the standards that are to be maintained; monitor these aspects and performance against the objectives; and update actions in the plan as necessary. Much of this is carried out by industry, which must report monitoring data to the collaborative group in order to facilitate the cooperative identification of any shortfalls in meeting targets and standards, and develop actions to remedy them (VEPA, 2002a, pp9–10). The EIP foregrounds the local knowledge of residents – the guidelines encourage residents to alert the committee to problems and issues that need to be remedied.

Overlapping with this 'adaptive' approach is a second 'process-based' approach to promoting learning and adaptation. Process-focused approaches assume that more will be achieved by influencing attitudes and creating a framework for better environmental organization than by detailed prescriptive standards (Parker, 2002). The focus is on developing systems for managing environmental performance *across an organization as a whole*. The negotiated plan is to include a range of minimum requirements. For EIPs under AL, these requirements are prescribed in legislation (*Environment Protection Act 1970* (Vic), s 26B(2)(c)). However, for other voluntary EIPs, the content is established according to VEPA guidelines. These generally include undertakings to comply or go beyond compliance with licences and regulations; emission and waste production standards; monitoring of compliance; audits; provision for upgrading of plant; assessment of new and emerging technology; emergency and contingency plans; assessment and monitoring; review, reporting and updating; enhanced response to community complaints; community relations, health and safety issues; and community reporting requirements on progress (VEPA, 2002a, p9; VEPA, 2004a, p2). In sum, the EIP is designed to encourage industries to change their behaviour in response to new information and opportunities about its operations and environmental impacts so as to achieve 'continuous improvement' (VEPA, 2002a, p1; Fiorino, 2004, pp402 and 415).

Finally, to ensure that industry and its collaborators contribute to (rather than pervert) environmental improvement, the EIP has been designed to employ a range of 'new' forms of accountability. As is characteristic of NEG's 'new' forms of accountability (Freeman, 1997, p96; May, 2007, p11), the EIP is intended to supplement traditional hierarchical accountability relationships (e.g., industry to VEPA) with more horizontal ones (e.g., industry to local residents). It is designed to take advantage of the involvement of private actors (such as industry, auditors and local residents) so as to enhance accountability for performance.

With EIP's process-based approach, accountability is centred on whether industry has an acceptable plan, rather than on the basis of its environmental outcomes (May, 2007, pp10 and 13). Industry's 'professional accountability' is vital here. This involves, among other things, making use of an industry's professional expertise in designing accountability systems (Manring, 2005, p61; May, 2007, pp10 and 13). Accountability is to be delivered through VEPA oversight of the plan, supplemented by independent experts' auditing. Public and private actors are to determine 'whether the EIP has been adequately implemented and is operating properly to manage environmental performance, rather than assessing the actual environmental performance of an organization (through environmental monitoring)' (VEPA, 2002a, pp9–10).

Overlapping with process accountability is a suit of mechanisms designed to ensure industries are held accountable for their performance. The core of this approach includes recommendations and requirements for industries (in negotiation with the others in the collaborative group) to set measurable objectives. For example 'Ensure no offensive odours are discharged beyond the boundaries of the premises' or 'Reduce the volume of sludge wastes by 20 per cent within the next two years' (VEPA, 2002a, p7). These objectives must meet a number of broad recommendations and requirements that include 'improve[d] environmental performance' by meeting or going 'beyond-compliance' (*Environment Protection Act 1970* (Vic), s 26B; VEPA, 2002a, pp1 and 4–11; VEPA, 2004a, pp1–3). A core feature of this approach is the intention of enabling stakeholders to 'blow the whistle' if decisions and actions fail to achieve targets.

These horizontal accountability and third-party auditing mechanisms are supplemented by the traditional command technologies. The VEPA retains a right to amend and approve plans to ensure that targets are appropriate. If slippage in a target is evident, the VEPA has recourse to its traditional regulatory powers (e.g., to impose more stringent licence conditions or to pursue prosecution) (Gunningham and Sinclair, 2002, p163; Meek, 2004, p4).

Although the EIP is underpinned by the command and control powers of the VEPA, its approach represents a significant departure from conventional rule-based regulation. Its focus on greater industry self-management sets it apart from prescriptive regulatory approaches that demand adherence to fixed rules. Also apparent is a shift away from a traditional bipartite relationship between the regulators and the regulated, to a 'tripartite' approach that involves disclosure of information to, consultation with and empowerment of local communities.

Neighbourhood Environment Improvement Plan

In 2001, the VEPA introduced the Neighbourhood Environment Improvement Plan (NEIP) as a new tool to address complex local environmental problems (Garbutt, 2000, p2). In contrast to a focus on single industry sites, the NEIP is designed as a 'place-based' approach at the 'neighbourhood' scale that involves multiple industrial, residential, commercial and/or agricultural causes of environmental problems. Like the EIP, the NEIP discards command and control for broad-based 'community' decision-making that seeks to engage the entire gamut of public and private actors who contribute to environmental problems at neighbourhood levels (VEPA, 2002d, p1).

The introduction of the NEIP instrument formed part of a wider shift in environmental governance and policy, intended to develop new tools for addressing complex environmental problems (Hirsch, 2001). These so-called 'second generation' environmental problems include issues such as the cumulative impact of multiple sources of pollution at a local level, which often have an overall environmental impact far exceeding that of the 'traditional villain', namely large industrial enterprises (Groundwork Trust, 1998). As we saw in Chapter 1, traditional regulatory approaches to these problems have often been ad hoc, lacking in integration and were largely ineffective in resolving these issues (VEPA, 2002d, p2).

The Victorian Minister for Environment and Conservation, in 2001, made the case for a more holistic, locally based governance approach. NEIP was introduced into Victoria's *Environmental Protection Act* (see *Environment Protection (Liveable Neighbourhoods) Act 2001* (Vic)) and was described as a statutory mechanism to enable those contributing to and those affected by local environmental problems to come together in a constructive forum. In this forum, the members of the local community, including residents, industry and local government, can agree on the environmental priority issues for the neighbourhood. They can then devise a plan to address their agreed environmental issues in a practical manner (Garbutt, 2000, p2; VEPA, 2002d, p1; *Environment Protection Act 1970* (Vic), s 19AD).

Two types of NEIP were introduced: a directed, and a voluntary NEIP (ss 19AD, 19AE and 19AH of the Act). In general terms, a directed proposal refers to a process whereby the VEPA directs a local government or some other 'protection agency' with responsibility for the environment to submit a proposal document to the VEPA for endorsement (*Environment Protection Act 1970* (Vic), ss 19AF, 19AG and 19AH). There have been no directed proposals and none are anticipated, in the short to medium term.

Any interested member of a local community can initiate a voluntary NEIP (VEPA, 2002d). The process for establishing a NEIP is initiated by a proposal. The proposal identifies objectives and actions for improving the local environment. A NEIP cannot be developed without identifying a 'sponsor' (*Environment Protection Act 1970* (Vic), s 19AE). A 'sponsor' can be an actor from a state, region or a local governmental agency, known as a 'protection agency', which has powers or duties under legislation with respect to the Victorian environment (s 4(1) of the Act; VEPA, 2002d, p7). The role of the sponsor can, and does, vary. It may include taking a leadership role, providing funding or support, or merely acting as one of the many participants. The sponsor is required to act 'on behalf of the neighbourhood community to take the proposal through the formal stage of gaining VEPA endorsement' (VEPA, 2002d, pp7–8; *Environment Protection Act 1970* (Vic), s 19AE). Once endorsed, the sponsor and the collaborators must then use the proposal to guide the development of a final plan.

Steps for both the development of a proposal and a plan include: the community and sponsor drawing a 'neighbourhood' boundary around an issue; identifying where the problems are, and what the possible solutions may be; engaging and obtaining formal sign-on of so-called NEIP 'partners', such as business and community groups, and government agencies; establishing a steering committee made up of key partners; determining a 'vision'; determining how the vision may be achieved through the efforts of the whole community; identifying the financial or other resources needed to fund the development of the NEIP plan; identifying the likely nature of involvement and resource commitments to be made by the partners; detailing the proposed process for developing the plan; and ensuring that the process is open to all parts of the community (VEPA, 2002d, pp4–6; s 19AI(3) of the Act).

Once the final plan is approved by the VEPA, the NEIP is intended to 'improve the quality of the local environment' through multiple public and private stakeholders collaborating together to address a shared and complex local environmental problem (s 19A(1) of the Act; Garbutt, 2000, p2). The NEIP does not have any direct regulatory authority beyond those who sign up to the plan, nor does it provide significant resources to fund, coerce or offer incentives for others to take action.

The NEIP programme, like the EIP, shares a family resemblance with many international NEG experiments. For example, the NEIP echoes elements of 'civic environmentalism' (John and Mlay, 1999, p361) and other similar experiments in the USA (Steinzor, 2000). It is particularly closely related to the, now defunct, NEG experiment of Community Based Environmental Protection (subsequently replaced by the Community Action for a Renewed Environment) developed by the United States Environmental Protection Agency (US EPA) (see www.epa.gov/ocem/nacept/cbep97/cbep_charge.htm; Nickelsburg, 1998, pp1372–1373). Like the US experiment, the NEIP programme aims to achieve 'top down support for bottom up community initiatives' (John and Mlay, 1999, p361; US EPA, 1999; see, generally, Weiland and Vos, 2002, pp123–124; US EPA, 1994; US EPA, 1997). Both are 'place-based' approaches designed to encourage collaboration between local stakeholders to addresses complex and cross-media environmental problems.

The NEIP involves the telltale features of NEG, including: (i) *collaboration* between multiple public, private and non-government actors within a local neighbourhood; (ii) *participation* of local residents and non-government actors and *deliberative* decision-making; (iii) 'adaptive management' and what can be termed 'systemic' processes of *learning and adaptation*; and (iv) many *'new' forms of accountability*, including mutual accountability, contractual agreements, and a performance-based accountability regime.

Broadly consistent with VEPA's collaborative approach to regulation, the NEIP has been designed to facilitate voluntary collaboration and 'partnerships', which are a central feature of its environmental governance (VEPA, 2002d, pp6 and 8–9; VEPA, 2004b, p10). NEIP was designed to address severe and complex environmental problems, 'which require concerted shared action' especially where this is accompanied by 'community concern' with the status quo (VEPA, 2003b, p7; Garbutt, 2000). A defining assumption is that collaboration will be better suited to addressing complex and multifaceted issues than traditional regulation (for example, see Cohen and Sabel, 1997, p326). Benefits are to be delivered through a NEIP collaborative group that can be any size, but must include the sponsor, 'those groups, businesses or people contributing to the environmental problems' in the neighbourhood, as well as 'those concerned about it and with the responsibility to act on it' (such as the VEPA) (VEPA, 2002d, pp7–8).

This collaborative group is to be responsible for developing both the proposal and subsequent plan. Upon the plan being approved by the VEPA it becomes a living document (*Environment Protection Act 1970* (Vic), s 19AI(4)). As with EIP, collaboration is intended to be ongoing and long term and subject to regular review, which can lead to plan amendments, and, over the longer term, a total review and redraft of plans (*Environment Protection Act 1970* (Vic), ss 19AI(3)(f), 19AJ and 19AI(e)(f)).

Again, as with the EIP, the NEIP forms a central plank in community empowerment. Indeed, the NEIP was expressly designed to 'operate on the basis of community agreement and participation' (the community being defined broadly as including 'the people who live, work and play' in the neighbourhood) (Garbutt, 2000, p4; VEPA, 2002d, p1).

Once again, as in the EIP programme, NEIP was designed to ensure that the members of the collaborative group contribute to its participatory and deliberative goals. This is done by encouraging and requiring that the group meet procedural criteria regarding inclusiveness, representativeness, and deliberative decision-making processes. These criteria include requirements for NEIP to be 'open to all parts of the community' and the use of 'negotiation' and 'mediation' processes to make decisions (VEPA, 2002d, pp4–6, 8 and 9; *Environment Protection Act 1970* (Vic), s 19AI(3)(d)).

The third NEG approach embodied in the NEIP is the intention to foster learning and adaptation. As with EIP, this approach is consistent with a 'passive' style of adaptive management. NEIP groups are to set measurable targets and objectives, develop milestones and measure progress against them. The aim is to ensure the NEIP will be well equipped to cope with the likely uncertainties and dynamic nature of complex second generation environmental problems (Ruhl, 2005, p28).

NEIP is intended to establish a process of information-sharing and learning that is broadly consistent with the first of two broad elements of pragmatic and democratic experimentalist ideas of 'systemic learning' (Karkkainen, 2002/2003, p243), namely: (i) the sharing of information and innovations between local collaborations (Paton et al, 2004, p262; Sirianni and Friedland, 2001, p86); and (ii) the continual modification of explicitly provisional, government policy determinations (Sabel et al, 1999; Karkkainen, 2006a, p238). This approach to learning was entirely absent from the aspirations in EIP.

This learning approach falls short of the full blown democratic experimentalist processes often associated with new governance. One reason for this is that there is no intention to use the information gained from collaborations to revise the rules that frame NEIP (Karkkainen et al, 2000, pp693–694). Nonetheless, the NEIP shares with experimentalists and other theories an appreciation for processes that diffuse information and innovative ideas between collaborative groups (Freeman, 1997, pp28–29; Fung and Wright, 2003b, pp21–22; Karkkainen, 2003a, pp959–960).

Finally, the NEIP is designed to deploy a range of 'new' forms of accountability to try and ensure the accountability of collaborators' governing local environmental issues (VEPA, 2002d, p3). Like EIP, the NEIP employs not only traditional hierarchical accountability mechanisms, but also horizontal ones that seek to capitalize on the roles that its collaborators can play in holding each other to account (Freeman and Farber, 2005, p904). Central to this approach is the use of contractual controls to enhance accountability. These features are designed to make the programme responsive to the VEPA, as well as the more immediate neighbourhood community (Freeman, 1997, p96).

Consistent with many NEG initiatives, these new forms of accountability are deployed within a performance accountability regime. This involves being held accountable for the achievement of broad environmental targets (e.g., 'Improvements in environmental quality and amenity' of a creek or 'improving neighbourhood sustainability', VEPA, 2002d, p6) to 'improve the quality of the local environment' (Garbutt, 2000). The collaborative group is expected to conduct self-monitoring and report to the VEPA (*Environment Protection Act 1970* (Vic), ss 19AI and 19AJ).

As with many NEG experiments (Freeman, 2000b, pp198–201; Dana, 2000, p36), the NEIP uses a form of contractual arrangement as a means to foster accountability. Once the plan is approved by VEPA, it is gazetted as a statutory document, making the actions in the plan legally binding (*Environment Protection Act 1970* (Vic), s 19AI(4)). Consistent with the voluntary approach to collaboration, a partner's decision to commit to actions in the plan is voluntary in nature and they must formally sign-on to the plan to demonstrate their willingness to do so (VEPA, 2002c, p6; *Environment Protection Act 1970* (Vic), s 19AH). However, those who choose to participate in this way legally bind themselves through a contractual agreement. The consequences of subsequent withdrawal, or failure to fulfil the contractual terms, have been designed to involve a breach of law (although this remains untested in practice) (Gunningham et al, 2007).

This contractual mechanism is intended to provide a number of accountability and transparency benefits, including improving the capacity of collaborators to hold each other to account by enhancing their capacity to shame and bring other forms of pressure onto under-performers (VEPA, 2002d, p1). In a similar vein, NEIP has been designed to provide VEPA with powers to hold the collaborative group to account. It has the power to amend, impose conditions and approve the NEIP proposal and plan to ensure targets set are credible (*Environment Protection Act 1970* (Vic), ss 19AH(2) and 19AI(2)) and that they 'improve the quality of the local environment' (VEPA, 2002d, p1; Garbutt, 2000, p2).

Like the EIP, the NEIP pursues an NEG approach to governance. However, the way in which it embodies these characteristics is different: it addresses more complex environmental problems; involves a broader mix of public and private actors in collaboration; seeks learning gains through a process of systemic learning; and is focused exclusively on a performance accountability regime.

Regional Natural Resource Management

The final NEG programme we will consider is the Regional Natural Resource Management (RNRM) programme. This programme involves the federal and state governments committing literally billions of Australian dollars of funding to what is perhaps the most ambitious and substantial NEG initiative in Australia and one of the more ambitious anywhere (Moore, 2005, p121; Lane et al, 2009).

Many factors contributed to the introduction of RNRM, including the rise of a 'sustainable development' discourse in Australia and the wider shifts in the roles of government and civil society in governance as discussed in Chapter 1 (Head, 2005a, p140; Moore, 2005, p121). However, perhaps the most influential factors were a perceived need to find an alternative to the limitations of more traditional regulatory approaches, and the shortcomings of three older innovative reforms in the governance of natural resources, namely Integrated Catchment Management, Landcare and the Natural Heritage Trust (NHT).

Both Integrated Catchment Management and Landcare emerged during the 1980s and 1990s and both were important in laying the groundwork for the emergence of RNRM. Integrated Catchment Management emerged primarily at the state level in response to growing concerns about the failure of traditional approaches to provide an integrated and holistic approach to managing natural resources. But, while each state made some attempt to manage natural resources more holistically under Integrated Catchment Management, each also suffered from weaknesses that constrained its success – including lack of funding, problems of representation, the limits of the supply of volunteer efforts, and a general lack of legislative backing and mandate, which reduced the influence of catchment groups over broader public policy (Margerum, 1999, p157; Curtis and Lockwood, 2000, p66; House of Representatives Standing Committee on Environment and Heritage, 2000; Buchy and Race, 2001, p303; Bellamy et al, 2002; Carr, 2002, p403; Ewing, 2003, p393).

Around the same time as Integrated Catchment Management was being rolled out at the state level, the National Landcare Programme emerged at the federal level. This collaboration between government and rural communities involved limited government funding for demonstration and trials of new farming practices and education to assist farmers to become more skilled, informed and adaptive land managers (Curtis, 2003, p446; Lockie, 2004, pp43–44; Moore, 2005, p122). This programme had its share of successes, including mobilizing extensive numbers of the rural communities (Lawrence, 2005, pp145–174). However, it soon became apparent that local Landcare groups, working with limited resources, were unlikely to effect the landscape changes necessary to protect critical natural resources assets (Curtis, 2003, p454; Paton et al, 2004, p262; Moore, 2005, pp122–123). As a result the federal government sought to address this problem by, in part, committing more funds to Landcare for on-the-ground works (Curtis, 2003, p446).

These funds were released through a new federal programme known as the Natural Heritage Trust (*Natural Heritage Trust of Australia Act 1997* (Cth)), which was supported by a reserve of A$1.25 billion (which, at the time of writing, was US$1.27 billion). This was later expanded to A$1.5 billion (approximately US$1.52 billion) over six years (Curtis, 2003, p454). This five-year programme, introduced in 1996/97, is commonly referred to as the 'first phase' of the Natural Heritage Trust (that is, NHT 1). NHT 1 was implemented through partnership agreements with the states to ensure effective planning and service delivery (Head, 2005a, pp142–143). The focus of the programme was primarily on funding conservation used to address water, seas, coasts, sustainable agriculture and natural resources management (*Natural Heritage Trust of Australia Act 1997* (Cth), s 3, part 3; Moore, 2005, p123). The National Landcare Programme was one of the programmes funded under NHT 1 (Curtis, 2003, pp446–447).

NHT 1 grants supported more than 12,000 projects around Australia and involved an estimated 400,000 Australians (*Natural Heritage Trust of Australia Act 1997* (Cth), s 3; see generally www.nht.gov.au). The monies invested in the NHT Reserve also provided funding for a National Land and Water Resources Audit (Government of Australia, 2007) that collected and collated primary data and information related to Australia's natural resources and their management.

Despite NHT 1's significant impacts, reviews of the programme at the end of the 1990s pointed to substantial shortcomings (Environment Australia and the Department of Agriculture, Fisheries and Forestry, 2000, pp2 and 14; see Australian National Auditing Office [ANAO], 2001). Three of the most significant weaknesses identified were that government investment tended to be piecemeal, that the programmes lacked adequate performance indicators and that government had failed to be sufficiently strategic in targeting national and state natural resource problems (Council of Australian Governments [COAG], 2000b, p6; Natural Resource Management Standing Committee [NRMSC], 2003, p3; Paton et al, 2004, p259; Head, 2005a, p143). In response, the federal government began contemplating how to develop a more strategic approach to resource management and began moving towards a system of regionally focused environmental governance (Natural Resource Management Taskforce [NRMTF], 1999, pp1, 29 and 39–43).

The first step in this shift to a regional system was the announcement in 2000 of a new programme, the National Action Plan for Salinity and Water Quality (NAP) (COAG, 2000b). The programme involved a federal and state commitment of A$1.4 billion (approximately US$1.42 billion) for seven years – A$700 million (approximately US$709 million) from the states and A$700 million from the Commonwealth. Its focus was on achieving 'place-based', regional natural resource management solutions that delivered on nationally agreed goals, namely preventing, stabilizing and reversing salinity; and improving water quality for human use and the environment (Intergovernmental Agreement, 2001, cl 5). The programme was managed by the Commonwealth and the states through bilateral agreements. It was focused on 21 'priority regions' across Australia.

Investment was delivered into each priority region via a community/stakeholder-based regional body (including local land managers, local communities, NGOs and other ground-level stakeholders) to manage and protect the region's natural resources (Intergovernmental Agreement, 2001, cl 13 and 14; Head and Ryan, 2004; see Intergovernmental Agreement, 2001, cl 16). Regional bodies were expected to develop a regional plan in consultation with the regional community that identified regional priorities and regional targets that accord with nationally determined 'matters' (e.g., soil condition) (Natural Resource Management Ministerial Council [NRMMC], 2002a, ss 4–11) and that contribute to national identified outcomes (e.g., the impact of salinity on land and water resources is minimized, avoided or reduced) (NRMMC, 2002a, ss 4–11 and Table 1).

Regional plans and a supporting 'regional investment strategy' identify actions to deliver on these targets. The state and federal government invested in these actions and projects, which were to be carried out by the regional body itself or by other sub-regional catchment management groups, farmers, science bodies or other stakeholders.

As the roll out of NAP commenced, the Commonwealth government announced in its May 2001 budget that it would invest a further A$1.5 billion (approximately US$1.52 billion) in a revised version of the NHT programme for a further five years. This 'second phase', NHT 2, provided a strategic shift in delivery (NHT, 2002). The focus and approach of NHT 2 was threefold: (i) investment relating to national priorities; (ii) investment across 56 regions – as with NAP these were to rely on regional bodies and regional plans; and (iii) investments at the local level through the Australian Government Envirofund (see www.nht.gov.au). Our work focused on the regional component.

This component followed the format of NAP and created multi-stakeholder regional bodies across Australia. State and territory governments agreed to match, either directly or in kind, the Commonwealth's investment. Regional bodies were required to develop a plan to guide this investment and deliver regional outcomes that contributed to national goals relating to biodiversity conservation, sustainable use of natural resources, and community capacity-building and institutional change.

NHT 2 and NAP were subsequently aligned and jointly delivered their funding streams through regional bodies (NHT, 2002, cl 3). Additional funding has since been made available by governments – extending both programmes into 2008 (Moore, 2005; Farrelly, 2005). With a change in federal political parties in 2007, NAP and NHT have since been replaced by the broadly similar Caring for Our Country Programme, however our empirical focus in this book remains on the joint NHT 2 and NAP approach to RNRM (not least because there was substantially more experience with this approach in practice) (NRMMC, 2006; Australian Government, 2010).

Like the other programmes we have reviewed, RNRM shares a family resemblance to NEG initiatives internationally (Head, 2005a, p139; Lawrence, 2005), including collaborative regional ecosystem efforts in Chesapeake Bay, San Francisco Bay Delta, and the multiparty, regional landscape-scale Habitat Conservation Plans (HCPs) (what Karkkainen classifies as 'Type II HCPs') under the *Endangered Species Act of 1973* in the USA (Karkkainen, 2003b, pp211–212). While all share a broadly similar collaborative and regional ecosystem-focused approach, there are also some differences. As we saw above, RNRM primarily relies on dedicated government investment to provide incentives and support to underpin the formation of collaborative groups, planning and implementation. In contrast, HCP's overall approach to regional collaborative ecosystem governance depends less directly on government investment and more on legal incentives and mechanisms, particularly the operation of a 'penalty default' style rule (a type of rule that imposes harsh outcomes to create incentives for parties to bargain around the rule by undertaking a self-initiated alternative deemed a satisfactory substitute). This approach encourages and compels landowners, local governments and others to collaborate and engage in landscape-scale ecosystem planning (Ayres and Gertner, 1989; Thomas, 2003, pp145–150; Karkkainen, 2003b, pp213–214; Karkkainen, 2006b, p297).

RNRM is also distinct from the Bay Delta and Chesapeake Bay experiments. Both these experiments emerged in response to limitations of traditional approaches, citizen movements that demanded improvements in the Bays and longstanding conflicts between key stakeholders. They have since developed their own unique and lengthy history, which has involved a great deal of institutional innovation and evolution to address the problems plaguing their regional ecosystems (Freeman and Farber, 2005, pp854–857; Karkkainen, 2004b, pp81–82). In contrast, RNRM stands as a far more structured and ambitious attempt to roll out a government-designed regional ecosystem programme across an entire country.

A final comparison can also be made between the approach of RNRM and NEG experiments, such as the Open Method of Coordination in Europe (OMC), with both seeking to 'combine the advantages of decentralized local experimentation with those of centralized coordination' (Sabel and Zeitlin, 2008, pp271–327). In the case of RNRM, its decentralized regional approach seeks to grapple with the fact that regional ecosystems are diverse, dynamic, contextual, and interconnected with human systems and stakeholders (whose capacity and resources to manage them are likely to vary between areas/ecosystems). By giving regional bodies the freedom to identify issues and develop management responses that reflect their aspirations, the RNRM programme aims to ensure that the different social, economic and environmental dimensions of regions are fully considered and the programme is accordingly adapted to respond to their specific circumstances (Bilateral NHT, 2004, Attachment E, p57). At the same time, RNRM seeks to take advantage of centralized government coordination and its ability to ensure that common national goals are achieved. It does this through the government framework of guiding national outcomes, matters for targets (and employing a range of performance monitoring and other controls, discussed below). As the guidelines note, regional planning is 'an effective way to engage all stakeholders and to build on activity at the property and local levels, while also complementing state and national activity' (Bilateral NHT, 2004, Attachment E, p57).

The OMC approach conducts a broadly similar process to RNRM but does so in the context of the European Union, where the pursuit of the Union's common objectives are achieved through a system that respects the diversity of member countries in implementation and standard setting. Notably, the OMC appears to employ slightly different forms of formal coordination than RNRM, including requiring countries to carry out benchmarking and multilateral surveillance (Porte, 2002; Trubek and Trubek, 2006/2007; Scott and Holder, 2006, p212).

While RNRM has several features that set it apart from other NEG initiatives, it also shares much with them (Frieder, 1997; Margerum, 2007). In particular it shares four key similarities: (i) *nested collaboration* between multiple public, private and non-government actors; (ii) *participation* of regional communities/non-government stakeholders and *deliberative* style decision-making; (iii) adaptive and systemic processes of *learning and adaptation*; and (iv) *'new' forms of accountability*. Our analysis of similarities and differences is based on our case study of a Queensland-based regional body.

As with many NEG experiments, including NEIP and EIP, the RNRM programme is premised on the assumption that a collaborative approach is better suited to governing complex, severe and increasingly urgent environmental problems than more traditional approaches (COAG, 2000b, pp3 and 5). Building on initiatives such as Landcare and Natural Heritage Trust, collaboration is regarded as offering an effective process for 'negotiating trade-offs, resolving conflict' at the regional level, as well as enhancing capacity to address natural resource problems by 'bringing together the efforts of individuals, communities and governments' (Bilateral Agreement NHT, 2004, Attachment E, pp57 and 73).

This objective of involving partnerships between individuals, community and governments was intended to give this programme a distinctive collaborative character. While EIP and NEIP involve a single collaborative group of public and private stakeholders, RNRM is designed as a nested arrangement, involving collaboration at several 'levels'.

At the national level, the overarching body is the Natural Resource Management Ministerial Council. This body is composed of Commonwealth and state ministers and oversees the development and implementation of national natural resource management programmes, including NAP and NHT 2 (see, generally, www.mincos.gov.au/about_nrmmc). Also at the national level, is the Natural Heritage Ministerial Board, comprising the Commonwealth Minister for the Environment and Heritage and the Commonwealth Minister for Agriculture, Fisheries and Forestry, who are responsible for administering the NHT funding account (*Natural Heritage Trust of Australia Act 1997* (Cth), s 40). At the Queensland state level, the key organization is the Joint Steering Committee (JSC), which is predominantly composed of multiple representatives from different Queensland and federal government agencies. This body has primary responsibility for overseeing implementation of regional and state arrangements in Queensland and is the main vehicle for supporting regional bodies, authorizing payments, bilateral decision-making and making recommendations to the Ministerial Board and state ministers regarding investment and planning approval (Bilateral Agreement NHT, 2004, ss 37–43; Bilateral Agreement NAP, 2001, s 22).

Below the JSC are four Regional Coordination Groups (RCGs) composed of senior management-level representatives from governmental agencies. These groups operate at the meso or regional level, having responsibility for one of four areas into which Queensland is divided. These bodies are designed to support regional-body operations, foster strong community–government partnerships, coordinate the whole of government processes and resolve policy inconsistencies at the regional level (see www.regionalnrm.qld.gov.au). Nested below the RCG are regional bodies and more localized stakeholders, such as local-level farmers, Landcare groups or other sub-regional collaborative bodies. There is no single form that a regional body must take, however, they are required to meet several criteria so as to be 'designated' as regional bodies – these include incorporation, community members must constitute a majority of the body, and appropriate stakeholders (such as indigenous groups and local government) must be included (Bilateral Agreement NHT, 2004, s 68(b); Bilateral Agreement NAP, 2001, s 7.1(b)).

The regional body, in consultation with the regional 'community', is responsible for developing a plan and an investment strategy. The former sets targets and actions to improve natural resources, while the latter provides a prospectus of government financial support required to support this agenda (Bilateral Agreement NHT, 2004, ss 87 and 93; Bilateral Agreement NAP, s 13.1). The RNRM programme imposes requirements for the regional body to develop a plan and a Regional Investment Strategy. The plan must:

- cover the full range of natural resource management (NRM) issues
- be underpinned by scientific analysis of natural resource conditions, problems and priorities
- have effective involvement of all key stakeholders in plan development and implementation
- focus on addressing the underlying causes rather than symptoms of problems
- include strategies to implement agreed NRM policies to protect the natural resource
- demonstrate consistency with other planning processes and legislative requirements applicable to the region
- set targets at the regional scale
- identify strategic, prioritized and achievable actions to address the range of NRM issues and achieve the regional targets, including an evaluation of the wider social, economic and environmental impacts of such actions, and of any actions needed to address such impacts
- provide for continuous development, monitoring, review and improvement of the plan. If the plan is accredited, a Regional Investment Strategy must also be developed by the Regional Body, in consultation with government, community and key stakeholders (Bilateral Agreement NHT, 2004, s 87, Attachment E, pp59–60).

Once approval is secured, government funding is provided and the work of the regional body then begins.

RNRM is emblematic of the 'Third Way' approach to environmental governance (Moore, 2005). This is clearly evident in the collaborative language used in launching this programme. John Howard, the Australian Prime Minister at the time, had this to say about the programme: '. . . the states and communities will develop plans to restore the natural environment in each area and then communities will be funded to do the work . . . importantly it seeks to marshal everybody in the community' (Howard, 2000).

This collaborative lexicon was similarly replicated in national guidelines and in the Bilateral Agreements between the Commonwealth and the Queensland government that set up this programme in this state (Bilateral Agreement NHT, 2004, ss 1 and 13, Attachment E, pp57 and 62):

> The active involvement and participation of rural and regional communities is the cornerstone of this Plan . . . we seek to enable communities to take responsibility for planning and implementing natural resource management strategies, in partnership with all levels of government, that meet their priorities for sustainable development and ongoing viability.
>
> (Bilateral Agreement NAP, 2001, p2)

By fulfilling these participatory and deliberative aspirations, RNRM, like the NEIP programme, was designed to connect residents, farmers and other stakeholders with regional resources to ultimately assist regional communities to 'become self sufficient in managing their natural resources in the longer term' (Bilateral Agreement NAP, 2001, p57; Cannon, 2000, pp421–422).

A further feature of NEG embraced by RNRM is learning and adaptation. Like most NEG experiments focused on managing ecosystems, RNRM was specifically designed to follow an adaptive management approach to implementation (Karkkainen, 2005, pp70–72). Indeed, the Queensland Bilateral Agreements (Bilateral Agreement NHT, 2004, ss 106 and 137(e); Bilateral Agreement NAP, 2001, s 30, Attachment 3, p38), specifically refer to 'adaptive management' (NRMTF, 1999, p13) and define it as a process that enables '. . . lessons learned to be realized . . . and to make necessary adjustments in response . . . utilis[ing] monitoring and evaluation activities to form a feedback loop in order to make necessary adjustments' (Bilateral Agreement NHT, 2004, Attachments C and K, cl 1, p118).

This is also evident in the guidelines, which state that:

> . . . there will need to be regular reviews of targets to implement an adaptive management approach. Reviews will also enable targets to take account of improving information and scientific understanding about trends in resource condition and about ecosystem function.
>
> (Bilateral Agreement NHT, 2004, Attachment H, p82)

Nationally the RNRM is designed to pursue an adaptive process across the programme as a whole (Commonwealth and Queensland, 2004a, s 7.3; Bilateral Agreement NHT, 2004, Attachment K, p108). Regional monitoring data is to be aggregated 'on broader scales to describe the progress being made on NRM issues throughout the country' (NRMSC, 2003, p7; Bilateral Agreement NHT, 2004, Attachment K, p108). This data is intended to contribute to periodic reviews and evaluations at key decision points throughout the life of the programme. These evaluations are intended to assess the appropriateness, effectiveness and efficiency of the programme in the achievement of its objectives and intended outcomes at all levels (Bilateral Agreement NHT, 2004, Attachment K, p108). Regional bodies are subsequently required to respond to and implement the findings of the evaluation (Bilateral Agreement NHT, 2004, pp68–69; Commonwealth and Queensland, 2004a, s 8.2.6).

These periodic evaluations are designed to be used to identify best practice across regional bodies. Further, regional body monitoring and reporting is intended to provide higher governmental levels with data on regional body performance (Bilateral Agreement NHT, 2004, pp145–151). While not stated in the guidelines, this information may be used to assist regional bodies to relate and coordinate activities across the region (Cohen and Sabel, 1997, p335).

Not surprisingly, given the billions of Australian dollars invested in RNRM, accountability was of particular concern to the architects of the programme (NRMMC, 2002b). The RNRM architecture seeks to achieve this through various 'new' mechanisms and forms of accountability, including an embryonic form of 'destabilization right' (see below) and a performance-based regime, which seeks to replace traditional accountability notions with an understanding of accountability that accords more with adaptive management. RNRM is designed to utilize collaborators' capacities to deliver democratic accountability, as well as to fulfil self-monitoring and reporting tasks. Compared to the other two programmes, RNRM places far heavier reliance on delivering accountability through hierarchical, bureaucratic monitoring requirements and fixed parameters of the programme via government frameworks (NRMMC, 2002b; NRMMC, 2002a) and monitoring and reporting strategies (Commonwealth and Queensland, 2004a; Bilateral Agreement NHT, 2004, Bilateral Agreement NAP, 2001).

Commencing at the regional level, and working our way up the nested structure, RNRM is designed to utilize the skills and capacities of regional bodies to contribute to programme accountability. This includes requiring regional bodies to conduct extensive monitoring, evaluation and reporting to government on progress against management action targets (below) (Bilateral Agreement NHT, 2004, s 94; Bilateral Agreement NAP 2001, ss 14 and 30.3), outputs, finances (Commonwealth and Queensland, 2004a, ss 6.2.1–6.2.3) and changes in resource conditions (the latter in conjunction with the state government who contributes to monitoring) (Bilateral Agreement NAP, 2001, s 24; Bilateral Agreement NHT, 2004). Regional bodies are required to have a communications strategy that will contribute to transparency (Bilateral Agreement NHT, 2004, pp62–63). Mutual accountability between different regional body stakeholders (who must balance production and conservation interests) is also intended as an important ongoing check against performance and the application of government investment, although the guidelines do not explicitly raise this role (Commonwealth and Queensland, 2004a, ss 5.2–5.2.3 and 7.1).

At national- and state-government levels there are multiple accountability responsibilities. For example, there are a variety of controls on how government investment and accounts are to be managed (*Natural Heritage Trust of Australia Act 1997* (Cth), s 19; Bilateral Agreement NHT, 2004, s 6, Attachment J), as well as multiple reporting requirements between the different state and national bodies, leading back to ministers and the Ministerial Council (Bilateral Agreement NHT, 2004, ss 153 and 154, Attachment J, s 8.1; *Natural Heritage Trust of Australia Act 1997* (Cth), ss 41 and 43).

In terms of ensuring accountability for performance of the programme, RNRM follows similar designs to other performance-based NEG approaches, but establishes more detailed controls over the type of targets that can be set and the outcomes upon which they are to deliver. Targets must be consistent with other planning processes and legislative requirements and meet overarching objectives and boundaries for targets (Bilateral Agreement NHT, 2004, Attachment E, p64).

This involves requiring regional bodies to set relevant regional objectives against a minimum set of matters (such as land salinity and nutrients in aquatic environments) that contribute to established national outcomes (to do with such matters as soil and water quality, biodiversity and the condition of ecosystems). When setting targets, regional bodies are required to formulate three different types: aspirational, resource condition and management action. These broad requirements are intended to ensure that the targets and subsequent actions taken by regional bodies will contribute to outcomes relevant to the nation. Regional bodies are to be held accountable for achieving their targets.

The RNRM has also been designed to use various forms of 'non traditional' mechanisms to ensure accountability. These include contractual-based 'partnership agreements' between the state government and regional collaborative bodies, which spell out expected outcome and performance milestones and other accountability responsibilities and expectations of regional bodies (Bilateral Agreement NHT, 2004, ss 71 and 94, Attachment J, s 8.5; Bilateral Agreement NAP, 2001, ss 8.1 and 14.1).

The RNRM programme has been designed to give the JSC a role that resonates with the democratic experimentalist concept of an administrative 'destabilization right' – a right to intervene and destabilize collaborative efforts that provide evidence of chronic underperformance and/or procedural defects. This is intended to create an opening for a fresh start under new arrangements that are prescribed in detail from above, but are fashioned by stakeholders in response to a critique by an oversight agency (Karkkainen, 2006b, pp318–320).

This nascent 'destabilization right' – albeit within what would likely be considered a more prescriptive and government dominated regime than envisioned by a democratic experimentalist such as Karkkainen (2006b, p317) – gives the JSC, on evidence of underperformance or financial impropriety (gained through regional body monitoring and reporting), the intervening power to:

- stop funding the regional body and conduct an evaluation (Commonwealth and Queensland, 2004a, s 7; Bilateral Agreement NHT, 2004, s 137; Bilateral Agreement NAP, 2001, s 30)
- critique accountability procedures, skills capacities of representatives (Bilateral Agreement NHT, 2004, ss 67, 68 and 71, Attachment D, p56; Bilateral Agreement NAP, 2001, s 7.1(b)) or the arrangements of regional body membership
- leave the details of the response to the regional body stakeholders, under ongoing monitoring from JSC (Bilateral Agreement NHT, 2004, ss 67, 68 and 71, Attachment D, p56; Karkkainen, 2006b, p317).

In summary, RNRM offers an example of NEG that departs significantly from often ineffective traditional regulatory approaches. It also seeks to rectify weaknesses in some not so traditional resource management approaches (such as NHT 1) so as to offer a more strategic, innovative and wide-scale programme that balances a decentralized and centralized approach with the aim of addressing some of the most intractable environmental and natural resource problems.

BOX 2.1 NEW ZEALAND DEMONSTRATION CASES: LIVING STREAMS PROGRAMME; COLLABORATIVE CATCHMENT MANAGEMENT PROGRAMME; AND CANTERBURY WATER MANAGEMENT STRATEGY

Our demonstration studies involve three programmes from the Canterbury region of New Zealand that were designed by its elected regional council, known as Environment Canterbury (ECan). This council has responsibility under legislation (*Resource Management Act 1991* (NZ), s 30) for the control and management of natural and physical resources in their region. Although the council's powers are predominantly command and control based, they have been developing a nested system of governance employing a wider spectrum of governance tools, including NEG. Their new governance approach was stimulated by recent legislation that requires regional councils to achieve sustainable development (as defined by community outcomes) via government, industry and community collaboration (*Local Government Act 2002* (NZ), ss 10, 14, 77–81 and 91; Palmer, 2004, pp752–856).

As explained by the council's then chief executive, these new requirements have contributed to the council developing a model of 'collaborative community engagement', designed to reflect common NEG principles including 'decentralisation', 'participatory processes' and 'mutual learning and decision making' (Jenkins, 2008). From around the year 2000 onward, this NEG model has been applied at a number of geographic levels.

At the most acutely local subcatchment level is the Living Streams Programme. This governance initiative has been designed to maintain and

continued . . .

BOX 2.1 *. . . continued*

improve the health of small waterways by addressing diffuse source rural pollution. To achieve this aim, the Living Streams Programme develops 'working partnerships' between local farmers, the regional council and local communities who together plan and implement actions to improve the condition of the stream and its riparian margins (ECan, 2009b, p2).

At the larger catchment scale is the Collaborative Catchment Management Programme. This programme involves the regional council developing non-statutory catchment management plans in partnership with government agencies and voluntary catchment-based community groups. This collaborative approach aims to address specific issues, such as the diffuse pollution of urban estuaries, rural lakes and water quality downstream of dams (Jenkins, 2007a, p3; Jenkins, 2009).

The final programme we examine operates at a much larger regional ecosystem scale. This programme, known as the Canterbury Water Management Strategy, was at the time of research a 'once-off' regional collaboration involving a number of work streams, including water quality and quantity. In the absence of a region-wide strategic planning framework, one key aim was to develop an effective water policy by harnessing the knowledge of the regional community, while also fostering agreement among them to reduce conflict and thus enhance the chances of successful implementation. Designed by ECan in partnership with other local councils in the region, the strategy involved four stages. Stages 1 and 2 were technical studies primarily focused on water availability. Stages 3 and 4 involved other technical investigations and progressively introduced multi-stakeholder engagement, public consultation and a new regional collaborative Steering Group that contained representatives of local, regional and central governments and community interests. Utilizing information generated throughout the four stages, this group was to develop and recommend a water management strategy to ECan and the local councils, who were then responsible for organizing its implementation (Canterbury Mayoral Forum, 2009, pp18–19; Jenkins et al, 2010).

Having explicated the specific goals of the three programmes with respect to each of the defining features of 'good' NEG, we now explore the extent to which the programmes realize their design goals of *collaboration*, *participation and deliberation*, *learning and adaptation*, and *new forms of accountability*. Our principal focus in doing so will be an investigation of the institutional arrangements of each programme in order to identify the conditions and mechanisms that may have an impact on the achievement of these goals in practice.

3

COLLABORATION

Introduction

Under what conditions can good NEG be achieved? This is the question that has guided us as we reviewed the findings of scholars on collaborative governance and engaged with the analysis of the programmes that are our own empirical focus. In this chapter we advance this analysis by turning from programme intentions to programme practice and to examining the first of the defining features of NEG, namely, collaboration.

The primary objective of many NEG processes is to form a multi-stakeholder collaborative body that develops a plan to guide policy implementation. Realizing this objective is no small undertaking, given familiar problems of collective action and free riding (whereby individuals attempt to benefit from the public good collaboration provides without contributing to its provision) (Olson, 1965; Hardin, 1968, p1244). Yet, despite the magnitude of the various cooperation dilemmas (Olson, 1965) confronting would-be collaborators, cooperation has become increasingly common (Raymond, 2006, p37). The question that will concern us here is: *under what conditions is cooperation possible* (Ostrom, 1990; Raymond, 2006, p37)?

Unfortunately, though we are hardly the first to raise this question, relatively little empirical exploration has been undertaken to answer it (Karkkainen, 2002/2003, pp225–238; Orts and Coglianese, 2007, pp302–304). The research that has emerged so far tends to be limited in its generalizability, not least because it focuses largely on watershed management partnerships (for example, Sabatier et al, 2005a), and/or regional natural resource management (NRM) approaches (e.g., Habitat Conservation Plans, the Chesapeake Bay Program and CALFED Bay-Delta Program) (for example, Wondolleck and Yaffee, 2000; Koontz et al, 2004; Heikkila and Gerlak, 2005), as opposed to the many other types of NEG institutions, such as pollution control or diffuse urban issues. Crucial unresolved questions include:

- What institutional design conditions best overcome transaction costs (Wilson and Weltman, 1999, p14; Coglianese, 2001, pp106 and 110; Gaines, 2002/2003, p17; Karkkainen, 2004b, p91; Margerum, 2007, pp137 and 140; Menkel-Meadow, 2008, pp847–850; Solomon, 2008, p833; Floress et al, 2009, pp1352–1353; Robinson et al, 2009, pp245)?
- What is the role and importance of trust in achieving successful collaboration (Gaines, 2002/2003, p17; Raymond, 2006, p37)?
- What is the nature and impact of consensus 'decision-rules' common to collaboration (Coglianese, 2001; Karkkainen, 2002/2003, p240, fn 116; Karkkainen, 2004b, p91)?

We will engage in each of these questions in our empirical enquiry below. As we proceed, we remain mindful of the need to distinguish between aspirations for collaboration and the mechanisms designed to achieve it and to explain the sometimes substantial gap between aspirations and achievements.

Our focus will be on the institutional design specific to each programme and the ways in which this design was translated into action. There is inevitably a blurred boundary between collaboration and the participatory and deliberative aspirations of NEG. In negotiating this boundary we have defined collaboration as requiring two or more stakeholders to pool knowledge, understanding and/or resources (e.g., information, money, labour, etc.) and to address problems they find difficult to resolve alone (Gray, 1985, pp912; Gray, 1989, p10). This means that we will not examine representativeness and power differentials (Head, 2005a, p138) until Chapter 4.

Fostering Collaboration: The Design of Programmes

In life there are few guarantees that our plans will be realized. So it is too with collaboration (Heikkila and Gerlak, 2005, pp583–584). Free riding, fear of future defection and high transaction costs can all undermine collaboration (Heikkila and Gerlak, 2005, pp583–584; Raymond, 2006, p39; Margeum, 2007, p137). Each of our programmes confronted these difficulties in different guises. Nevertheless, while potentially fatal, these challenges were often overcome or at the very least, mitigated (Axelrod, 1984; Libecap, 1989).

Designers and programme implementers, aware of these potholes on the road to collaboration, sought to develop mechanisms that would avoid or minimize them (Wilson and Weltman, 1999, p14; Dana, 2000, p54; Coglianese, 2001, pp106 and 110; Gaines, 2002/2003, p17; Karkkainen, 2002/2003, p229; Karkkainen, 2003b, p966; Karkkainen, 2004b, p91; Margerum, 2007, pp135 and 137).

Mechanisms 1 and 2 – funding and incentives

A central concern of our programmes was to design relevant incentives to bring parties to the table. The design of RNRM, for example, offers access to significant pots of government funding, which may act as an important inducement for interested actors to collaborate on regional boards and through this mechanism advance their natural resource management initiatives (*Environment Protection Act 1970* (Vic), s 26B(2)(c)). Other programme incentives included reputation benefits and less prescriptive regulatory requirements (e.g., reduced licence fees) for leading performers in the EIP's AL approach (VEPA, 2002a, p1).

Negative incentives – to increase transaction costs for not collaborating – were also invoked. For example, the EIP encouraged the use of community pressure to bring industries to the table to engage in collaborative arrangements (Gunningham and Sinclair, 2002, p163; Karkkainen, 2003b, pp989–990; Karkkainen, 2006b, p296). These pressures included legal objections by communities to development applications and the use of the media to shame industries and to challenge their 'social licence' (Gunningham et al, 2003). In addition, the VEPA was able to invoke the threat of more stringent and costly licence conditions, audits, and prosecution (Environment Protection Act, 1970, s31C; Gunningham and Sinclair, 2002, p162).

NEIP, however, in contrast to the EIP and RNRM, did not provide either form of incentive. It was neither directly underpinned by regulatory rules that could be used as a credible threat to induce cooperation from reluctant parties, nor did the VEPA offer any significant inducement to NEIP partners to encourage volunteers to collaborate (VEPA, 2002d, pp8–9).

Beyond incentives, all three programmes offered relief from transaction costs (Interview 237, VEPA). For example, under EIP, VEPA provided information about regulatory standards and acted as a broker between industry and community. The industry partner, in turn, was often persuaded to offer in-kind support to the community (VEPA, 2002a, p10; VEPA, 2004a, pp1, 3 and 5), such as providing meeting rooms, minute taking and drafting the EIP plan (VEPA, 2001a, p5).

Both the NEIP and RNRM programmes were designed to provide some government support to volunteer collaborators (for example, see John and Mlay, 1999, pp362–363; John, 2004, pp230–242; Freeman and Farber, 2005, p890), to assist them in meeting the costs of their consultative obligations (Bilateral Agreement NHT, 2004, ss 80–93; Bilateral Agreement NAP, 2001, s 12.7). NEIP's financial and in-kind support included small (A$10,000 to A$30,000, which, at the time of writing was approximately US$10,100 and US$30,400, respectively), short-term seed funding for administration and organizational tasks. NEIP was also designed to harness government agencies as 'sponsors' to assist with operational costs (VEPA, 2002d, pp1–5 and 7–10; John, 2004, pp239 and 241–242). The support provided for in the RNRM programme included:

1 a rebate (A$1000 to A$5000 per annum – approximately US$1012 and US$5060 respectively) for regional body collaborators (covering costs, such as time and travel)
2 'foundational' and 'priority' funding to support the process of establishing regional bodies, and consultation to involve stakeholders in plan development

and drafting plans (Commonwealth and Queensland Interim Agreement, 2003, s 51; Bilateral Agreement NHT, 2004, s 95; Bilateral Agreement NAP, 2001, ss 9 and 24; Farrelly, 2005, p396)

3 in-kind support from government officers (Bilateral Agreement NHT, 2004, ss 40–42, 83 and 101).

Such support was administered through RNRM's nested model of collaboration, which itself served to reduce transaction costs by creating opportunities for interaction that might otherwise have required considerable investment of time and resources (Margerum, 2007, p144). For example, a structured collaborative forum at the state level often reduced the time spent by agencies consulting each other. Similarly, local-level groups gained from nested arrangements because they interacted within a single regional forum (Margerum, 2007, pp144–146).

At the same time however, the nested model, with its many levels, necessarily involved collaboration costs (Margerum, 2007, pp144–146). In particular, a major challenge for nested models was to achieve collaboration between different agencies and governments (Ewing, 2003, p406; Paton et al, 2004, p263; Farrelly, 2005, p400; Freeman and Farber, 2005, pp900–901; Head, 2005a, p145; Margerum, 2007, pp144–146).

Mechanism 3 – building trust

The benefits of building trust to solve collective action problems is asserted in the social capital, alternative dispute resolution and NEG literatures (for example, see: Olson, 1965, pp44 and 49–50; Freeman, 1997, p924; Fung and Wright, 2003b, p15; Kahan, 2003, pp71 and 88–89; John, 2004, pp232 and 235; Head, 2005b, p57; Sabatier et al, 2005b, pp186 and 189; Raymond, 2006, p42). In our analysis, we define 'trust' as that which exists when people are confident that others will keep their promises, treat each other fairly and show concern for the welfare of others (Sabatier et al, 2005b, p187; Thomson and Perry, 2006, p28). Trust, it is argued, promotes greater cooperation, and an increased likelihood of agreement and implementation by partners (Freeman and Farber, 2005, p801).

Each of our programmes assumed that mistrust between stakeholders was likely to undermine collaboration. All were designed to involve a range of negotiation, mediation and facilitation processes to build trust. The broad intention appears to be that such processes, and the opportunities they afford for assisting parties to show respect, contribute their fair share to discussion and iteratively demonstrate reciprocity (Kahan, 2003, pp88–89; Raymond, 2006, p42), will achieve 'better relationships . . . and social networks' (VEPA, 2002d, pp3–6) and ultimately build trust and resolve conflict among stakeholders in the development of their plans, or other outputs (COAG, 2000a, p10; VEPA, 2001a, pp1–5; VEPA, 2002a, pp1–2 and 7; VEPA, 2004a, pp1–6; Bilateral Agreement NHT, 2004, s 121, Attachment E, p57; Commonwealth and Queensland, 2004a, pp4–5).

Mechanism 4 – a consensus approach

Consensual decision-making is regarded by many as likely to enhance collaboration. Consensus, it is argued, is associated with shared understandings about the causes and consequences of environmental issues and increases the likelihood of effective implementation and compliance (Coglianese, 2001, pp96, 102 and 106; Karkkainen, 2004b, p91; Lubell, 2004, p551; Lubell et al, 2005, p275; Karkkainen, 2006a, pp228–229).

Both the EIP's and NEIP's guidelines stated that decision-making should 'be by consensus' (VEPA, 2002d, p5; VEPA, 2004a, pp1–6). While RNRM did not directly speak of 'consensus' its design refers to 'close partnerships and cooperation' (NRMTF, 1999, pp13 and 27).

There are a variety of different decision rules that can be used to encourage consensus – for example, unanimity and majority voting (O'Leary et al, 2004, pp330–335). None of our programmes, however, defined precise decision rules for achieving consensus, preferring to leave these processes to parties, their negotiator and mediators (Innes, 2004, p7, fn 4). Nonetheless, all our programmes were designed to encourage what might be thought of as a cooperative approach that avoided veto options for parties other than government agencies – much in the manner of what Karkkainen terms a 'mixed' consensus (Karkkainen, 2002/2003, p240). VEPA in EIP and NEIP and the Joint Steering Committee (JSC) in RNRM could veto plans, proposals and investment strategies (VEPA, 2002a, pp2, 7 and 11; VEPA, 2002d; *Environment Protection Act 1970* (Vic), ss 19AH, 19AI(1) and 19AI(3)(B); Bilateral Agreement NHT, 2004, ss 80–84). In the remainder of this chapter we define consensus in the above terms rather than in a stricter sense implying total agreement.

Just what this cooperative approach meant in practice is a question to which we now turn, by examining each of the three programmes.

Environment Improvement Plans – Collaborating without Trust and with Little Cause

Within EIP, the path to collaboration tended to follow two distinct routes (Raymond, 2006, pp46 and 47). To make clear what these routes involved we distinguish between two types of business enterprises: those who were environmental 'leaders', and all others – that is, 'good', but not excellent, and 'poor' environmental performers.

The first route involved only the latter group. The catalyst to collaboration with regard to cases involving non-leaders was the occurrence of severe environmental problems (or at least problems perceived to be severe by residents whose amenity and/or health were affected). All industrial enterprises, except environmental leaders, were vulnerable to severe environmental problems (though, unsurprisingly, good performers were less likely to encounter them than poor performers). Typically such problems involved severe noise, persistent strong odour, or other pollution impacts on local residents. Residents' initial attempts to approach industry had often stonewalled, while their complaints to VEPA and/or local government typically engendered only cumbersome, slow and/or ineffective responses. Negative incentives were used with considerable success to induce such enterprises to collaborate.

'Good' industries tended to be particularly sensitive to their public image and brand name. Unsurprisingly, when frustrated local stakeholders began opposing industry expansion (Interview 15/62, Local Resident) and drumming up bad publicity in the local media (Interview 121, VEPA), they saw this assault on their social, economic and/or regulatory viability as an unacceptable cost and looked for ways to bring people together to identify and solve the problem. As one VEPA respondent put it: '. . . bad publicity is the best thing. Not a prosecution. Bad publicity is the turning point for a lot of these industry changes' (Interview 121, VEPA).

While similar community pressure emerged in cases involving poor performers, this was typically not enough to tip the cost-benefit equation for these less reputation conscious industries. In response, VEPA ratcheted up regulatory threats, warning industries that harsher licence conditions, compulsory EIPs, and audits and prosecutions, would be imposed if a change was not forthcoming (Interview 181, VEPA; Interview 161, Industry). These threats were sufficient to motivate most poor performers to collaborate (Gunningham and Sinclair, 2002, ch 8). As one VEPA officer expressed it: 'there is still that arm-twisting in the background. The classic one would be: "Right, if you don't agree with this we'll just put it in your licence". So there's the easy way or the hard way' (Interview 121, VEPA). The utility of such arm-twisting as a means to persuade collaboration-averse stakeholders to engage in new governance was confirmed in our New Zealand demonstration programme known as the Living Streams Programme (LSP) (see Box 3.1).

Even so, our findings in the EIP programme also suggest that the shadow of the law will not always be sufficiently threatening or credible to motivate *all* stakeholders to commit to new governance. Indeed, arm-twisting was insufficient in a few cases where industry management and owners were largely antagonistic to good environmental practice (Gunningham and Sinclair, 2002, p162). In such cases the VEPA had to break out the handcuffs to force industry to collaborate via court orders or by inserting EIP conditions into licences (Interview 184, Industry). Once an industry was brought to the table using negative incentives (or the direct force of law), there was little trouble generating interest from other local stakeholders and engaging with a diverse mix of interests.

Route two involved leading environmental performers exclusively (see Table 3.1 below for an illustration). The experience of collaboration here was in stark contrast to that under route one, which had involved pressure from and the active engagement of the local community, coupled with VEPA pressure for business enterprises to come to the table. In contrast, environmental leaders were typically motivated to voluntarily initiate an EIP in order to secure an Accredited Licence (discussed in Chapter 2) and its reputation benefits (Interview 151, Industry). Given that leading enterprises, by definition, had exceptional environmental performance, they had only very minor or highly infrequent environmental impacts on the local area (Interview 15/62, Local Resident). Without any 'severe' problems, local stakeholders unsurprisingly identified few benefits in collaboration. In consequence: 'industry has major problems getting attendance at their committee meetings because they don't annoy anyone' (Interview 113, VEPA; Interview 151, Industry). For these reasons, route two, which we have termed 'collaboration with little cause', was far less successful in achieving collaboration than route one.

Under route two, environmental leaders and the VEPA had to invest considerable time and effort in persuading *any* civil society actors to come to the table (Interview 153, VEPA). This often involved VEPA drawing on its contacts with non-government actors in other EIP collaborations. Accordingly, even to the extent that they were successful in persuading some civil society actors to come to the table, these actors rarely had any involvement with the local area where the problem (such as it was) was situated. The best that could be said was that these actors were interested in the general environmental performance of industry and/or wanted to make a broader 'public contribution' (Interview 161, Industry).

With each set of cases having overcome the initial challenges in bringing stakeholders together (albeit with little success in leading industry cases) the next stage of the journey was rising to the challenge of developing a plan.

With few exceptions the EIP design adequately supported the costs of those involved in collaboration. It was indeed extremely rare for people to disengage during plan development due to excessive transactions costs. Further, the small size

BOX 3.1 NEW ZEALAND DEMONSTRATION CASE: LIVING STREAMS PROGRAMME (LSP)

This acutely local demonstration case aimed to maintain and improve the health of small waterways by addressing diffuse source rural pollution through 'working partnerships' of local farmers, the regional council and local communities (ECan, 2009a, p2).

To foster collaboration, the programme was designed to provide in-kind officer support to offset collaborative transaction costs. Like the Australian EIP programme, LSP was also designed to harness ECan's regulatory powers (e.g., inspect, control and enforce pollution of in-stream water quality) as an incentive to get stakeholders to participate (ECan, 2005; *Resource Management Act 1991* (NZ), s 30). While direct regulation remained prominent where practicable, persuading farmers to come to the collaborative table (albeit in 'the shadow of the law') offered ECan a less costly and conflict-ridden mechanism with which to achieve its environmental regulatory goals.

continued . . .

BOX 3.1 *. . . continued*

Our findings revealed that LSP was able to foster a very successful collaborative process. Government support and small affected populations of around a thousand people kept transaction costs down and ensured collaborative groups captured 'a cross section of who should be there' (Interview NZ332, Farmer). And having engaged all key stakeholders, an agreement on a plan of action was quickly reached. This collaborative achievement appeared to *fundamentally* depend on two conditions, namely, peer pressure available within the small communities, and regulatory pressure. In terms of the former, while the LSP had few troubles bringing concerned townspeople and altruistic farmers to the table to address 'dirty, very unappealing, foul smelling streams' (Interview NZ331, ECan), a key stumbling block had been engaging with the numerous, reluctant farming polluters. To ensure that *all* farmers agreed to cooperate, ECan sought to leverage potential pressure from incensed farm and community peers. With a small population it was a straightforward process to identify and shame the main polluters, using existing community networks (normally less than 20 farms, along a 15km long stream, within a 5000ha area). One government officer illustrated how this was achieved:

> . . . the farmers were pretty antagonistic for a while . . . and I said 'there's a lot of photos there that you probably wouldn't like shown at a public meeting' and they said, 'you show your photos to whoever you like!', but, then they rang back a fortnight later and said, 'look we've thought about it, we'd like to work with you' . . . the threat of peer pressure worked really well there.
>
> (Interview NZ331, ECan)

Peer pressure was not, however, an adequate technique for some of the more recalcitrant farmers. Accordingly, analogous to VEPA's strategy in the EIP programme, ECan routinely resorted to a second strategy, namely using direct or tacit threats of costly enforcement and penalties under the traditional regulatory framework to motivate farmer engagement. As one ECan respondent voiced it: 'I said, "okay you've got a choice, you can either work with me . . . or we'll send our enforcement people in and you'll be facing abatement notices or potential environment court fines. It's your choice"' (Interview NZ331, ECan). As our farming respondents summed up, this use of regulatory and peer pressure ultimately ensured that LSP: 'had 100 per cent buy-in . . . there's been no one sort of saying, "Oh, no, that's a load of bullshit, bugger off"' (Interview NZ322, Farmer).

TABLE 3.1 Three Examples of Typical EIP Cases – Good, Poor and Leading Performers

	Good Performer	*Poor Performer*	*Leading Performer*
Overview	• Good performing industries generally maintained better performance records under their VEPA licence (e.g., infrequent licence violations). • However, they had pollution impacts that were problematic for local resident and/or non-governmental groups. • These impacts were often within licence requirements or were so infrequent that VEPA did not see it as a worthwhile use of resources to take serious action to address the problem.	• Poor performing industries often had persistent regulatory breaches, had been fined (or even prosecuted) and were under close scrutiny by VEPA for their environmental performance. • The impacts on local residents were often serious or outright breaches of licence. • However, in these cases VEPA actions to address the problem were extremely slow, cumbersome and often resoundingly unsuccessful.	• Leading industries had a really strong focus on the environment and from the VEPA's perspective, these industries 'more or less looked after themselves' (Interview 153, VEPA). • They rarely had major impacts on the local area and there were no specific complaints lodged. • Their EIPs were commenced as a component of the 'accredited licensing scheme'.
Key Cause and Problem	• Sewage treatment process, waste gas burning, effluent discharged into ocean. • Odour impacts on residents, declining water quality and beach conditions, health risks to beach users, declining marine ecology.	• Rendering of meat products release extensive odour. • Odour impact on residents, greenhouse gas, waste water, water utilization.	• Air emissions and noise from foundry and vehicle assembly, vehicle painting. • Minor noise and odour impacts near immediate industry boundary, stormwater contamination, wastewater generation and water consumption.

Source: Based on analysis of interview data and documents.

of the areas (on average estimated to be a few square kilometres) kept travel costs down for residents. VEPA officers also provided useful assistance by encouraging communication between stakeholders (Interview 111, Industry; Interview 181, VEPA). In addition, the incentives that brought industry to the table were effectively harnessed to cover the principal collaborative costs:

> . . . the [V]EPA would say to [an industry], 'you need to get an independent person and you need to pay for it, you need to have an independent location for the meetings and you need to pay for it, and by the way if the meeting is on at 6 o'clock at night and people are coming straight from work maybe you should put a bit of supper on' . . . and they did.
>
> (Interview 182, Community)

This support proved vital during lengthy negotiations – it could take anywhere between six months and two years to agree on a plan.

How the development of the plan took place differed across sets of cases – again the distinction between environmental leaders and all others is an important one. With the latter group (which includes both good and poor environmental performers), the historically adversarial behaviour of parties meant there was typically a high degree of mistrust and animosity. Despite repeated meetings and negotiations, mistrust was rarely overcome. 'Shouting and screaming', 'a lot of anger' and accusations of 'lying' were common (Interview 112, Community). One respondent reported:

> I didn't believe them for years and years and years, every night, they were telling lies and some of them have admitted that they have told lies . . . they were long and tiring, difficult meetings that we all absolutely hated going to, for years really.
>
> (Interview 162, Community)

Local residents showed little trust in the VEPA or in local government, whom they believed had not 'represented them to the degree that they expected' (Interview 174, Industry). Similarly, business enterprises were wary of regulators (Interview 121, EPA). Enterprises tended to reveal only the bare minimum of information and were 'tight lipped' in response to a mistrusting community (Interview 111, Industry). As one respondent explained:

> . . . the residents argued over every step of the way . . . because the relationship was so poor that nobody trusted each other. They argued over every single word. They spent hundreds and hundreds of hours drafting this document.
>
> (Interview 184, Industry)

The failure to significantly improve trust and reciprocity augmented the transaction costs of negotiating, and lengthened the time it took to draft a plan

(Interview 173, Local Resident; Interview 121, Industry; Interview 161, Industry). However, this was not fatal to the process, as the high benefits to be gained by local stakeholders and the background pressure on industry were sufficient incentives to keep people at the table (Interview 184, Industry).

The mixed consensus decision-rule designed by EIP sometimes involved VEPA exercising its veto to ensure that minimum regulatory standards and processes were met, but generally this set of cases achieved 'substantial' agreement among most of its stakeholders, including VEPA (Interview 211, VEPA). Such 'substantial' agreement among stakeholders is common to many cooperative processes (Innes, 2004, fn 4). These parties may oppose a proposal but are nevertheless willing to 'step aside' because while a specific issue or agreement does not serve their interests, it does not entirely harm them either (Interview 141, Industry; Innes, 2004, fn 4). Stakeholders are often willing to forego immediate goals on the understanding that these will be addressed more fully over the long term (Interview 142, Industry). As one industry respondent explained: 'I think one of the most important things we had to do is make them realize you couldn't just do that overnight, it had to be a 5–6 year program to do it [over a number of EIP plans]' (Interview 131, Industry).

Further, the cooperative approach also appeared to reduce the chances of parties defecting or undermining a plan's implementation. For example, after reaching agreement, local stakeholders typically stopped complaining to VEPA and gave industry 'a moratorium on complaints' so that they could get on with plan implementation (Interview 173, Local Resident). As one respondent summed it up:

> It's helped them see the relative merits of all these things and prioritized it. I think it's one of the things with any EIP that is really good, coming to consensus around the priorities . . . we've got good acceptance and congruence, and I think that's important because if you've got that agreement you can move forward.
>
> (Interview 121, VEPA)

Another had this to say: 'I think it's pretty good – it's not efficient and it's not conflict free, but it's a good working group that has actually achieved a lot' (Interview 161, Industry).

In contrast to all of the above (and to the experience of good and poor enterprises), in cases involving environmental leaders, the negotiation process was smoother. This was so because the absence of any pressing environmental problem meant that the stakeholders had less pre-existing animosity toward each other and were able to quickly establish trust. During negotiations, acts of good faith (such as VEPA and industry openly sharing information with community groups) broke down barriers and built trust. As one respondent noted: '. . . they came with the mindset that perhaps we weren't as open but that broke down very quickly . . . It was putting everything on the table . . . Just [by] proving we were honest' (Interview 151, Industry). Honesty improved relationships, quickly built trust and enabled partners to work together in coordinated, timely and effective ways. As one respondent explained: 'Every member . . . is very supportive' (Interview 151, Industry). As a consequence, the parties in these cases were able to agree upon a plan months earlier than in the case of EIPs involving non-leaders.

The improved relationships also enabled these cases to achieve almost unanimous agreement on the plan by following decision rules of 'substantial consensus', underpinned by VEPA veto (Interview 151, Industry). While this rule appeared to have achieved greater agreement on the sort of minor local problems that leaders experienced (Interview 151, Industry), its overall utility in terms of contributing to the production of an effective plan appeared to be minimal (Interview 15/62, Local Resident). Indeed, the plans produced largely reiterated existing industry targets, projects and priorities for both local and broader issues – plans that the industries were already committed to delivering on under their pre-existing environmental management systems: '. . . we already had a lot of our projects documented and set up in a way that worked with our ISO system . . . [so] we already had the projects anyway' (Interview 151, Industry).

The fact that most plans involving environmental leaders did not go beyond 'business as usual' was attributable to the fact there were no severe environmental problems to be addressed (rather than implying a flaw in the cooperative approach per se). For the most part, there were simply not that many gains to be made: '. . . whenever we suggest anything they've either tried it and failed, but they'll try again, or they've taken it on board and they get it done straight away' (Interview, 15/62, Local Resident).

To summarize, the two distinct routes to collaboration that have been examined in this section reveal that collaboration is contextual in nature, with success depending on the circumstances in which the EIP institution is applied.

In cases of EIPs involving non-leaders, collective action barriers were largely overcome. Yet contrary to conventional wisdom (and much of the literature) this was achieved *without* building trust (Raymond, 2006). The key to achieving 'cooperation without trust' and overcoming collective action barriers (Raymond, 2006, pp40–41 and 54) was a combination of factors. These were: the presence of a severe problem to engender stakeholders to cooperate; 'negative' incentives (and even direct force of law) to compel industry to collaborate and make meaningful commitments; adequate in-kind support from VEPA officers and industry to reduce transaction costs; and consensus decision-rules that improved agreement on issues and contributed to increased likelihood of implementation.

When trust was easily built and evident, collaboration was certainly easier. Since environmental problems, when involving leading enterprises, often bordered on the trivial and certainly lacked severity, it is perhaps unsurprising that it proved very difficult to engage external stakeholders, particularly local communities. Outcomes that did not go beyond business as usual were the common result. Here we find collaboration 'with little cause' – the problems here were not severe enough to encourage much change.

NEIP: Flawed Design and Limited Success

In contrast to the EIP programme, NEIP addressed more complex second-generation problems across a larger area, and involved a greater number of stakeholders. For these reasons there have been fewer collaborations than under the EIP programme: only seven operational NEIP collaborations have arisen over its seven-year life, compared to 35 collaborations that were commenced over the EIP programme's first seven years of operation (see www.epa.vic.gov.au; Raymond, 2006, p45). However, the existence of these seven collaborations demonstrates that at least some stakeholders have begun to overcome the barriers to collective action to address neighbourhood environmental challenges. Our analysis of three of the most advanced NEIP collaborations (our cases) demonstrates that the path to collaboration again followed two distinct routes.

The success of the first and most common route involved a subgroup of stakeholders coming together to agree on a plan but being thwarted by a significant flaw within the NEIP design: an absence of incentives either to encourage and sustain other stakeholders to engage or to ensure meaningful commitments, particularly where those commitments would prove costly to deliver on. The Degraded Creek case and the Sustainable Township case (two formal 'pilots' of the NEIP programme), both described below, were examples of this first route.

The second route (illustrated by the Water Supply case) demonstrates the importance of context in collaboration outcomes. Here, a NEIP with the same design flaw as in the above two cases, nevertheless resulted in a successful collaboration. As we will see, this was achieved because of three conditions *external* to the NEIP institution – small population size, high and direct stakes for local actors and external funding.

In terms of the first route, the Degraded Creek case focused on an urban creek that had long been used as a drain and was contaminated by diffuse sources, in particular, pollution from multiple industries and small- and medium-size enterprises (SMEs). The Sustainable Township case focused on the even more complex problem of developing a 'sustainable town' in a diverse coastal environment threatened by a range of diffuse problems, including air pollution and habitat impacts from a local coal mine and power station, development pressure and household and business resource use.

In both cases, *to commence the collaborative process,* the local governments that had nominated their neighbourhoods as cases to VEPA took on the role of 'sponsors', and committed a small amount of resources to the collaborative endeavour. These sponsors saw the NEIP as 'a way forward' (Interview 213, Local Government) to resolve many of the above environmental issues and they received short-term 'seed' funding from the VEPA, and smaller contributions from other partners (Surf Coast Shire Council, 2004, p28; Maribyrnong City Council, 2004, p17). This funding (A$20,000 to A$30,000 in total – approximately US$20,200 and US$30,400 respectively) was used by sponsors to employ a coordinator for the two to three years that it took to develop a proposal and plan (Interview 211, VEPA). These

\coordinators were widely regarded as an effective and vital means of overcoming the transaction costs associated with bringing parties together, bargaining and keeping stakeholders connected in the relatively small local neighbourhoods (20km^2 or less): 'I think initially to get a project up and going and build momentum, you definitely need someone in a paid position . . . to build that initial enthusiasm, involvement, and commitment, get runs on the board' (Interview 221–1, Coordinator).

With these coordinators' support, local government and VEPA officers began engaging partners and seeking broader stakeholder engagement by consulting within the neighbourhood, and holding initial meetings, multiple public workshops and conducting surveys (Maribyrnong City Council, 2004, p16; Interview 222, Local Government). The pre-existing community concern about environmental problems ensured relatively high participation at these meetings: between 100 and 200 people from neighbourhood populations of approximately 10,000 in each case (see Surf Coast Shire Council, 2004, pp9 and 12; Gunningham et al, 2007). These meetings in turn led to significant stakeholder engagement – one to four industry collaborators, five to seven government collaborators, five to six non-government groups and two to 11 residents. However, the strikingly low number of polluting businesses that chose to participate is noteworthy, and an issue to which we will return.

Having engaged a number of diverse stakeholders, the next stage was to build trust among them, an enterprise that was led by the local government, the coordinators and VEPA. This they did by convening numerous multi-stakeholder negotiation and mediation forums over many months of planning and decision-making, ultimately to establish environmental targets, actions and a vision for the neighbourhood. While we examine the detail of these negotiation processes in Chapter 4, at a broad level, the face-to-face interactions, information-sharing and reasoned discussion among stakeholders reportedly led to a marked improvement in trust with 'none of this us and them thing' anymore (Interview 221–1, Community; Interview 213, Local Government). As our respondents explained, facilitating discussion among otherwise unacquainted community and government stakeholders 'managed to build those relationships . . . I think without that, you're always going to have that bit of cynicism and a bit of lack of trust' (Interview 221, Community). Others pointed to the fact that relationships and trust had substantially improved between businesses and local non-government groups because 'those conversations [were] open rather than the [local business] for example just being totally hostile to the [community group] and seeing them as just a bunch of greenies' (Interview 213, Local Government).

This trust was viewed as enabling participants to work together strategically in a more coordinated and effective way and to move beyond their previously fragmented responsibility and interests: '. . . it's making it a bit more effective and that's been a really good outcome, even identifying, well, hey, we're doing this. Let's join up together' (Interview 211, EPA).

While these are all positive achievements, there were significant limits to the success of the collaborations in terms of improved environmental outcomes.

Crucially, respondents drew attention to a lack of 'buy in' from key industry stakeholders (primarily polluting industries) who were the primary contributors to the local environmental problems.

This weakness was most dramatically illustrated in the Degraded Creek case, where over 200 industries and SMEs lined the polluted creek and were a major source of environmental degradation. The sponsor and VEPA tried to engage industry through workshops and sending out 400 letters to industry managers. However, only 15 industry members attended the workshops and not one response was received from the letters (Maribyrnong City Council, 2004, p17). The VEPA accordingly tried to use tacit regulatory pressure. However, a lack of staff resources and limited leverage over SMEs restricted such pressure to a few large, licensed industries. The result was that very few companies signed on to the plan: one business representative group and three industries. Our respondents were clear about the reason for this:

> I don't think the NEIP has the capacity to engage with industry. I think with industry, if they're abusing the creek, then they will choose not to be engaged . . . the only way they will become engaged is through regulation [that is through government pressure].
>
> (Interview 216, Industry/Business Association)

The absence of adequate incentives to persuade industry to participate was a serious flaw. Industries that had polluted the waterway for many years without penalty were more than happy with the status quo and the structure of the NEIP gave them no reason to change their behaviour. It also meant that those who did engage (such as larger enterprises with a reputation to protect but for whom pollution control nevertheless represented an unwanted expense) had little motivation to share information or make anything other than token commitment (Interview 212, Local Community; Karkkainen, 2006b, p296). Indeed, none of the four industry enterprises who did participate made any commitment to improve environmental performance (Gunningham and Sinclair, 2002, p150): '. . . they did attend some meetings but nothing's actually happened with them. They haven't formally committed to anything' (Interview 212, Local Community).

The conclusion of many of our respondents was that without increased industry participation *and commitment* there were substantial limits on what The Degraded Creek case could achieve in terms of improving the creek's water quality. In short, while the NEIP process brought about collaboration between *some* stakeholders, improved relationships between them and built trust, it generated little effective action because there was no incentive for other stakeholders (primarily those responsible for environmental degradation) to come to the table or to change their behaviour.

The incentive structure in the NEIP programme's design (or lack thereof) also produced difficulties for the Sustainable Township case. Although the sustainability agenda of this NEIP was wide in scope, threats to the local airshed and habitat were largely the result of the activities of one company (Surf Coast Shire Council, 2002, p1; Surf Coast Shire Council, 2004, p12). With only the one industry to contend with, the local government sponsor was able to successfully focus its efforts on persuading this industry to come to the table (Interview 223, Industry). However, again, respondents reported that, once at the table, the NEIP design did not provide the necessary tools to encourage positive action (Interview 223, Industry). Indeed, aside from helping with a workshop and participating in a town clean-up day, the industry had committed to few NEIP actions:

> I smile, I suppose, when you look at [Town] and you sort of say, 'okay, yeah, we want to be a sustainable, ecologically friendly town', and then you look out the back and you see this dirty rotten big mine . . . I don't think we'll have as much of a chance getting them to change their output. I think that's a bit beyond the NEIP.
>
> (Interview 221, Local Resident)

The lack of incentives built into the design of NEIP extended beyond the issue of industry partners and stakeholders to the incapacity to induce even other government agencies to participate in a meaningful way. In particular, there was a lack of dedicated funding to encourage and enable government parties to make commitments that went significantly beyond 'business as usual' (Interview 213, Local Government):

> . . . there's no central source of funding . . . that meant that they committed to a lot less than they would've committed to . . . that money wasn't there so they couldn't agree to anything where they didn't have it.
>
> (Interview 212, Environmental Group)

This failure to go beyond business as usual, that we noted earlier with some cases in the EIP programme, is a common criticism of many 'consensus-building' processes (Coglianese, 2001, pp107–110). However, with NEIP the problem appeared to be more the lack of incentives (a condition that is external to the consensus decision-rule) and less the collaborative approach per se.

Indeed, while commitments from government parties may not have gone far enough in the immediate term, the mixed consensus decision-rule used to agree on the plans typically emphasized 'substantial' consensus among stakeholders, which appeared to ensure that government agencies had at least accounted for and sought to meet other parties' interests over the longer term (i.e., over a number of plans). As one respondent pointed out, while budget limitations had prevented one agency from undertaking infrastructure works to restore the flow of the creek under the five-year NEIP plan, the agency and stakeholders were able to reach an agreement on long-term commitments to complete these works over a 30- to 40-year time frame. As the respondent put it 'we're prepared to be patient' (Interview 215, Local Government).

Broadly akin to the EIP programme, this consensus approach saw the VEPA influence, but not directly veto, decisions made by the group. Further, even though there was seldom unanimity among stakeholders (Interview 227, Local Resident), the cooperative approach did lead parties to set objectives, targets and actions that focused on important environmental issues, albeit often hampered by lack of industry involvement (Interview 223, Industry). The cooperative approach reportedly increased the likelihood of implementation (Interview 224, VEPA) and assisted parties to improve their understanding and agreements on the nature of environmental problems, allowing them to create a shared agenda. As one respondent put it: '. . . we're clearer on our own areas of direct responsibility and shared responsibility and we have an improved understanding of the broader issues and the greater challenges' (Interview 213, Local Government).

In short, the cooperative approach in the Degraded Creek and Sustainable Township cases offered a number of benefits for the success of the collaboration. However, as suggested above, the external design conditions, the existence of many small industries or one large one, who lacked incentives to participate or change their behaviour, undermined the chances of the plan delivering successful environmental improvements. However, this was not an inevitable outcome, as route two, encapsulated by the Water Supply case, reveals.

The Water Supply case commenced shortly after the Degraded Creek and Sustainable Township cases and was not considered a pilot case. It focused on a creek under threat from diffuse sources of pollution and was located in a rural community. The findings on the emergence of collaboration in this context corresponded closely with those of our other two cases on many issues, including the positive role of the local government sponsor, effective seed funding (A$20,000 – approximately US$20,200) (Towong Shire Council, 2006, pp37–38), cooperation-enhancing trust building (Interview 234, Local Government; Interview 232, Water Trust) and a similar cooperative decision-making approach (Interview 324, Local Government; Interview 235, VEPA). However, in contrast to the Degraded Creek and Sustainable Township cases, the Water Supply case was far more successful in engaging, and obtaining commitments from its 'problem' stakeholders as well as other parties in the collaboration. This was due primarily to three conditions.

First, stakeholders had a greater stake in the environmental problem in the Water Supply case than in the other two cases – a condition for success we identified in EIP. The polluted creek not only provided irrigation for local dairy and other farming industries, it was also the sole water supply for the population of a hundred people in the catchment, including a rural township that had no wastewater system. However, this water was not treated and was below Australian drinking water standards. While some residents suggested that they had 'built up a bit of an immunity', personal health concerns were evident, particularly for visitors to the town, with noted cases of tourists becoming sick from drinking the water (Interview 236, Community Group). These issues raised economic – tourism and future development – as well as public liability issues (Interview 237, VEPA; Interview 135,

VEPA). Such direct health and economic stakes for local actors meant a greater number of stakeholders who saw significant benefits in engaging and committing to the collaboration than for either of the other two cases. As one respondent stated: 'This NEIP collaboration is very different to the others . . . because the core issue is the water supply which affects everybody' (Interview 237, VEPA).

The second reason why the Water Supply case was able to achieve greater success than either the Degraded Creek or Sustainable Township case was the difference in population size. With only around a hundred people in the neighbourhood, 'every single person knows every single person', which provided a high level of networks on which to build cooperation (Interview 234, Local Government). This fact, combined with the small catchment area, kept transaction costs much lower than in the other cases, and engagement rates proportionally higher (Interview 237, VEPA). Further, sponsors were able to engage a larger proportion and mix of significant stakeholders (18 local residents/farmer representatives, 13 government and three non-government groups, and one collaborative Landcare body). These stakeholders included two-thirds of the key problem stakeholders, namely the dairy farming industry (Interview 237, VEPA).

Interestingly, our New Zealand research also revealed that a small population can provide a very solid foundation for collaboration. As demonstrated in Box 3.1 above, the small populations involved in the Living Streams programme were reported to have provided very supportive conditions for successful collaboration, including existing networks and low transaction costs.

In addition to a small population, the ability of the Water Supply case to engage with its problem stakeholders arose from a third and final reason why this case was the most successful collaboration: the availability of resources, an external condition. Specifically, the town water supplies, and the management of rural resources, were both issues that were the subject of significant external government funding (Interview 241, VEPA). Unlike the Degraded Creek or Sustainable Township cases where stakeholders had to rely on their own limited resources or small grant programmes to fund their commitments (Maribyrnong City Council, 2004, p25; Surf Coast Shire Council, 2004, p23), these external funding sources brought with them more than A$700,000 (approximately US$711,510) in investment over four years. This funding enabled partners to make significant commitments to realize plans for developing wastewater and water supply systems, as well as to undertake waterway restoration projects. Perhaps most importantly this funding was used to provide incentives that encouraged local farmers to engage with and contribute to farm improvements. As one respondent noted: '[Landowners] wanted all of their waterways fenced out, they wanted all the willows removed, they wanted it all revenged, and they saw that as being a real bonus, a real benefit, and they were very committed to that' (Interview 231, CMA).

While the NEIP programme appears to have been less successful than EIP in fostering successful collaboration, our analysis suggests that all the NEIP cases were able to facilitate the mustering of a diverse set of public and private stakeholders for the first time to agree upon a plan and make collective commitments to address significant environmental issues at neighbourhood level. As with the poor and good performers in the EIP programme, these achievements are attributable to the presence of a severe problem, sufficient subsidies for transaction costs (in this case through a sponsor and seed funding) and a cooperative decision-making approach. However, with the cases under the NEIP programme, trust-building proved to be more important.

But crucially, the success of the NEIP programme under route one was qualified by what proved to be a fundamental design flaw: a lack of incentives capable of engaging effectively with important stakeholders and persuading them to modify their behaviour. And this, in turn, severely constrained their potential to achieve significant environmental improvements.

The lack of incentives built into the NEIP design appears to share a genealogy with new governance endeavours internationally that similarly aim, somewhat optimistically, to achieve successful collaboration through purely voluntary approaches. Box 3.2 below provides a demonstration of one such case in New Zealand that, similar to the NEIP programme, struggled to persuade or enforce affirmative engagement from key stakeholders.

Yet, notwithstanding such weaknesses, it is also clear that there is more to fostering successful collaboration than just designing 'the right' institution. Indeed, the NEIP design, despite its flaws, clearly was successful under the right conditions. As with EIP it was clear that collaboration was context bound. As the Water Supply case amply illustrates, collaborations were more likely to succeed with a small population, with high stakes in an environmental issue – particularly where funding was available to effectively fill the 'incentive gap' in the NEIP design.

BOX 3.2 NEW ZEALAND DEMONSTRATION CASE: COLLABORATIVE CATCHMENT MANAGEMENT (CCM)

This catchment-based demonstration case was designed to develop non-statutory catchment management plans through partnerships between government agencies and voluntary catchment-based community groups to address specific issues, such as the diffuse pollution of urban estuaries and rural lakes.

To foster collaboration, the programme was designed to provide an annual allocation of government funding (NZ$30,000, approximately US$22,000 as at the time of writing) and in-kind government support to offset collaborators' transaction costs. However, unlike its LSP cousin, CCM had not been designed to harness available regulatory pressure. This was largely because, facing numerous and diverse diffuse polluters and sometimes extremely large catchments (e.g., 276,000 hectares), such a strategy seemed costly if not

continued . . .

BOX 3.2 *. . . continued*

impossible for ECan. Instead, much like the Australian NEIP programme, the designers hoped to succeed through purely voluntary collaboration. As one CCM document points out:

> The draft community strategy has no legal status; that is, at the present time, none of the actions can be enforced . . . The expectation is that those identified as having a responsibility will work together co-operatively to achieve the targets contained in the strategy.
>
> (WET, 2004, p3; Memorandum of Understanding, 2003, cl 3)

Perhaps predictably, our findings revealed that such pure voluntarism limited the overall effectiveness of the programme. Certainly, CCM had gone a long way towards bringing together actors into a new forum to agree to a substantial plan of action. Central to this success was the fact that the programme had focused on water resources 'in crisis' that had fallen through the cracks of government regulation and were of significant community concern. A range of concerned stakeholders were accordingly quick to engage in the collaborative process. Supported by government funding and in-kind officer assistance, the collaborators invested considerable amounts of their own time in negotiations and agreed to a management plan for their water resources. However, a lack of leverage and incentives to persuade or enforce affirmative action, limited CCM's effectiveness, and environmental improvements fell substantially short of aspirations.

As we will see in Chapters 5 and 6, this included an inability to ensure partners took action to deliver on their commitments. More importantly, from the perspective of the present chapter, were the reports by respondents regarding their lack of leverage to secure buy-in from key industry stakeholders responsible for polluting water resources upstream. As one catchment collaborator pointed out:

> . . . the industry or the developers they are an important group of people that should be in the [collaborative process] . . . but I'm not sure how you would pull people in without putting a lasso round their foot . . . I think they should be there, because we all know that's where all that stuff is leaking from.
>
> (Interview NZ212, Government Body)

The result was that the failure of the collaborative process to deter free riding (and the absence of any credible form of leverage) has seriously limited the extent of environmental improvement.

RNRM – the Challenges of Nested Arrangements

Collaboration in RNRM is somewhat different to EIP and NEIP, as its nested model requires cooperation at more than one institutional level. Collaboration must occur between (i) federal and state governments to negotiate bilateral agreements; (ii) state government agencies to support delivery; and (iii) local and regional stakeholders across 14 different regions to negotiate and cooperatively agree upon plans and investment strategies (Head, 2005a, p144).

We found that stakeholders achieved substantial cooperation at all of these levels. However, at each level problems were reported. These included drawn-out conflicts between federal and state governments; agency 'turf wars' at the state level; vague guidance and insufficient support for regional bodies; and difficulties achieving consensus and trust between regional community and government. None of these problems were fatal to collaborative arrangements. Nonetheless, they served to diminish their overall success.

In this section we first examine the challenges confronting collaboration under the nested model of RNRM. We then describe how that model was rolled out despite the challenges, and managed to gain buy-in from a substantial range of rural stakeholders, although questions about inclusiveness and balance of interests remain. Finally, we show how some of the obstacles to collaboration, while demonstrably not insurmountable, nevertheless served to limit its success in a number of ways.

The primary issue for RNRM's nested approach was state and federal governments agreeing to provide the strategic framework for the state's RNRM. Consistent with suspicions of some RNRM commentators and NEG authors (Paton et al, 2004; Margerum, 2007, p149), conflict rather than cooperation was evident at the outset. This meant that the transactions costs of negotiating bilateral agreements proved to be extremely high – negotiations were problematic, lengthy and repeatedly stalled (Interview 3210, Science). This was particularly the case regarding the more expansive NHT 2 bilateral (NAP being limited to only four 'priority' regions in Queensland). Indeed, following announcements that NHT and NAP would be implemented together (Head and Ryan, 2004, pp16–17), the NAP Agreement was reached relatively quickly in 2002, but negotiations continued on the NHT Agreement until 2004.

A number of factors contributed to these difficulties. First, respondents pointed to state/federal conflicts and the lack of trust culturally entrenched in a federal system: '. . . you know what the states are like they are always paranoid about the feds . . . "If its federal driven it must be crap, those bastards, they are just pushing us around"' (Interview 334, Regional Body). Second, the federal government had assumed that states would see resource benefits arising from collaboration and would willingly participate for this reason. This proved to be incorrect since the federal resources available were reportedly too little to motivate states to change their stance. As one respondent put it:

> . . . [the federal government] think they've so much money to run this [RNRM] that the state will click and dance. Well it started to click and dance and then it decided well no, get nicked . . . there's not enough money . . . so you had a failed system to start off with.
>
> (Interview 3210, Science)

This conflict not only weakened the foundation of RNRM's collaborative process but reduced its overall success by delaying funding support and providing uncertain guidance for lower regional levels.

Exacerbating these problems was an ongoing conflict *within* the Queensland government. Akin to the turf warfare among administrative departments that had plagued earlier NEG experiments (Ewing, 2003, p406), state agencies reportedly struggled to reach agreement regarding their collective approach to RNRM. While some agencies with direct responsibility for RNRM reportedly wished to pursue a collaborative and 'whole of government' approach (Interview 334, Regional Body), others were resistant to sharing their power, leading to what in other contexts has been termed a 'disintegrated government system' (for example, see Zammit et al, 2004; Interview 334, Regional Body). As one respondent put it, this uncertainty and conflict 'was a tragedy because . . . the whole of government solidarity sort of fell apart' (Interview 334, Regional Body).

Nonetheless, the governments pressed ahead and rolled out RNRM at the regional level, operating under the NAP bilateral and interim NHT arrangements (Interview 342–2, Sub-regional Body). Building on pre-existing groups (Head and Ryan, 2004, pp16–17) and following numerous meetings with the regional community, government officers facilitated the development of a collaborative regional body. This included five sub-regional collaborative groups (Catchment Management/Landcare groups), two science interests, two indigenous interests, two local government members and four non-voting government advisors.

Why did these stakeholders want to collaborate? At the broadest level, stakeholders were interested in participating because they were concerned about the region's severe natural resource problems (Burdekin Dry Tropics Natural Resource Management [BDTNRM], 2005a, pp29–33). Indeed, since the 1990s, rural communities had manifested concern and involvement in catchment or Landcare groups. These had sought to manage diverse natural resources that were reportedly threatened and degraded by a range of intensive resource uses, such as grazing, cane farming and urban development (BDTNRM, 2005a, pp1, 8 and 29–33). Not surprisingly, the five existing sub-regional groups were the most motivated stakeholders. For some of these groups, an additional incentive for participation was the potential to obtain and/or control government funding. Put simply: 'they nominated these people to make sure that they got some money for their organisations' (Interview 341, Regional Body).

Although valid questions exist about the inclusiveness and balance of interests on the regional body (not least that a number of stakeholder groups were not represented there), the membership of the sub-regional bodies went some way toward bringing a diverse mix of key stakeholders into the regional collaboration, including Landcare, local government, environmental and agricultural interests. A particularly beneficial feature of the involvement of the sub-regional groups was that the regional body nested approach took account of the geographical spread of catchments (Gilbey, 2002). In particular, through their direct representation, this structure ensured that existing sub-regional groups were not forgotten or overlooked in the shift to broader regional arrangements (which emerging RNRM research has shown was a noted problem in other areas) (Interview 342, Sub-regional Body; Gilbey, 2002; BDTNRM, 2005a, p8; Whelan and Oliver, 2005).

This nested arrangement helped reduce transaction costs in ways broadly consistent with hypotheses in the literature (Margerum, 2007). For example, it provided a forum that reduced the costs of disseminating government information and guidance down to the multiple sub-regional groups (BDTNRM, 2005a, p187). Dividing the workload among these groups served to reduce the time and resources spent by the regional body in consulting within the wider region.

The 'foundational funding' obtained by the regional body was in part devolved to the sub-regional bodies to hire coordinators (BDTNRM, 2005b, p15; Gilbey, 2002). As in the NEIP programme, these coordinators proved to be vital in assisting sub-regional groups (BDTNRM, 2005a, pp185–187) to support some of the transaction costs of consulting and bargaining regarding critical NRM assets, targets, actions and prioritizing in each sub-region (Interview 342, Sub-regional Body). This consultation fed up to the coordinating regional body, where the remaining foundational funding was vital in enabling it to rent an office and employ support and planning staff – including three additional technical support coordinators and a consultant to complete the supporting regional planning documents (BDTNRM, 2005a, p197).

These were undoubtedly very positive achievements in the development of plans and strategies. However, the success of collaboration was limited in a number of ways. First, because of the ongoing bickering between state and federal governments over the overarching bilateral agreements, government guidance was often vague and changing (Farrelly, 2005, p399). As one government advisor explained:

> . . . the regional bodies have been evolving at the same time as the infrastructure has been . . . The administrative arrangements [and] the guidelines . . . we haven't necessarily provided them with the framework or the support to be able to achieve what we want them to achieve.
>
> (Interview 327, Government Agency)

This did little to reduce transaction costs, and may have even augmented them, as regional bodies continually had to adapt and readapt to changing requirements (e.g., the form of their organizational structure) (Interview 327, Government Agency). Our findings suggest this lack of firm guidance was detrimental to the overall success of the process, with regional bodies often failing to connect effectively with key stakeholders (Interview 327, Government Agency). As one respondent reflected: '. . . we have got some major coal and gold mines in the area. Not one of the mining industries has even been talked to' (Interview 341, Regional Body).

The second issue that undermined the success of regional collaboration was the reported delays in government funding to mitigate transaction costs. These delays were created by the ongoing disagreement between federal and state governments. This increased the time it took to complete plans and made it more difficult to engage local stakeholders. As one respondent explained:

> I see the [Queensland]–[Federal] crunch as incredibly negative. It's stopped us getting funding when we needed our funding . . . and then that flows through to the community, through the committee to the community, so there is all this negative stuff that comes out as friction at the top end.
>
> (Interview 342, Sub-regional Group)

Augmenting these difficulties was the sheer task of collaborating across such a large regional scale. Challenges of scale are, of course, not unique to RNRM. There are many large new governance institutions across the globe, including our New Zealand demonstration case known as the Canterbury Water Management Strategy (CWMS) programme. This programme not only relied on considerable public investment to offset the transaction costs of bringing stakeholders together across a large region, but also experimented with online technologies. Indeed, Box 3.3 (below) provides a unique illustration of a growing international trend in the use of online collaborative tools to try and avoid the high transaction costs imposed by such large scale collaborative endeavours.

Although RNRM utilized web pages and databases, online collaborative tools were not explicitly harnessed in the RNRM programme. Instead it was left to funding and volunteers. However, on all accounts there were significant insufficiencies in the funding. As one respondent frankly stated: 'the biggest deficiency is that it is hopelessly under resourced' (Interview 337, Local Government).

Even with volunteers putting in 'thousands of hours' (Interview 342, Sub-regional Group), the funding did not sufficiently equip the sub-regional groups to overcome transaction costs and cooperative barriers that arose in the extremely large geographic region (almost 130,000km^2). Indeed, respondents reported that they lacked the time and resources to engage with a range of peak industry bodies who were reportedly wary of new regional bodies and saw them as 'a threat' to their influence over rural issues (Interview 323, State Agency). Even more problematic was the failure to 'tap into all of the farming structures' in the region (Interview 314, Industry Body) – in particular 'average' farmers as opposed to those who were already involved in existing sub-regional Landcare or catchment bodies. As one respondent put it:

> . . . we have had a group of most probably 30 landholders, commercial beef property people have been involved fairly heavily in doing all this consultation process for the planning, but the majority haven't engaged.
>
> (Interview 344, Sub-regional Body)

BOX 3.3 NEW ZEALAND DEMONSTRATION CASE: CANTERBURY WATER MANAGEMENT STRATEGY (CWMS)

Our third demonstration case operates at a much larger regional ecosystem scale and was a 'once-off' regional collaboration involving a number of workstreams, including water quality and quantity, that sought, inter alia, to develop an effective water policy by securing the input and buy-in of the regional community. Facing an extremely large regional population and area (500,000 people in 42,200km^2), the programme provided significant government funding to cover the costs of collaborating across multiple stages and forums of decision-making. To a large extent, this funding was successful in significantly offsetting transaction costs and obtaining a high level of stakeholder buy-in and agreement to a water management strategy that many respondents believed would limit future litigation. Of particular interest for this chapter is the unique and novel web-based mechanism the CWMS utilized to try and address the high costs and challenges of collaborating at a large regional scale.

This web-based tool was designed to foster direct participation in online dialogue and decision-making about water storage options and water management issues. Akin to international attempts at harnessing information technology (Coglianese, 2006), this web-based technology was intended to reduce the transaction costs of collaboration across the large region by providing 'a structured framework so that people could participate in a variety of ways without having to bring all parties together at the same time and place' (Jenkins, 2007a, p4).

Astute to possible barriers of poor computer skills preventing access to and use of the web tool, pilot tests with stakeholders and an assistance 'clinic' were conducted. Despite these precautions, respondents were unanimous that the online tool had not lived up to its expectations. In essence, as one government respondent pointed out, 'the [online tool] didn't produce the result that we wanted' (Interview NZ101, Regional Resident).

Certainly some respondents reported that there had been benefits of the online approach. In particular, the tool enabled content-rich information to be stored and summarized in a structured framework, which enabled decision-makers to distil the principles that now underpin the CWMS (*Environment Canterbury (Temporary Commissioners and Improved Water Management) Act 2010* (NZ)). However, it was clear from the large majority of interview responses that on the crucial test of facilitating and increasing engagement levels and fostering constructive decision-making by stakeholder groups or

continued . . .

BOX 3.3 *. . . continued*

their members, the online process had fallen significantly short. To illustrate: after a public call for input on a range of issues gleaned from earlier CWMS processes, only 31 people/organizations across the region responded. Of those, only a very small minority actually engaged in detailed discussions. Respondents attributed this failure and an overall lack of engagement to the time and costs of reading through reportedly dense information on the website and 'getting up to speed' on water issues more generally. As one regional non-government collaborator explained: 'members of my [stakeholder group] haven't got a show . . . other than the website . . . but first of all they wouldn't read it . . . secondly, it's just too voluminous' (Interview NZ109, Peak Body). Notably, the engagement gaps left by the online tool were subsequently filled by extensive 'on-ground' collaborative meetings across the region.

However, the above findings should not be seen to imply that this or any other specific online tool will inherently fail. The online tool used in CWMS is reportedly flexible and can have other uses. Nonetheless, our findings highlight that policy designers must be careful in over-optimistic assumptions of the benefits of internet technologies for dealing with large-scale new governance collaborations. Indeed, policy designers must ensure that such tools are applied in the right context and in the right way, paying particular attention to how information will be displayed and how complex issues will be dealt with through the web interface.

These vital stakeholders had not engaged in the regional collaborative process for a number of reasons. These included 'cynicism' about government programmes (Interview 311, Industry Body); anger that previous 'on-ground' funding (e.g., NHT phase 1) had largely ceased, while RNRM plans were being developed (Interview 345, Sub-regional Group); and most prominently, the fact that some farmers had to drive many hours to attend meetings (Interview 345, Sub-regional Group). This reduced the overall success of the collaborative process and the effectiveness of the plan that was produced.

However, those who did engage were able to agree on a plan and supporting documents (BDTNRM, 2005a, pp66 and 197). Repeated interactions and negotiations to develop these – while far from conflict free (Interview 341, Regional Body) – helped build stronger relationships, reduce mistrust and ensured agreements were reached with greater ease. As our respondents explained:

> . . . successfully facilitating multiple planning forums and technical workshops at the local and regional level actually allowed people and allowed our facilitators to work much more closely with the landholders and it allows

> them to basically develop a relationship with that community, because trust is the biggest thing . . . the only way you can get through all the planning and legislation and decisions is to just to keep the dialogue going and to actually demonstrate that, yes, something will come out the end of this.
>
> (Interview 351, Regional Body)

Another 'science respondent' reflected after a number of negotiated meetings with farmers, local government and peak industry bodies: '. . . you know when you have some sort of break in the log jam . . . there was just a level of honesty about presentations by all sides that got it away from the hostility' (Interview 331, Science).

Having built trust over time, how did the parties reach agreement on the planning documents? Although the RNRM legislative design did not specifically emphasize a consensus approach, in practice the planning process sought to use the ongoing consultation and negotiation processes as a way 'to work towards consensus' (BDTNRM, 2005a, p49). What is different about these arrangements in RNRM, compared to the other two programmes, is that RNRM was not so much about a single group of stakeholders who were relatively contained in number and followed a consensus approach to agree to a plan. Rather, it involved multiple groups of stakeholders at the sub-regional, regional, and other levels making decisions that were designed to contribute to some form of overall regional agreement. Of course, NEIP also involved multiple consultation forums; however, this was typically carried out by members of a single collaborative group and their coordinator (as opposed to different sub-regional groups, technical teams and a regional body all reaching agreement on multiple issues).

For example, in one RNRM sub-region alone a facilitated workshop of sub-regional stakeholders reached agreement on issues for the sub-region, while a select group of these stakeholders then agreed on the priority of these issues and decided which would have targets set for them. This was followed by smaller technical teams agreeing to targets for each of the priority issues, and notice and comment consultation processes. Finally, a regional forum involving regional and sub-regional stakeholders reached agreement on which of the targets had regional value, which was then followed by planning staff and regional body negotiating with government agencies and other key industry stakeholders to draft and agree to a plan (BDTNRM, 2005a, pp68–69 and 187–190).

As one may expect, these different processes threw up a host of different decision-rules, ranging from 'substantial' agreement among sub-regional group stakeholders, majority voting (both in sub-regions and the regional body) and agreement by a small representative group of stakeholders or by a technical advisory team (BDTNRM, 2005a, pp68–69, 187–190 and 193; Interview 323, State Government). As with the cases in the NEIP and EIP programme, unanimous agreement in any forum appeared to be rare, with particular disagreements regarding scientific information and targets (Interview 341, Regional Body; Interview 334, Regional Body).

What was clear from a regional body perspective was that these processes involved 'decision-making that promoted mutual education' and 'increased knowledge of resource issues' (Interview 342, Sub-regional Body; BDTNRM, 2005a, p49). Respondents reported that reaching consensual agreement had helped increase the chances of implementation from regional and local stakeholders who had signed onto the plan:

> It's their plans, their targets . . . we sat there and we work-shopped the growers with the work . . . it creates ownership if the plan sits there and these targets if they know they helped write them they understand why we are achieving or why we are driving for targets, and they can achieve them, then they are more likely to actually engage in it.
>
> (Interview 311, Industry Body)

Despite this, some respondents felt that the fact that a consensual decision could be, and was, trumped by the governments' (that is, the Joint Steering Committee's) exercise of its veto, undermined the process. In defence of the possibility of a veto one government official had this to say: '. . . from our point of view, we said "No. From a government point of view, as the funder of the groups, you've got to address these issues"' (Interview 323, Government Agency). Our findings suggest that this veto power had detrimental effects, especially in mobilizing support at the implementation stage. As one respondent expressed it: 'Your opinion is irrelevant basically or that's the way it seems' (Interview 242, Sub-regional Body). On the other hand, the government veto and associated oversight of the programme had the virtue of ensuring that credible targets were set and that one did not simply get trade-offs between stakeholders, for example, between agricultural and environmental interests.

> . . . if we were to hold a meeting here of local community people in the region and you go in with a blank sheet of paper, I don't think that is altogether helpful. You end up with such compromise . . . it is lowest, common denominator outcome . . . that means no outcome quite often. So you need to have some broader policy guidance as to how that might be applied.
>
> (Interview 328, Government Agency)

The regional plan that emerged contained several ambitious targets. These ranged from soil issues (e.g., by 2024, achieve a 10 per cent improvement in soil health in extensive and intensive agricultural areas) to biodiversity issues (e.g., by 2015, ensure 90 per cent of all threatened flora and fauna species in the region will be represented in conservation reserves or under voluntary conservation agreements) to coastal and marine issues (by 2025, connectivity between and within fresh water and marine ecosystems will be restored) (BDTNRM, 2005a). As we will see in Chapter 5, some respondents questioned the science behind these RNRM targets. However, this weakness was not seen to arise from the approach to decision-making itself.

In sum, RNRM has been successful in enabling federal, state and a range of regional non-government stakeholders to come together through a nested set of collaborative arrangements. Broadly similar to elements of some EIP and NEIPs, our findings suggested that what encouraged this success were several key conditions – severe natural resource problems, monetary incentives to engender interest from key regional stakeholders, government support (albeit insufficient) to reduce transaction costs, a trust-building and a consensus-building orientation to decision-making.

However, like the NEIP programme this success was qualified by a host of difficulties in securing key stakeholders' input into the planning process. While nested arrangements certainly assisted in reducing transaction costs, given the region's size, conflict and uncertainty at higher levels created an unstable foundation for the RNRM programme, delayed financial support and reduced effective guidance from government to regional bodies.

Conclusions

Although collective action barriers remain a 'theoretical thorn in the side' of NEG (Hornstein, 2005, p952), our findings suggest that under the appropriate conditions collaboration is possible. This finding makes clear that it is a gross oversimplification to rely on 'tragedy of the commons' arguments to conclude that cooperative solutions within NEG are impossible (Steinzor, 2000; Gaines, 2002/2003; Karkkainen, 2002/2003, pp231 and 233).

Nevertheless, it is also clear that achieving collaboration is far from easy. Realizing stakeholder collaboration is both time and resource intensive and provision for this (including significant sums of government money) has to be built into NEG processes if they are to be successful (Coglianese, 1999; Coglianese, 2001, p13; Karkkainen, 2002/2003, p225; Karkkainen, 2004b, p91; Lane, 2006). Our findings also revealed varying degrees of success between processes designed to enhance collaboration. At a broad level, the EIP programme appeared more successful than the other two programmes, with most cases having engaged a majority of key stakeholders in developing plans that took substantial steps toward resolving local environmental issues. This success, as we noted, was in part attributable to the fact that the EIP programme faced comparatively 'simple' point-source pollution problems, harnessed negative incentives to engage industry and required fewer key parties to make direct commitments. With NEIP and RNRM, the environmental problems were more complex and involved many more stakeholders. Within NEIP the most successful collaboration took place within the Water Supply case, where there were high environmental stakes for a small number of local actors and significant external funding was available.

At first glance these conclusions appear to support sceptical arguments that successful collaboration in NEG is limited to narrowly constrained or unique circumstances (Cannon, 2000, p428; Gaines, 2002/2003, p17) – for example, less complex settings involving fewer parties, such as the cases in the EIP programme or, small communities closely tied to environmental conditions as in the Water Supply case, and the LSP in New Zealand (Gaines, 2002/2003, p17; Karkkainen, 2004a, pp476–477). However, such a conclusion places too little weight on the significant achievements made in our other programmes and cases.

In our view a more sensible conclusion to draw from the relative success of these programmes is that collaboration is highly contingent and contextual (Schlager, 2004, pp164 and 169). Understanding these conditions is vital to understanding NEG and its potential. Our analysis suggests that these conditions can be grouped under five principal themes: the severity of environmental problems; incentives (both negative and positive); structures for subsidizing transaction costs; consensus decision-making; and trust. For each, our findings provide important lessons for NEG theory and for policymakers.

Commencing with the issue of problem severity, for the most part our programmes dealt with problems perceived to be severe by key stakeholders, be they odours, a degraded urban creek, or degraded natural resources. Where this condition was absent, we found that few gains were achieved (Sabatier et al, 2005b, p181). The common theme here is that successful collaboration is more likely to emerge where problems are perceived to be severe (Heikkila and Gerlak, 2005, p586; Lubell et al, 2002, p148). From a policy perspective this suggests that if environmental problems are not severe there may be few gains to be made from collaborative initiatives (Cannon, 2000, p408).

The findings provided insights into the use of incentives to increase the likelihood of successful collaboration (Karkkainen, 2002/2003, p241). It is widely acknowledged in the regulatory literature that the strategic use of government funding and/or authority (or even harnessing pressure from third parties) can be an effective spur to cooperation and affirmative self-regulatory behaviour (Karkkainen, 2002/2003, p229; Karkkainen, 2006b, p296). We found that social and economic pressure from non-government stakeholders can indeed prompt effective cooperation, at least where large reputation-conscious corporations or stakeholders are involved (Gunningham et al, 2003). And as we saw in the LSP, peer pressure can be an effective tool for bringing polluters to the table where they live in small, close-knit communities. However, the proviso here is the very real limits to third parties' capacities to pressure players who place little value on their public image.

A key question in terms of incentives is what is likely to shift the cost-benefit calculation of stakeholders? We found that the 'shadow of the law' (or a similar economic incentive) is vital to successful collaboration (as was the case in EIP and LSP). Without it, new governance will likely face severe difficulties engaging polluters (as was the case in some NEIP cases and the CCM Programme in New Zealand). We also found that the shadow of the law alone may not be sufficiently menacing to compel even the most recalcitrant actors to collaborate. Here direct legal compulsion may need to be used. The use of such coercion on a wide scale, however, needs to be balanced against the possibility that it may engender resistance and produce less efficient results (Ayres, 2006, p589). Such coercion, however, remains an important string in the regulatory bow.

In addition to incentives, our findings also shed light on the issue of transaction costs. Many authors in the literature have suggested that sufficient support to collaborators to enable them to reduce transaction costs is vital to successful collaboration (John and Mlay, 1999, pp362–363; John, 2004, pp230–242; Sabatier et al, 2005b, p181). Our findings strongly support these claims (Sabatier et al, 2005b, p181). In addition to transaction costs, we found that it was crucial to provide for the costs of facilitation in the form of funding for a coordinator. Here our findings suggest that such support may need to be quite substantial to be effective (Farrelly, 2005, p402; Head, 2005a, p145). We also found that sponsors played an important role in facilitating collaboration. This supports John's (2004, pp239–242) findings in the USA. An important characteristic of sponsors is their ability to provide direct and in-kind support to reduce the transaction costs of collaborative processes (John, 2004, p239). In addition our findings suggest that a third way of reducing transaction costs is to harness the resources of well-resourced industries. Incentives to these industries include both sanctions and economic incentives (Selin and Chavez, 1995, pp189–195; Karkkainen, 2002/2003, p228; Raymond, 2006, p48).

We also found evidence to suggest that appropriate institutional design, particularly at larger regional scales, can mitigate transaction costs. This included an illustration of the use of internet technologies in the CWMS and the use of nested structures. While the former is clearly no 'magic bullet' (as some may profess), the latter can reduce transaction costs by tapping into existing institutional resources to divide and conquer collaborative tasks at lower local levels, while receiving guidance from government in a structured manner through higher regional forums (Bonnell and Koontz, 2007, pp161 and 163; Margerum, 2007, pp144–146). However, the potential of nested designs can be undermined where guidance is ineffective and uncertain, and where funding support is not forthcoming. We found that one cause of this was a desire to 'get on' with programmes before fully overcoming the resistance of agencies and governments to share power (Freeman and Farber, 2005, pp900–901; Head, 2005a, p145; Bonnell and Koontz, 2007, p161; Margerum, 2007, pp144–146).

This suggests that achieving cooperation at these higher levels poses one of the greatest challenges to the effectiveness of nested collaborative models and their potential to reduce transaction costs. At a policy level, the implication is that, rather than trying to develop collaboration at multiple institutional levels simultaneously, the success of nested models may depend upon proceeding in a more staged manner. Further, as the findings revealed, inadequate funding was one of the major impediments to a state's willingness to collaborate with federal governments, suggesting that significantly more funding may be required to generate greater cooperation at these higher levels (Freeman and Farber, 2005, pp901–903; Margerum, 2007, pp149–150).

Our findings also provided insights as regards the virtues or otherwise of a cooperative or consensus approach. For many authors, decision-rules that foster consensus are vital to effective collaboration. Our findings by and large confirmed this. The findings from EIP and NEIP indicate that their mixed consensus rules often assisted stakeholders to reach agreement on environmental and resource problems and that this in turn increased the likelihood of implementation (Margerum, 1999, p158). Our findings with regard to RNRM were broadly similar.

Finally, as regards the role of trust, our findings were somewhat at odds with the conventional wisdom. With the NEG and related literatures it is often argued that building trust will make it easier for stakeholders to cooperate and achieve successful collaboration (Stewart and Jones, 2003; Fung and Wright, 2003b, p15; John, 2004, pp232 and 235). We too found this to be broadly true. However, the findings in the majority of EIP cases require a nuanced understanding of the issue of trust. Consistent with the findings of a handful of empirical studies in other NEG jurisdictions, we found that complex agreements can be reached, and successful collaboration achieved, in the absence of trust (Lubell et al, 2005, p275; Raymond, 2006, pp37, 40–41, 50 and 54; Leach and Sabatier, 2005; Cook et al, 2005).

The evidence from our studies indicates that trust operates differently in different contexts, and at least in some, may be largely irrelevant to successful collaboration (Lubell et al, 2005, p277). The implication of this finding for policy is that in NEG programmes it may, in some cases, be wise to devote less time and energy to trust-building and to focus instead on designing incentives and institutional mechanisms that encourage cooperation between adversarial stakeholders (Raymond, 2006, p54).

4

PARTICIPATORY AND DELIBERATIVE

As we have seen, all our programmes share broad participatory and deliberative aspirations. In particular, they seek to develop processes that will deepen the ways in which non-governmental actors are able to contribute to the governance of human impacts on their environment (Fung and Wright, 2003b, p5). To realize these aspirations our programmes included design features directed at ensuring that participation was inclusive and representative and conformed with deliberative ideals. These processes vary across NEG experiments and our programmes are no exception.

Inclusiveness

The question of inclusiveness relates to the issue of who is eligible to participate (Fung, 2006, p67). As with most NEG approaches, all three of our programmes sought in principle to include all non-governmental actors who were 'affected' (Cohen and Sabel, 1997, pp15–16, 18; Freeman, 1997, p22; Karkkainen, 2004b, p75; Leach, 2006, p101). Each programme defined 'affected' actors in terms of general and/or specific geographic criteria (e.g., local community in EIP; a neighbourhood in NEIP; a regional community in RNRM). None excluded the possibility of 'affected participants' being outside an affected geographic area – for instance, 'people who may have an interest or be potentially affected', such as NGOs (EIP), those who may 'work and play' in the neighbourhood (NEIP) or 'relevant stakeholders' (RNRM). The broader objective was to encourage equality in participation and to encourage participation from any affected group or person, including the socially disadvantaged. Mobilizing 'average' citizens was regarded as vital to meaningful participation, and these would include residents in EIPs, individuals and householders in NEIP and community representation in RNRM (VEPA, 2002a, p2; VEPA, 2002d, p8; Bilateral Agreement NHT, 2004, pp67–68).

There was also an effort to include affected green and conservation interests (VEPA, 2001a, p2; VEPA, 2002d, p8; Bilateral Agreement NHT, 2004, pp67–68), which can be seen as potentially giving a voice to future generations and 'nature' (Moore, 2005). The aspiration here was that these voices would reduce, and perhaps even neutralize, the power advantages of powerful industries (Fung and Wright, 2003a, p260).

Representativeness

The second criterion – 'representativeness' – intersected with the first, and was directed at mitigating differences in power and capacity that limit who participates in policy forums (Parkinson, 2006, p23). While our programmes were short on specifics, they shared a common aspiration to be 'representative', especially with respect to non-governmental stakeholders. This is evidenced in requirements for representation to 'reflect the demographic' so as to include the 'range of different community interests and perspectives' (EIP) (VEPA, 2001a, pp2–3, 6); 'capture and represent the views' of a 'cross section of the community' (NEIP) (VEPA, 2002d, pp5 and 8); and include 'majority community membership' so as to encourage a 'balance' of conservation and production interests among 'relevant' stakeholders (RNRM) (Bilateral Agreement NHT, 2004, ss 67–68, Attachment D, p56).

Designing Inclusion and Representation

To achieve these inclusive and representative ideals, each programme was designed around flexible processes that encouraged voluntary, self-selecting participation (as opposed to a formal mechanism such as an election) (VEPA, 2001a, p4; VEPA, 2002a, p10; Bilateral Agreement NHT, 2004, Attachment D, p56). While there is considerable scepticism within the NEG literature about the possibility of realizing these ideals (e.g., Steinzor, 2000, pp19–20; Tushnet, 2003, p170; Lane, 2006, pp7–8; Hatzopoulos, 2007, pp325–326), similar objectives are to be found in many NEG theories and experiments (Fung, 2003, p342; Fung, 2006; Leach, 2006; for a discussion of other concepts see Renn and Schweizer, 2009, pp176–180). One primary reason for this scepticism is the perception that the contribution of volunteers is often substantially limited as a result of the transaction costs of participating (Abers, 2003, p207; Fung, 2003, p342).

The time and financial costs of participating were certainly likely to be significant barriers in our programmes, as well as their heavy reliance upon the skills and resources of volunteers. For example, all three programmes expected volunteers to attend regular collaborative meetings – as well as to develop and negotiate complex plans and documents – followed by ongoing monitoring and implementation. The demands in NEIP and RNRM were particularly taxing as volunteers were expected to contribute to wider consultations within their neighbourhood and regional communities (VEPA, 2002d, pp2–6; Bilateral Agreement NHT, 2004,

Attachment F, pp74–75). They were also expected to contribute to drafting two intricate and detailed planning documents (VEPA, 2002d, pp4–6; *Environmental Protection Act 1970* (Vic), s 19AI(3); Bilateral Agreement NHT, 2004, Attachment E, pp59–60).

Unlike EIP and NEIP, the RNRM made the capacity of participants to fulfil programme requirements a necessary consideration within the programme. This arose through the power that the programme afforded to state governments to 'designate' a regional body as being suitable. This effectively gave states the authority to appoint representatives, albeit in consultation with the regional community (Bilateral Agreement NAP, 2001, ss 7.1(f) and (g), Attachment D, p56; Head, 2005a, p145). While RNRM does not specify any *specific* skill requirements for representatives, it does suggest that the selection process should not compromise merit, and that the representatives as a whole must have the capacities and skills to advance the objectives of the programme and fulfil its accountability responsibilities (Bilateral Agreement NAP, 2001, ss 7.1(f) and (g); Bilateral Agreement NHT, 2004, ss 67, 68(b), 71, Attachment D, p56).

The onerous nature of these time and skill requirements across the programmes was in part offset by: (i) sharing tasks among the collaborators; (ii) government assistance, such as technical information; (iii) RNRM government funding for the regional body and modest rebates to cover travel costs (Bilateral Agreement NHT, 2004, s 95; Bilateral Agreement NAP, 2001, ss 9 and 24); and (iv) short-term seed funding in NEIP (VEPA, 2002a, p10; VEPA, 2002d, p9; VEPA, 2004a, pp1, 3 and 5; Bilateral Agreement NHT, 2004, s 101).

In addition, our programmes were designed to establish a range of procedural checks intended to identify and resolve representation deficits. For example, both the EIP (VEPA, 2001a) and NEIP (VEPA, 2002d, pp5 and 9) programmes included procedural requirements with respect to organizers of the collaborative group that encouraged them to promote inclusion (e.g., publicly advertising meetings). Both programmes relied on VEPA officers to enforce these requirements and to assist the group to ensure representativeness (e.g., contact parties directly to see if they would be interested in volunteering) (VEPA, 2002a, p11; VEPA, 2002c, pp3 and 5–6; VEPA, 2004a, pp2–3; *Environmental Protection Act 1970* (Vic), s 19AI(1)). In a similar vein, the RNRM design made funding conditional on groups meeting representation requirements (Bilateral Agreement NHT, 2004, Attachment D, p56).

Deliberative Processes

In addition to inclusiveness and representativeness, decision-making processes themselves were also of considerable importance to NEG – deliberation being a close sibling of participation and inclusiveness.

All of our programmes involved complex processes of decision-making – some took months or years to develop a plan that then might require years of adaptive implementation. The design of both the EIP and NEIP programmes emphasized processes of negotiation, mediation and similar forms of deliberative, cooperative and collaborative decision-making (VEPA, 2001a, pp4–6; VEPA, 2002d, p5; VEPA, 2004a, p4; Bilateral Agreement NAP, 2001, s 7.1). With RNRM, the fact that regional bodies were required to be incorporated (Bilateral Agreement NHT, 2004, s 68; Bilateral Agreement NAP, 2001, s 7.1) meant that decision-making was governed by rules that required some form of discussion, deliberation and, at times, voting.

While specific procedures and criteria for deliberation were not spelled out in the legislation or guidelines, the community empowerment aspiration they shared encouraged jargon-free communication, shared decisions and fairness. This reflects an aspiration to avoid adversarial, zero-sum negotiations and the fostering of processes that enabled government and non-governmental stakeholders to give their free and informed consent to plans of action (Trachtenberg and Focht, 2005, pp60–64; Fung and Wright, 2003b, pp23–24).

Designing Deliberation

Major challenges to equal and fair forms of deliberation are imbalances in power and capacity. Our programme designers were alert to such issues and sought ways of ameliorating them. For example, they provided government support, such as office assistance, (VEPA, 2002d, p9; VEPA, 2004a, p5; Bilateral Agreement NHT, 2004, s 101) and, in RNRM, government funding (Bilateral Agreement NHT, 2004, s 95; Bilateral Agreement NAP, 2001, s 24.2) to assist non-governmental representatives to gain scientific, legal or other technical information. Government support was particularly emphasized in the EIP programme where VEPA officers were able to act as brokers in support of local residents negotiating with the better-resourced and knowledgeable industry representatives (VEPA, 2001a, p4; VEPA, 2004a, p5). The EIP framework also contained other 'power balancing' features recognized in the NEG literature (Fung and Wright, 2003b, p23), including sanctions (for example, the use of VEPA's legal power along with community pressure on industry to negotiate and reveal information).

The design of the three programmes also recognized the potential of government actors to dominate decision-making unreasonably (Karkkainen, 2002/2003, p240; Fung and Wright, 2003b, p34; Head, 2004, p31; Head, 2005a, pp148–149). For example, VEPA officers and government officers of the RNRM Regional Coordination Group were entrusted to assist – but not unfairly use their knowledge of technical or regulatory issues to dominate – non-government actors in negotiations (VEPA, 2002a, p11; *Environmental Protection Act 1970* (Vic), ss 19AH(2); Bilateral Agreement NHT, 2004, ss 80–81, 89; Bilateral Agreement NAP, 2001, ss 7, 12). Nonetheless, there were many ways in which government actors could dominate or unduly influence the decision-making process. For example, the VEPA and RNRM Joint Steering Committee had, as we have noted, formal vetoes over plans (and in RNRM directly controlled not only how regional boundaries were established but also subsequent funding) (*Environmental Protection*

Act 1970 (Vic), s 19AH(2); Bilateral Agreement NHT, 2004, ss 69, 71, 80–81 and 89; Bilateral Agreement NAP, 2001, ss 7 and 12). Similarly, requirements in the NEIP programme for a sponsoring government body to submit proposals and plans to the VEPA effectively give these sponsoring agencies a more powerful 'voice' in the planning process than other organizations. While these powers may be vital for issues such as accountability, they also enabled government actors to exercise control over key decision-making stages. These provisions placed government bodies in a privileged position from which they had the potential to dominate non-governmental actors (*Environmental Protection Act 1970* (Vic), ss 19AH, and 19AI; John, 2004, p239).

We turn now to the question of how these tensions in terms of inclusion, representation and negotiation, played out in practice. Specifically, we will explore whether our programmes were able to realize a balance of interests and perspectives.

Findings – Inclusion and Representation

Our findings reveal that non-government actors and stakeholders were the largest group of participants. Nevertheless, many respondents reported a lack of genuine inclusiveness. For example, our respondents pointed to the under-representation of green and conservation interests. This included having no 'environmental representative' on the regional RNRM body. The same applied to five of the eight cases in the EIP programme and the Water Supply case in the NEIP programme. Gaps in environmental group engagement were also reported in our New Zealand demonstration programmes, although not to the same extent (see Box 4.1 below).

Consistent with the hypotheses of scholars regarding environmental groups in NEG (Fung and Wright, 2003a) the environmental interest groups represented in both our Australian and New Zealand cases were not traditional national or state 'peak' NGOs, but local environmental groups, either 'home-grown' in the area or local branches of state and national environmental groups.

A second deficiency was a lack of equality in terms of representation. Although there was little reliable and detailed demographic data of the newly defined local, neighbourhood and regional *demoi*, respondents consistently pointed to a range of affected, but typically socially disadvantaged interests that lacked representation. For example, across all three cases the number of women represented was proportionally smaller than men; however, there were no hard opinions as to why this was this case. Women made up approximately one-third of representatives in EIP cases, less than one-third of the membership in the RNRM case, and less than half across the NEIP cases. The findings in RNRM appear roughly consistent with the findings across Queensland, where one-fifth of regional bodies' members were women (Whelan and Oliver, 2006, pp31–32). Further, in the EIP and NEIP programmes, migrant populations, who sometimes comprised up to 20 per cent of the local demographic group (Interview 211, VEPA; Maribyrnong City Council and Stony Creek NEIP Partners, 2004, p86), lacked any direct representation, while in the RNRM programme, Indigenous Australians were under-represented across

Queensland (Whelan and Oliver, 2006, pp31–32). However, in our RNRM case Indigenous interests were thought to be adequately represented by two Indigenous individuals on the Board. Similar gaps in Indigenous engagement were also evident in our New Zealand demonstration programmes detailed in Box 4.2 (further below).

A third, and final, representation deficiency related to the desire to obtain a 'rough balance' of all affected interests. With the exception of a handful of cases from the EIP programme involving environmental leaders, all three programmes lacked any significant representation from outside their immediate local geographic area. This included state and national environmental groups, regular visitors to the area, such as recreationalists/tourists in NEIP (the impacts of tourism being an identified environmental problem in the Sustainable Township case) and, in the RNRM case, urban interests or consumers of agricultural products (Interview 212, Local Resident; Interview 338, Local Government).

In the EIP programme, the majority of cases involving non-leaders (i.e., good and poor performers) also lacked representation from groups who lived away from the industry, but reportedly experienced its impacts (e.g., occasional noise or odour events). As one respondent explained: 'There's a few live out there past us . . . They say "we smelt it" but they don't want to get involved' (Interview 173, Local Resident). While a higher level of involvement in these cases had been attained from the neighbouring local community, some respondents questioned whether these actors were sufficiently representative. Those who participated frequently included retired individuals and technically trained people (e.g., ex-engineers) with an interest in the industry or pollution issues. Such persons were rarely considered to reflect the wider demographic of the local affected community (Interview 161, Industry).

Despite these shortcomings, a positive finding in the EIP programme was that most cases had significant success in attracting 'ordinary citizens'. Indeed, the majority of EIP cases came close to reaching the recommended number of five community/ resident representatives. Most of these residents had no previous connection to organized community groups or any previous influence over decision-making regarding industry environmental performance. As one resident put it, prior to the EIP: 'The residents had no idea at all about any EPA regulations, noise limits or the right boundaries . . . we just used to ring the [V]EPA' (Interview 112, Local Resident).

These findings can be contrasted to the Degraded Creek and Sustainable Township cases in the NEIP programme. Here, in addition to a failure in the Degraded Creek case to obtain sufficient representation of industry stakeholders, non-government representatives tended to be limited to the 'usual suspects' – namely, local residents and other participants who were already active and networked in relation to the environmental issue at stake (Taylor, 2003, p133; Parkinson, 2006, p57). These participants were not seen as typical of the communities from which they came, and were not seen as representing a cross section of the community or 'ordinary citizens'. As one NEIP participant put it: '[The NEIP] has been preaching very much to the converted. The engagement has been very much among the people who were already involved in a lot of similar activities (Interview, Industry, from Environment and Natural Resource Committee, 2005, p124; Interview 215, Local Government).

Similar 'usual suspects' were prominent in EIP cases involving environmental leaders. Here there was a noticeable lack of representation from ordinary citizens, local residents and industry 'neighbours' (Interview 151, Industry). In an effort to bolster group numbers, these industries had often engaged experienced and interested representatives from other EIP groups that lived some distance from the industry. As one respondent described these representatives, they were 'semi-professional . . . they're actually not [local] residents' (Interview 161, Industry).

A similar pattern was evident in RNRM. Here ordinary citizens, such as urban residents or 'average' farmers from the region, were not represented on the RNRM body. Instead, representation was dominated by existing sub-regional catchment management association groups (CMA groups) and Landcare groups that were already active and networked around natural resource management issues and had previous input into NRM decision-making. These stakeholders comprised almost half of the requisite 'community' membership. This appears to be consistent across many other regional bodies in Queensland (Whelan and Oliver, 2006, pp31–32).

While the regional body had successfully obtained representation of scientific interests, respondents reported that the body had otherwise failed to meet its requirement for balanced representation of stakeholders' interests. This included reported gaps in representation of affected mining and tourism interests (which employed the most people within the region) (BDTNRM, 2005a, p34; Access Economics, 2005, at II), a lack of specific representation of all affected Landcare or CMA groups from the various sub-regions and a dominance of production interests in sub-regional group membership. As one respondent put it: 'If you look at the make-up of the regional board I see such a strong lobby from agriculture and pastoral industry' (Interview 341, Regional Body).

Contrary to the above findings for the majority of our cases, respondents in the Water Supply case in the NEIP programme reported largely equitable and 'balanced' representation from affected non-government stakeholders. Further, a cross section of the neighbourhood community had been obtained – save for environmental interest groups. According to respondents, affected interests in urban areas and rural areas were represented almost equally (Interview 235, VEPA). Representatives from central businesses, community groups and other collaborations had also been obtained (Interview 231, CMA). While some local resident representatives were considered by some to be 'the outspoken people' (Interview 235, VEPA), many were ordinary citizens who had not previously been active nor had any influence over relevant decision-making on the issue.

What can we learn from the above findings? It is to this question that we now turn.

Explaining patterns of representation

A range of interrelated and overlapping factors contributed to the various patterns of representation across our programmes. Consistent with the expectations of some NEG scholars, the under-representation of potential 'countervailing power' environmental interest groups reportedly arose due to at least three factors. First was the well recognized problem of insufficient funding for public interest groups, which prevented many of these NGOs (particularly peak groups distant from decentralized NEG forums) covering their costs of engaging in the collaborative processes. Second was their absence from 'local' areas and third their adversarial attitudes (Fung and Wright, 2003a, p283). Environmental interests were particularly absent in rural areas, such as the Water Supply case and in the RNRM programme. As one government respondent explained: '[Regional Body] can't get a greenie on their committee because no one will stand up and say I'm a greenie and so they have a void there' (Interview 321, Government Agency).

Other respondents from the EIP and RNRM programmes argued that the under-representation of localized and state environmental groups arose from their adversarial nature and their 'deeply entrenched attitudes and belief systems' (Interview 318, Environmental Group). Similar explanations for the lack of environmental engagement in new governance were offered in our New Zealand demonstration programmes (see Box 4.1).

BOX 4.1 NEW ZEALAND DEMONSTRATION CASES: ENVIRONMENTAL INTEREST GROUPS

As was the case in Australia, all three of our New Zealand demonstration programmes – the Living Streams Programme, Collaborative Catchment Management and the Canterbury Water Management Strategy – aimed to engage environmental interest groups as members of their decentralized collaborative groups (ECan, 2009a, p2; Jenkins, 2007a, p3; Canterbury Mayoral Forum, 2009, pp18–19).

Only the Collaborative Catchment Management (CCM) and the Canterbury Water Management Strategy (CWMS) successfully accomplished this goal, but they did so in very different ways. Much like the Australian programmes, CWMS had engaged an existing local chapter of a peak environmental group. This chapter was composed of volunteers rather than the professional staff common to the centralized peak organization.

In contrast, the novel approach taken by the CCM programme involved the development of new environmental groups in the form of Local Charitable Trusts (Trusts). These Trusts represented the environmental concerns of the affected local catchment communities in the wider CCM collaborative process.

continued . . .

BOX 4.1 *. . . continued*

Interestingly, these Trusts sometimes absorbed the membership of existing local environmental groups in the catchment area, with the latter choosing to dissolve and join the new charitable Trust. However, as discussed below, some pre-existing groups chose both to maintain their operations and remain largely outside the collaborative process.

In contrast to CCM or CWMS, the Living Streams Programme (LSP) had very little success engaging environmental interests – only one of the three LSP collaborative groups we examined secured an environmental interest group representative. Again this was a volunteer-based local chapter of a peak group.

The reasons for these engagement gaps in LSP, and the unwillingness of some local groups in CCM to engage appeared to mirror our findings in Australia. Common themes were limited resourcing for environmental interests generally (LSP and CCM), the absence of organized groups in, or geographically near, localized and predominantly rural locales (LSP) and the adversarial and autonomous nature of existing environmental groups (CCM). As one respondent explained, such fierce independence and desire to maintain a 'pure position' was the primary motivator for a pre-existing environmental group to remain outside of the CCM process:

> I think a big factor motivating people remaining in the [existing environmental group] . . . was understanding that the [new environmental group] was in a situation that it's got a cooperative agreement with the poacher – the council. The constitution of [the existing group] doesn't have any inhibitions or prohibitions . . . it speaks for its own interests and its common shared interest is the wellbeing of the estuary and good functioning of the catchment.
>
> (Interview NZ214, Environmental Group)

BOX 4.2 NEW ZEALAND DEMONSTRATION CASES: INDIGENOUS POPULATIONS

Contrary to many government agencies in Australia, regional councils in New Zealand have very specific statutory responsibilities to take account of their local indigenous people, the Māori. This involves recognizing and providing for the Māori relationship with the environment and taking into account the

continued . . .

BOX 4.2 *. . . continued*

principles of the Treaty of Waitangi (hereafter the Treaty). The Treaty sets a framework in relation to resource ownership in New Zealand – both in terms of the treaty itself and in relation to customary authority exercised in an identified area (*Resource Management Act 1991* (NZ), ss 6, 8, hereafter RMA). Our research focused on the Canterbury region, which lies in the area of one tribe, the Ngāi Tahu (ECan, 2007, p2; *Ngāi Tahu Claims Settlement Act 1998* (NZ)). In practice, the Canterbury regional council is required to consult with a statutory body known as Te Rūnanga o Ngāi Tahu, who represent the tribal collective that holds customary authority over the Canterbury area. This obligation was augmented by the introduction of the *Local Government Act 2002* (NZ) (hereafter the LGA), which requires the council to facilitate the participation of Māori in local government decision-making processes (*Local Government Act 2002* (NZ), ss 4, 14, 81).

Pursuant to both the LGA and RMA, the regional council has endeavoured to engage Māori in their new governance approaches. Our findings, however, revealed only partial success. The Canterbury Water Management Strategy, for example, had successfully secured the participation of Te Rūnanga o Ngāi Tahu in regional decision-making to develop a water management strategy. However, the more decentralized programmes, involving both decision-making and implementation responsibilities appeared to face greater challenges. The three cases we studied in the Living Streams Programme, for instance, had no direct Māori participant, although all had certainly remained open to the participation of any interested Māori stakeholders.

The experience of the CCM and its efforts to engage Māori representatives is of particular note. One of our CCM cases involved a large lake, whose bed was owned by the Ngāi Tahu tribe (as part of its 1996 treaty settlement). However, there was a noticeable gap in representation by Māori interests in this case, and so too in our other CCM case that was focused on an estuary. Although the CCM cases had consulted with *tāngata whenua* representatives for short periods during the CCM planning stage, they and their statutory representative had progressively scaled back their engagement and stopped attending meetings. Despite considerable ongoing effort to secure wider Māori representatives, little success was achieved (for further on this issue, see Ruru, 2010). This was attributable to two key challenges. First, even with small amounts of government funding to support the CCM process, the time and cost demands were simply too much for either volunteer collaborators (who lacked the time to identify an appropriate local Māori representative), or for potential Māori stakeholders (many of whom were already overstretched as representatives across other governance initiatives). As one respondent

continued . . .

BOX 4.2 *. . . continued*

explained: 'We've struggled with [Māori] representation and their organisations have struggled to have the stability to actually get involved in this, it's a resourcing issue' (Interview NZ227, Government Body). The second challenge that stymied wider engagement was that many local Māori representatives and Te Rūnanga o Ngāi Tahu believed that acting as one of a number of community stakeholders in the CCM process did not adequately reflect their rights under the Treaty of Waitangi as resource managers and/or owners. Accordingly, they chose not to engage with new governance processes, and instead act under other statutory management mechanisms, including a joint statutory management plan with the Crown regarding the Lake (*Te Waihora Joint Management Plan*, 2005; Interview NZ221, Māori Stakeholder).

Beyond environmental interest groups, the above patterns arose from specific preconditions, such as how pressing the environmental problem was and the stake local actors had in it. For example, the higher rates of participation of ordinary citizens in EIP programme cases and the Water Supply (NEIP) case appeared to result from the urgency of the problem and the high stakes these non-government participants had in it (Abers, 2003; Fung, 2003, pp342–343, 352). Ordinary citizens living near polluting industries were particularly attracted to participating in EIP as it provided an avenue for them to resolve industry's direct impacts on their daily lives (Fung, 2003, p359). The motivations and passion of local residents to resolve such impacts is evident in the following anecdote from one industry respondent:

> We called a public meeting to discuss the issue. About 50 local residents showed up . . . at the meeting we were given the rounds of the kitchen. The focus was on the past. Many of the residents had been round here before the company, they gave us a potted history of the business, and they vented their spleen on the company's past and the problems. We were big brother and they didn't trust us.
>
> (Interview 111, Industry)

In contrast, environmental leaders often had a negligible impact on the local area, giving affected neighbours little motivation to participate in the EIP. This left the door open for the 'usual suspects' to make up the numbers.

Similarly, respondents in the EIP programme (particularly in young EIPs) regularly reported that the *lack* of more balanced representation in their cases was attributable to the community's general disinterest in wider environmental issues. Indeed, because the public experienced few (if any) tangible impacts of industries' global environmental degradation (e.g., water and energy use) most had little motivation to collaborate. As one respondent explained; 'The [collaborations] are not totally representative and that can maybe be the process that we set up, and sometimes it can just be the general ambivalence or apathy that a lot of community members have' (Fung and Wright, 2003b, pp37–38).

In the NEIP programme, high stakes for ordinary residents were present in the Water Supply case where the personal health and/or income of average residents and farmers were impacted upon by an increasingly degraded water supply. Accordingly, residents had a particularly high stake in this issue because the risk of tourists becoming ill threatened the town's income and raised public liability issues. Again in contrast, the environmental issues addressed in the other two NEIP cases (a creek that largely served as a stormwater drain for urban and industrialized suburbs, and the broad issue of a sustainable coastal township) were considered comparatively less important to most ordinary people.

Ordinary urban consumers from within and outside the region in the RNRM programme appeared to be underrepresented for similar reasons. Indeed, the stakes of urban consumers in natural resource problems remained largely diffuse, not least because the RNRM programme was predominantly focused on rural problems, such as salinity and biodiversity, and 'most of the urban community wouldn't even know [RNRM] existed' (Interview 337, Local Government). The under-representation of average farmers in the RNRM programme may also be attributable to a similar lack of stake, given that, for most, their short-term economic interests were not impacted and the goals of the RNRM programme were essentially long term.

Another important impediment to participation was the time and skill burdens imposed by all three programmes (notwithstanding government support and funding). This was widely reported to be a serious obstacle to obtaining greater participation from ordinary citizens and farmers, as well as more equality and balance in representation from inside and outside the local area (Steinzor, 1998a, p142; Steinzor, 2000, pp19–20; Tushnet, 2003, p170; Thomas, 2003, p166).

In older EIP cases, the *ongoing* time and costs of participating had reportedly been too much for some participants, leading to a reduction in participation numbers and in the representativeness of the group (as we discuss in Chapter 6). In the Sustainable Township and Degraded Creek cases in the NEIP programme, respondents blamed the time and cost demands imposed by the NEIP, which were notably onerous: 'it's a big time commitment for individuals to put in . . . it's a big ask' (Interview 211, VEPA). The fact that participants saw the commitments required to participate in the NEIP programme as a bigger barrier than participation in an EIP (which only became a major problem over the longer term) may explain why the EIP's primary weakness was gaining more balanced representation, while in the case of NEIPs the struggle was primarily to secure participation from ordinary citizens. Respondents from both programmes also saw skills and time commitments as a particular barrier for migrants because they 'didn't have the language skills' (Interview 182, Local Resident) to participate in the process (Interview 211, VEPA).

Time demands were similarly reported as too much for ordinary farmers in RNRM: 'it's hard to get the real honest toilers to sit on these things because they're too busy earning a quid' (Interview 321, Government Agency). Indeed, although the RNRM programme provided a small rebate to representatives to offset what were often significant time and travel costs (approximately A$5000, which, at the time of writing is approximately US$5060) (BDTNRM, 2005c, p12), this was seen as largely incommensurate with demands and tasks expected of representatives (Interview 3210, Science). These demands appeared particularly insurmountable for more diverse industry sectors, such as the tourism industry, that were seen to be such a 'poorly organized, poorly structured industry' (Interview 338, Local Government) that they did not have the resources to put an appropriate representative forward. Other respondents also suggested that the responsibilities and skills associated with RNRM also may have prevented ordinary farmers from volunteering to participate: '[it] is sort of difficult for people . . . say practical cane farmers, if they can't resolve something over a cup of tea that night, well move on, better do something else you know' (Interview 332, Local Government).

Mitigating most of these apparent impediments were government 'checks' and support mechanisms. Some respondents certainly saw these as useful for seeking out and encouraging broader representation. For example, government funding was used to overcome barriers to Indigenous representation in the RNRM case (Traditional Custodians of Country in the Burdekin Dry Tropics Region, 2005, pp1 and 6; BDTNRM, 2005b, pp15–16).

Although one can speculate why Indigenous interests remained under-represented across regional bodies in Queensland (Whelan and Oliver, 2006), the data from one case revealed little evidence on the issue. Whatever the reasons, and despite the fact government agencies recognized the need and importance of ensuring adequate representation, one cannot but conclude that these, and the other representation inadequacies discussed above, were not adequately resolved by government oversight and government did not view such representation deficits as a reason for withholding support or delaying implementation. Indeed, despite the deficits in inclusiveness and representation across the cases, the VEPA approved all plans in EIPs and NEIPs and the Queensland government provided funding to all regional bodies (BDTNRM, 2005a, pp8–9; Head, 2005a, p148; Head and Ryan, 2004).

Explaining exceptions: the Water Supply case

The Water Supply case in the NEIP programme was exceptional in that (save for environmental interests) it achieved a balanced representation from affected non-government stakeholders as well as from a cross section of the neighbourhood community. One reason for this was the high stake local residents had in resolving the local environmental problem. However, other factors also played an important role.

In particular, this case involved a small affected population (approximately a hundred people), and this reportedly reduced the potential range of 'affected interests'. This made it comparatively easy to achieve balanced representation. Indeed, respondents suggested it had been relatively straightforward to identify and include not only those already known to VEPA, but also those that were 'missing' and to determine how they should be balanced. As one officer reported: 'we can go through every single person and I can tell you where they stood on [the NEIP issues]' (Interview 231, CMA).

Of course, this is not to claim that the Water Supply case had flawlessly met the idealized criteria for representation and captured all the interests and views of the hundred people affected in the area. However, when compared to the experience of the other cases discussed above, it achieved considerable success in including and representing key affected urban and rural interests, as well as incorporating a cross section of the views of average farmers, ordinary citizens and businesses.

The small size of the population also allowed government organizers to establish a credible and low-cost representation system that elected representatives from the community. This involved holding an initial town public meeting that reportedly included nearly the entire affected population. At the meeting an initial six of the total 18 local residents were nominated and elected as formal representatives (Interview 231, CMA).

Respondents suggested that those representatives who had been elected were happy with their role as a representative and that they maintained 'good communication' (Interview 235, VEPA) with non-participants. Because of the small size of the community, representatives were able to rely on existing community networks, open meetings and public notices (in the only general store in town) to generate effective two-way communication. As one respondent reflected on the difference between the Degraded Creek case and the Water Supply case:

> ... the other country ones, you've got a lot more of that connected community already ... which is why I think that the country ones are probably better – you've already got that community feel and things already established. So in the city it's more difficult.
>
> (Interview 211, VEPA)

In contrast to the Water Supply case in the NEIP programme, there was no evidence of formal election of representatives across the other programmes. However, there was *some* evidence of informal relationships fulfilling a similar de facto role, but not one that, for the most part, performed credibly (Mansbridge, 2003, p194; Cohen and Fung, 2004, p30; John, 2004, pp231–232; Trachtenberg and Focht, 2005, p59).

Certainly, most (albeit not all) representatives from organized groups (e.g., community, environmental and sub-regional CMA and Landcare groups) were reported to have maintained relatively effective communication and accountability with their membership. However, aside from the Water Supply case, informal relationships between individual local residents and people in the wider community were less common. This appeared to be attributable to both the practical cost and time limitations of an individual's capacity to maintain active communication with the wider community and the fact that most participants were often reluctant to take on a representative role. Indeed, nearly all local residents who had volunteered in the EIP programme, along with the 'usual suspects' residents in the Sustainable Township and Degraded Creek cases in the NEIP programme, reportedly did not 'take any particular responsibility and accountability back to anywhere else' (Interview 161, Industry).

While these findings are perhaps predictable, they do provide a valuable, empirical insight by pointing to what appears to be the very real limits of individual citizens taking on a role as an informal and accountable representative of those who do not directly participate in NEG (Mansbridge, 2003, p194).

Findings – Deliberative Processes

NEIP, RNRM and the problem of power imbalances

Decision-making in our NEIP and RNRM programmes involved various public, private and community stakeholders engaging in multiple negotiation and mediation processes to try and reach agreement on complex planning documents. As we will see, the presence of skilled mediators ensured that non-government actors had opportunities to express their views and opinions in processes of non-adversarial decision-making. Despite this success, these negotiators were unable alone to sufficiently offset an imbalance in skills and capacities between non-government and government stakeholders and/or prevent government from utilizing the legal framework to control decision-making. Further, in the NEIP programme in particular, our respondents raised concerns about the independence of the negotiators. Together, these three issues ultimately undermined the input of non-government stakeholders and saw government agencies dominate the deliberative processes.

Although government and non-government actors were often at the same negotiation table, for heuristic purposes, we focus first on the negotiation process between non-government actors, before turning to consider the more problematic interaction between non-government and government actors.

Respondents in both NEIP and RNRM programmes noted that their decision-making processes had at times involved conflict and self-interested bargaining between non-government parties, often arising from power imbalances between different non-government stakeholders (Interview 214, Government). For example, one respondent in RNRM suggested that the over-representation of agricultural and primary industry interests on the regional body might have influenced the consultation process during plan development. However, most of our respondents reported that the presence of skilled negotiators and mediators in decision-making forums had largely overcome these challenges to foster genuine reasoned discussion among themselves.

In the NEIP programme, for example, negotiators who had been hired by VEPA or sponsors, had reportedly done an effective job in facilitating community forums, encouraging 'lots of talking over the issues' (Interview 212, Local Resident), and 'significant negotiations' between non-government stakeholders (Interview 213, Local Government). Over time these negotiators were vital to moving stakeholders forward from simple strategic argument and preconceived positions towards discussing, reasoning, sharing information and ultimately adjusting their positions to 'agree on something' (Interview 235, VEPA; Thomas, 2003, p159). As one respondent reflected on the role of their negotiator during various negotiations and meetings that occurred to develop their plan:

> . . . all of us now understand a bit more about where everyone else is . . . they'd say 'Let's think about this, what do people want to see? Let's see if we can do that' . . . they sat down around the table and up on the whiteboard, talking through the issues, they narrowed it and said 'what do you think?'
> (Interview 211, VEPA)

Similarly in RNRM, respondents variously pointed to the key role of negotiators in forums, and workshops at both sub-regional and regional levels to ensure genuine processes of 'negotiating with the property owners' (Interview 341, Regional Body; Interview 327, Government Agency), 'negotiation between community sectors, stakeholders and individuals' (BDTNRM, 2005a, p197) and to foster 'negotiated solutions' among different sectors in the region (Interview 331, Science). In particular, respondents noted the important role these facilitators played in assisting productive discussion, and making parties comfortable in the process:

> . . . there were difficulties in bringing in people to open up, to feel comfortable that ideas that they really didn't like were coming through. I think there were one or two instances where people didn't want to be part of it anymore because they felt threatened too much, but again the facilitator was a very wise choice to make. [He/she] was somebody who could bring those people back in pretty non-threateningly and get them back on board.
> (Interview 348, Regional Body)

Ultimately, such facilitation (often combined with significant technical information and support as noted below) ensured non-government parties were able to negotiate and reach agreed positions on overarching regional targets:

> . . . the meeting that happened I reckon sorted this out, well no meeting actually formalized it . . . industry said 'yeah we are willing to admit that there are things that can be improved', so we got away from 'you are wrong you are wrong' situation to one of well 'what can we do?'
> (Interview 331, Science)

Despite this successful decision-making among non-government actors, many respondents questioned the overall level of fair and genuine deliberation achieved by the programmes. These questions arose because of power imbalances between government and non-government stakeholders, with the former regularly manipulating or overriding decisions made by the latter in ways that marginalized non-governmental interests, promoted government programmes, and/or simply eroded decisions. Echoing the reservations of some NEG authors, this domination arose from three sources.

First, the technical knowledge and skills of government officers who participated in the process often overwhelmed non-governmental stakeholders. This was most apparent only in the NEIP programme, where non-governmental stakeholders when asked to reflect on the decision-making, consultation and plan-writing process described it as 'mainly a place of agencies' (Interview 221, Local Resident), 'experts' (Interview 231, CMA) and 'people who were used to doing that sort of thing as part of their job' (Interview 227, Local Resident). The result was that 'it all became a bit high brow' (Interview 227, Local Resident) for non-governmental respondents, who – while they could express their point of view – felt that they could not 'drive' the decision-making and instead were 'sitting back and watching the process' (Interview 221, Local Resident). There were few similar concerns of such 'technical' dominance in the RNRM programme, most likely because regional bodies had been better supported by governments to conduct research and to form a technical advisory panel (including biophysical and socio-economic science from a range of academic, research institutions, government and non-governmental organizations) to assist them in their decision-making (BDTNRM, 2005a, pp12, 185–190 and 196).

There was also a second and more prevalent concern. In the case of the RNRM, this arose from the Regional Coordination Group and Joint Steering Committee utilizing other institutional opportunities to dominate decision-making. These groups reportedly played an important 'policing role' (Interview 3211, Government Agency): ensuring groups met standards and procedures set in the RNRM legal and policy framework, and approved plans accordingly. However, our findings indicated that government had used these powers to override a number of successfully facilitated decisions made by non-government regional groups (in consultation with the regional community) without providing them with any reasoning, opportunity for negotiation or cooperative discussion. As one respondent put it:

> . . . some of the [plans and targets] have been really good but then it gets down to the point that these targets are written, and it's something the group and the community agrees with, it goes to the JSC and the Commonwealth say that's not good enough, crosses it out, rewrites it, signs the plan off and sends it back.
>
> (Interview 311, Industry Body)

Similar problems arose in the NEIP programme regarding both local government sponsors and the VEPA who had privileged institutional and decision-making positions. Indeed, on all accounts the VEPA and local government used this power to 'drive' (Interview 231, CMA) the agenda of the NEIP planning and proposal process and dominate agenda setting (Interview 211, EPA). As one officer commented, 'it was driven by myself, [VEPA and another local government officer] . . . and all of the meetings and all the agendas and topics were really driven by us' (Interview 221, Coordinator).

Third and finally, the fact that government bodies controlled seed funding in NEIP meant that the coordinator they had employed to assist with the consultation and plan-drafting process was also often less than independent, and acted as another officer of government that often 'push[ed] the community into something they didn't necessarily want' (Interview 237, VEPA).

Transcending power disparities: the EIP model

There was a similar potential for government to dominate decision-making, and for power imbalances to jeopardize deliberative decision-making in the case of the EIP programme. However, respondents suggested that this was extremely rare. One reason for this is that, unlike the NEIP or RNRM programmes, where government agencies either commit to take actions and integrate their organization's goals and activities with non-governmental stakeholders (NEIP) or invest significant public funding (RNRM), in EIP the VEPA has a much lower 'organizational' stake in the programme. It invested no direct funds beyond officer attendance at meetings, made no direct commitments to take actions apart from existing responsibilities to monitor industry and attend the collaboration. Furthermore, the VEPA took a minimal role in holding groups accountable for substantive targets and rarely sought to intervene in this regard (Interview 141, Industry).

The result was that in the case of the EIP Programme the process for most stakeholders involved relatively fair and genuine negotiation to reach agreement on how to address *local* issues, such as noise, amenity, odour and dust impacts. As the following anecdote from one industry illustrates, this process involved reason giving, debate and discussion:

> . . . if we couldn't do something the community wanted we would agree to understand them and say look we are listening to you, but right now this is what we are facing and we would explain our rationale for our decision-making, we wouldn't say 'No! We don't want to!'
>
> (Interview 141, Industry)

These processes of negotiation resulted in residents and industry adjusting their pre-established positions based on the insights and new information they gained through the negotiation:

> . . . my line is now 'run the place and run it properly'. You know, it's about change . . . I understand their point of view now . . . 7–8 years ago I wanted to close them down.
>
> (Interview 111, Industry)

These findings may appear surprising given that, as we saw earlier, in many EIP cases industries blatantly abused their power over information by telling 'lies' about the nature and extent of their pollution impacts. Yet, despite the self interest and power of industry and its capacity to manipulate information, successful negotiation on local issues was nevertheless achieved. This was because a number of conditions were met that enabled the power disparities and informational asymmetries between the community representatives and the industry to be transcended.

First, echoing some NEG authors (Fung and Wright, 2003b, p23), most negotiation processes were underpinned by 'power balancing' mechanisms, including background rules, court orders, and subtler forms of VEPA persuasion and threats to reputation and social licence. These ensured that industry, at the very least, had been induced to come to the table, disclose some information and negotiate (Karkkainen, 2006b, pp295–296).

Second – again echoing recommendations in the dispute resolution and deliberation literatures – VEPA, local government or a hired mediator, reportedly assisted parties to reach a decision (O'Leary et al, 2004, pp332–333). These 'neutrals' were considered vital in cases characterized by high-severity problems and conflict. A minority of respondents raised concerns regarding the neutrality of professional mediators where they had been hired by industry (Interview 182, Local Resident). However, on the whole these and other types of mediators were considered to be 'very important' (Interview 162, Local Resident), 'effective' (Interview 174, Industry) and essential to 'control the debate' (Interview 174, Industry) and allow representatives to 'negotiate the high level objectives' (Interview 182, Local Resident).

In those cases involving lower-severity problems and less conflict, 'impartial' mediators were rare. Indeed, industries in these cases tended to be more reputation conscious, 'very open and transparent' (Interview 151, Industry; Interview 133, Local Resident/Environmental Group; Interview 132, VEPA), and built trust quickly with non-governmental actors. Under these conditions, non-governmental stakeholders and VEPA reportedly agreed to allow industry representatives to chair the meetings and suggested they were 'very fair' (Interview 133, Local Resident/Environmental Group; Interview 132, VEPA) and called 'a spade a spade even to [their] own staff' (Interview 132, VEPA).

Third, the risk of such industry chairs, or less than 'neutral' hired mediators, to act in a biased manner was reportedly checked by the presence of a VEPA officer. Indeed, consistent with expectations of some authors, this final condition was reported to ensure a degree of fairness to the process in both types of EIP cases (Freeman, 1997, p32). As one industry respondent explained, they saw the VEPA officer's presence as 'Mak[ing] sure that we're consulting and that we're being reasonable and listening and where opportunities for improvement are available that we take those on board' (Interview 142, Industry).

These three elements resulted in local residents being able to genuinely participate in decision-making, setting and consenting to targets, and shaping substantive agendas on local pollution issues, such as noise, amenity, odour and dust (Gray, 1989, pp8–9; Cohen and Sabel, 1997, p323). However, our findings suggested that such conditions for balancing power were not always effective in fostering fair negotiation processes. In particular, when it came to *broader and more technical issues*, such as greenhouse gas and wastewater, industry appeared to often dominate decision-making and overpower non-governmental actors' decision-making capacities (Farber, 1999, p24; Steinzor, 2000, p18). Three main reasons appeared to explain why this was so.

First, even though 'power balancing' mechanisms encouraged industry to reveal information to non-governmental actors about these technical issues, non-governmental stakeholders who were interested in such issues commonly reported that such information was 'too technical for us to say what to do' (Interview 162, Local Resident). VEPA officers confirmed this fact, suggesting: 'with technical details and the actual actions and improvements, the community has a very minor input' (Interview 181, VEPA).

Second, and closely related to the above, industry either consciously or unconsciously exploited their knowledge advantage. Indeed, consistent with some authors' fear (Farber, 1999, p24) one industry respondent suggested they could dazzle and placate local residents easily enough by using technical information and setting targets that were largely in the industry's interest – 'if you get out ahead of them, then they'll just sit there and listen' (Interview 184, Industry). However, such a direct intent to manipulate was the exception rather than the rule. Nonetheless, most industry respondents acknowledged that they made the majority of decisions on technical issues, with either cursory or no input from local residents – 'to be candid I would say most of the time about 85–90 per cent is generally prepared by us' (Interview 131, Industry).

The final reason that industry was able to exploit their technical knowledge advantage in their favour echoes concerns such as those expressed by Steinzor (2000, p19) and Fung and Wright (2003a, p265), namely, that government officers were either 'overwhelmed' or too passive in evaluating technical issues. Indeed, some VEPA officers characterized their role as little more than to 'sit there and watch and let the parties sort it out between them' (Interview 113, VEPA). Further, they reportedly provided little of the needed and expected technical support nor the training to improve the capacity of non-governmental stakeholders to meaningfully participate in the process.

Given these power imbalances in the EIP process, as well as problems raised in the RNRM and NEIP programmes, it is important to consider the impact of the environmental interest groups who engaged in our five cases from the NEIP and EIP programmes. Some scholars suggest that these interest groups can act as a countervailing power to level or reduce asymmetries in prior organization, knowledge, intensity of interest and capabilities and so create conditions for fairer collaborative decision-making processes (see e.g. Fung and Wright, 2003a, pp226 and 284).

Findings – countervailing powers

Our findings suggest that 'home grown' or local environmental groups sometimes possessed the necessary organizational competencies required to collaborate so as to create a countervailing base. Across the three cases from the EIP programme, local environmental groups concerned with nature conservation were able to directly engage with industry on certain technical and 'bigger picture' environmental issues, such as biodiversity, the impacts of sewage on oceans or impacts on the local fauna and flora. As one VEPA officer from an EIP case explained: '[The environmental groups] provide guidance to the [industry] about how to select the species and that type of thing, biodiversity is another one . . . So they do drive the company' (Interview 132, VEPA).

Although the dominance of industrial or development interests was of less concern in the Sustainable Township and Degraded Creek cases in the NEIP programme, the local environmental interest group was recognized as a non-governmental stakeholder who could engage more directly with government agencies on environmental issues, rather than 'sit back' as local residents had done. For example, as one VEPA officer noted: '[The government] organizations would put themselves forward, saying, "yes, we can do this" . . . and during that, you'd have [environmental group] going "well, how about this, can you do this?"' (Interview 211, VEPA).

However, the findings suggest that this countervailing power role was limited in two respects. First, some interest groups did not appear to have the skills or vision to represent the 'full' public interest, and tended to countervail predominantly on issues close to the group's heart, as opposed to the full range of technical issues or speaking for 'the environment' more generally (McCloskey, 1996; Farber, 2000, p75; Seidenfeld, 2000, p477; Defilippis et al, 2006, p684). As one respondent put it: '. . . sometimes these groups can be fairly single-issue focused and, as long as their part of the environment is doing all right, bugger the rest, if you know what I mean' (Interview 123, VEPA).

The second and overlapping constraint on the countervailing role of these groups was that collaboration sat uncomfortably with their traditional adversarial advocacy or 'outsider' roles (Sturm, 2006, p331). Although our findings are restrained by our limited data set, one group in the EIP programme reported becoming frustrated and excluded themselves altogether from the collaboration to pursue an advocacy role outside the group (Interview 121, VEPA). State-level representatives, for example, also noted the difficulties faced by the few environmental groups that were represented in regional collaborations – similarly suggesting the difficulty of 'walking the fine line' between collaborating and advocacy (Farber, 1999, p75;

Sturm, 2006, p331; Taylor, 2007, p312). Similar challenges were also raised in our New Zealand demonstration programmes (see Box 4.3 below).

These difficulties suggest the importance of asking: what other forms or ways of mobilizing countervailing powers may be available? The findings in the EIP programme and the RNRM programme pointed to the development of two potentially promising and novel structures for doing so (Sabel et al, 1999, p12).

BOX 4.3 NEW ZEALAND DEMONSTRATION CASES: COUNTERVAILING POWERS

Our examination of the environmental groups that had engaged in the New Zealand demonstration programmes revealed mixed success in their role as countervailing powers. Our respondents certainly offered a number of examples of environmental groups utilizing their local and technical knowledge to challenge and reduce the influence of economic and government interests relating to issues such as compliance with environmental laws and water management. For example, one environmental group from the CWMS programme stated:

> . . . we were feeling . . . manipulated by the agricultural types . . . they want[ed] to put a dam up at the River . . . so after we were coming up with evidence about this and the flows and so on, one of the people of a group that is very, very focused on irrigation and accessing water, he just stood up and said that he thought the dam was a no-go . . . and I realized that even though we were a small group, we were heard.
>
> (Interview NZ107, Environmental Group)

Despite such success, the majority of respondents in each case (save for the rare case discussed in Box 4.4 below) reported that the countervailing power role of environmental groups had been significantly constrained and diluted for two reasons. One of these, raised in the most locally-focused LSP programme, was that local groups tended to be parochial in their attitudes, concerned primarily with a single environmental issue and lacking in the skills or vision to represent the full public interest. As one respondent described a local conservation group: 'They're very focused and one eyed and they really don't understand that after a rain you've got a lot of tars and oils and all sorts of things wash off tar seal and . . . roads . . . They don't like being told these things' (Interview NZ322, Farmer).

Second, and characteristic of all three programmes, was balancing an advocacy/adversarial role with the novel collaborative politics of new governance. This was a major difficulty for environmental groups that were

continued . . .

BOX 4.3 *... continued*

supported by government funds for their operation and survival. As one non-government respondent pointed out: 'if the [Trust] really want to have a fight with the [government] they can't do it because it's biting the hand that feeds them' (Interview NZ212, Government Body). Even where the collaborative group was not substantially dependent on government funding, most respondents identified the cooperative decision-making and implementation approach inherent to NEG as a regular and significant constraint on an environmental group's capacity to fulfil a countervailing role. One environmental non-governmental organization (ENGO) representative summed it up as follows:

> Once we needed to lobby and write letters, but now [cooperative processes] are the way it is, so that's what the rules are now . . . [so] now I feel constrained, and I feel as my other colleague feels that when we were agreeing to things that we aren't very happy about, we are selling our souls and that's how we feel about it.
>
> (Interview NZ107, Environmental Group)

The first novel structure for mobilizing more effective countervailing powers emerged in a unique EIP case. This case involved a collaborative approach to managing odour and adverse effects on aquatic and coastal ecosystems caused by a sewage treatment plant and its ocean outfall. While the sewage treatment plant had engaged in collaboration with local residents, six local environmental groups, and the environmental regulator for a number of years, both the industry and regulator had been decidedly slow in taking action or requiring significant upgrades to the plant.

One local environmental group found this lack of action so frustrating that they began to engage in a public campaign against the industry and state government. However, such advocacy was difficult to reconcile with the EIP's collaborative approach, and the group chose to exit the collaboration.

Having excluded themselves, the group vigorously pursued campaigns, lobbied government and ministers and took legal action against decisions by the regulator. These actions were reportedly quite successful in generating public and political pressure on the regulator and industry to take serious action to upgrade the plant (something they and other local groups had not achieved from the 'inside' of NEG forums).

As may be apparent, the downside of acting solely on the 'outside' of the NEG forum was that this local group no longer had the same level of input and influence over the details of the upgrade. However, this deficit was readily compensated for by the local environmental groups who had continued to collaborate and could directly influence the details and actions taken to improve the plant's operations.

Perhaps most importantly, many collaborating local environmental groups felt that the external advocacy had allowed them to play a more effective countervailing role inside the NEG forum without damaging the collaborative relationship. That is, by pointing to the publicity and action outside of the EIP collaboration, the local environmental group collaborators could more effectively 'push' from the inside for meaningful changes and environmental improvements (Craig et al, 2004, p235). As one respondent from a participating environmental group described this success:

> . . . its actually good because [the 'outside' group] tend to use the stick approach. They'll hit 'em with a stick and say 'now that I've got your attention' and I think the industry and the government needed that . . . but our group they're enthusiastic but keen to get a positive approach to it . . . the [outside group] brought it to the public agenda and I think now it's up to us to get their point of view to the policymakers and it's time to look at long-term changes and to implement long-term strategies.
>
> (Interview 133, Local Resident/Environmental Group)

The resulting EIP case achieved a number of improvements over subsequent years of implementation, with the external local environmental group claiming a major victory as the industry, regulator and collaborative committee committed to a major upgrade of the plant and its processes.

Interestingly, we found a very similar productive relationship between insiders and outsiders in one of our New Zealand Collaborative Catchment Management (CCM) cases, as detailed in Box 4.4 below. What these two vignettes from the EIP and CCM programmes suggest is that it will often be easier for ENGOs to play a more effective countervailing role where the advocacy and cooperation tasks are shared between groups operating on the inside and outside of new governance forums. ENGOs on the outside are free to pursue more radical strategies in the knowledge that those on the inside will take care of the details. At the same time, their external advocacy supports those on the inside to have a strong countervailing voice, without the insider's actions being perceived as damaging to the cooperative relationship.

BOX 4.4 NEW ZEALAND DEMONSTRATION CASE: A NEW STRUCTURE FOR COUNTERVAILING POWERS

The difficulty local environmental groups appear to face in balancing advocacy with cooperation was sidestepped not only in the Australian EIP programme, but also in a unique CCM case where these roles were shared between a

continued . . .

BOX 4.4 *... continued*

new local environmental group that took the form of a charitable trust and an older local environmental group, which chose to remain on the outside of new governance.

This CCM case involved a district council that had responsibility for the disposal of sewage into a local estuary. The council and the environmental regulator had a history of battling with a local environmental group regarding the health of the estuary and there had been increasing public concern about the declining quality of the water. In response, the environmental regulator suggested that a CCM approach be pursued between themselves, the district council, and concerned local stakeholders, such as the local environmental group. However, rather than collaborate directly with multiple individuals and the environmental group, it was proposed that a new Local Charitable Trust be formed, whose brief would be to collaborate directly with the council and regulator.

While some members of the pre-existing environmental group decided to join the new organization, the majority kept their group operating outside of CCM because they were wary of the constraints imposed by the collaborative process (as discussed in Box 4.1 above).

As was the case in the EIP programme, the choice to remain on the outside of the new governance forum had its drawbacks, including difficulties in accessing information and updates from the council: '... the council keep leaving us out of the mailing list and we keep having to fight to get back on them ... you can get them brushing you out of existence ... it's very difficult to cope with' (Interview NZ214, Environmental Group). However, respondents were adamant that having one environmental group collaborating while another simultaneously operated outside of the CCM forum had significant benefits. Indeed, the older environmental group had reportedly pushed the council on some issues that the new Trust had neither been able or willing to do, including raising legal objections to council permits for the development of the estuary. This in turn assisted the Trust on the inside to harness this pressure and push for further changes in the management approach, without significantly upsetting the collaborative nature of the CCM forum. Those on the inside of CCM put it this way:

> ... you let the [old group] throw the rock so that it does damage which is helpful to everybody rather than being unhelpful, but it's a real art form ... when you need a shouter, they're quite useful but you've got to manage where they can do their shouting.
>
> (Interview NZ211, Environmental Group)

Largely because of this productive relationship between insiders and outsiders, the local groups were able to claim a number of successes, not least the relocation of the sewage outfall away from the estuary.

The second structure for mobilizing countervailing powers emerged at the Queensland state level in 2002 in the form of the 'Regional Groups Collective'. The Collective was a collaborative organization composed primarily of the chairs of each regional body in Queensland. It operated at the state, as opposed to the regional scale and thus created a 'higher' level nested governance arrangement (for a similar approach see Margerum, 2007, p143) that provided 'communication networks at a state level with key stakeholder organizations' (Interview 349, Regional Group Collective). This networking provided the opportunity for state-based sources of countervailing powers to emerge. Because the Collective was 'removed' from collaborative regional decision-making it enabled environmental groups to work with it, without becoming a formal member of a collaborative group. Similarly, because it operated at the state level the barriers of scale mismatches and adversarial framings that had prevented state groups from participating in RNRM were avoided.

The Collective accordingly was able to link with a state-based environmental group that had hitherto not participated in regional decision-making (Interview 318, Environmental Group). Through a government grant obtained through the RNRM programme to support the Collective, these two bodies were able to enhance the level of engagement of environment interest groups at lower regional levels (Margerum, 2007, p141). This support included flying environmental interest groups into regions to act as 'proxy' representatives on regional bodies that lacked environmental representatives. As the environmental group reported:

> . . . they've got people from the [city] flying into the [regional area] to engage with the [regional body]. We've got people from [environmental interest group in region A] going into [regional group C] to engage there as well.
>
> (Interview 318, Environmental Group)

At the time of research, the data remained limited in terms of how successful or sustainable these attempts to improve environmental representation had been, or whether the Collective had opened up other ways for state groups to be involved in RNRM. Nevertheless, these developments do provide a useful example of the sort of avenues that can be explored to provide opportunities for enhancing environmental voices in NEG processes. In this particular instance, the key elements of support for countervailing powers were (i) a nested collaboration approach and (ii) the availability of government funding to support under-funded groups.

Summary and Implications

In this chapter we have examined the conditions under which NEG can achieve meaningful participation and deliberation. Our analysis suggests that in all but rare cases, there were substantial difficulties in fully satisfying the participatory and deliberative aspirations of NEG (Samuelson et al, 2005, p166), with the challenges of negotiated decision-making and achieving 'balanced' representation and inclusiveness within a geographically defined area proving particularly onerous.

In line with research in other NEG contexts (Abel and Stephan, 2000, p625; Moore, 2005; Camacho, 2007; Robins and Dovers, 2007; for somewhat contrasting findings see Lockwood et al, 2009, pp177–178) we identified deficits in all cases regarding inclusiveness and representativeness, and pointed to the potential for NEG to largely disenfranchise environmental interest group stakeholders (McCloskey, 1996; Koontz and Thomas, 2006, p113). It was only in the exceptional Water Supply case in the NEIP programme that citizens and other interests were considered to have achieved a degree of balanced representation.

Critics of NEG might conclude from the above that their concerns are well founded (Steinzor, 1998a, pp142–143; Steinzor, 2000, p19; Tushnet, 2003, p170; Lane, 2006, pp7–9). However, although we identified substantial flaws in participatory and deliberative practices, it does not follow that the three programmes were completely undemocratic in their processes, entirely lacking in significant participation or wholly subject to the whims of the powerful (Lubell et al, 2005, p282).

On the contrary, it is important to remember that inclusive, representative and deliberative criteria are *ideals* that may never be fully realized in practice. All three programmes did include representation from a wide array of affected individuals, non-governmental organizations and private interests. Further, the deficits in the interests represented did not appear to arise from *calculated efforts* to exclude them. Indeed, the opposite appeared to be the case (Lubell et al, 2005, p282). Organizers and government officers all sought to widen representation but failed primarily due to matters of prior institutional design and/or other capricious factors beyond their control (Lubell et al, 2005, p282). Moreover, although negotiations and decision-making were often disproportionately shaped by powerful interests, non-government respondents in EIP, NEIP and RNRM were still able to input their views and influence decision-making.

More importantly, the weaknesses identified above do not imply that NEG's desires for enhancing participation and deliberation are necessarily a sham or somehow inherently flawed. Rather, our findings raise questions about how far the mechanisms and conditions for enhancing meaningful participation and deliberation might be reshaped so as to further contribute to achieving good NEG. We offer some directions for reshaping these conditions below, commencing with the issue of participation.

Our findings across the cases confirm that 'open door' policies are unlikely to be sufficient *in themselves* to even loosely approximate the representative ideal and that the deficits of this approach are not adequately resolved by government support, oversight and imposed procedural requirements (Abel and Stephan, 2000, p625; Marshall and Jones, 2005, p733; Bidwell and Ryan, 2006, p840). Beyond all else, these findings point to the importance of designing and contextualizing mobilization efforts to account for both the nature and impacts of the environmental issue and the relevant socio-demographic characteristics of desired participants (Marshall and Jones, 2005, p733; Fung, 2003, p342). For example, the findings suggest that time and skill demands act as significant impediments to representation from ordinary people, marginalized populations and other affected groups. They suggest a need for appropriate training, language support and/or funding (e.g., rebates more commensurate with time and skill demands) to reduce these barriers and impart the necessary foundational capacities (Taylor and Warburton, 2003, p331; Fung and Wright, 2003b, p29; Thomas, 2003, p166; Bidwell and Ryan, 2006, p840). Furnishing NEG with funding, however, introduces complicating factors. Among other dangers, the findings in the RNRM programme revealed that small reimbursement of volunteers' travel and organization costs may not be sufficient to overcome all representation deficits. While this suggests more investment in NEG is needed, policy designers must be careful not to create perverse incentives. As Taylor's work in the UK has shown, significant funding can often do more to reward 'usual suspect groups' than to encourage new and more representative participants (Taylor, 2003, p185).

Where interests are diffuse (such as in RNRM and the Sustainable Township and Degraded Creek cases) our results point to the importance of linking people's everyday concerns with the environmental and natural resource issues being addressed (Abers, 2003, p207). This may involve ongoing and extensive 'educational programmes' or similar 'community events' (Abers, 2003, p207; Marshall and Jones, 2005, pp733–734). Without these forms of assistance NEG participation may well be confined to 'usual suspects', rather than achieving popular participatory governance (Abel and Stephan, 2000, p625).

Turning to decision-making, in all three cases we found evidence of deliberative negotiation, albeit sometimes lapsing into strategic bargaining (Sturm, 2006, p331). However, the findings in the NEIP and RNRM programmes suggest that governmental agencies may often dominate decision-making processes. As in some other NEG studies (Whelan and Oliver, 2005, p133), this occurred because of an imbalance in skills and capacities and/or opportunities to control decision-making afforded by the legal framework. How far governments were willing or even capable of assuming the supportive and empowering role expected of them by NEG experiments is an open question (Abers, 2003, pp200–201; Defilippis et al, 2006, p684). Certainly power was at times abused by government to undermine genuine input of non-governmental stakeholders in decision-making (Paton et al, 2004, p263; Head, 2005a, pp30 and 148–149; Whelan and Oliver, 2005, p133). This was most common where government had a veto power over decisions.

Of course governments are often endowed with such veto powers for accountability purposes. However, in order to realize the ideals we have been exploring, alternative institutional designs and mechanisms for ensuring such accountability may be needed if government is to be disabused of the notion that it simply knows best.

In the EIP programme, where the VEPA had a much lower 'organizational' stake in the programme than government agencies in either NEIP or RNRM, the much larger problem was industry's dominance of *broader and more technical issues* due to knowledge imbalances between local non-governmental actors and technically trained industry members (Farber, 1999, p24; Steinzor, 2000, p9).

Our findings point to the importance of designing other mechanisms canvassed in the NEG literature to enhance the meaningful input of non-governmental stakeholders. For example, provision of education and training in deliberation and problem-solving may improve both government and non-government actors' adherence to ideals of negotiation (Fung, 2004, p26). Funding and technical support also plays an important role in reducing the capacity of government officers or of private industry to take advantage of informational asymmetries (Steinzor, 2000, p9; Fung, 2004, p26). As the experience of 'civic environmentalism' in the United States suggests, opportunities for non-governmental actors to input into decision-making seem more likely to arise under conditions where decision-making is centred around an 'independent' person who represents no particular substantive interest (John and Mlay, 1999, p360).

Our findings have also provided support for suggestions in the literature that the use of mediators, agency assistance and mechanisms, such as VEPA and community pressure, can effectively overcome or at least mitigate power imbalances. However, we found that although these conditions were effective for local issues, this was not the case when knowledge and capacity differences between non-governmental stakeholders and industry were amplified (i.e., more technical issues). In the latter circumstances, industry was able to exploit their technical knowledge and capacity to dominate decision-making and overwhelm government officers (Farber, 1999, p24; Steinzor, 2000, p19). Where knowledge imbalances are large (e.g., between industry and local resident) fair deliberative decision-making may require conditions such as funding for technical assistance, training in deliberation (as discussed above), and effective countervailing power (Steinzor, 2000, p19; Fung and Wright, 2003a, p265).

We also found empirical support both in Australia and in our New Zealand demonstration cases for a range of conjectures made in the NEG literature regarding environmental interest group participation. First, it was clear that national or state-located groups are typically adverse to or incapable of collaboration at local levels (Fung and Wright, 2003a, pp280–282). Second, local environmental groups were more inclined than state/national groups to participate in NEG (Fung and Wright, 2003a, p284), and in a number of cases played a countervailing role in offsetting the dominance of industry and government. However, echoing the concerns of other authors (Farber, 1999, p75; Seidenfeld, 2000, p477; Defilippis et al, 2006, p685), and empirical research in watersheds in the USA (Leach, 2006, p108), we also found that local groups were widely under-represented, largely because they lacked funding to cover the costs of engagement, were absent in locales or possessed cognitive frames incompatible with collaboration (Karkkainen, 2003b, pp962–963; Fung and Wright, 2003a, pp283–284). Further, the countervailing role of these groups was constrained by a narrow political vision and/or by the challenges of synthesizing a collaborative and advocacy role. This suggests that there may be limits to the capacity of local environmental groups to act as a countervailing power (Karkkainen, 2003b, pp962–963; Fung and Wright, 2003a, pp283–284). However, our findings in two novel cases from the EIP and CCM programmes suggest that a promising direction for resolving some of these issues is to foster active links and share cooperative and advocacy roles between environmental groups who have engaged (the insiders) and those who have remained on the outside of the collaborative forums.

As to how the lack of countervailing power (at both local and state level) might best be mitigated, the Regional Groups Collective example from the RNRM programme suggested two key factors. First, nested collaborative organization operating at multiple scales appeared to provide more opportunities for engaging state-based environmental groups that were typically mismatched with NEG in scale and framing (Margerum, 2007, p148). This engagement at higher levels can also have benefits for mobilizing countervailing powers at lower levels. However, for this to occur, the second key factor, namely government funding, was vital to support an under-resourced environmental group (Farber, 1999, p75).

5

ACCOUNTABILITY AND LEARNING

Introduction

In this chapter we continue our empirical investigation of the question: under what conditions can 'good' NEG be achieved? We do so by focusing on two further ideals of good NEG, namely, accountability and learning.

In principle, it is difficult to challenge the desirability of accountability in governance. Who, for example, would deny the need to prevent abuse by governing authorities, to ensure that resources are used appropriately, and to secure performance expectations (Bovens, 2007, p448; May, 2007, p11)? Similarly, the fundamental importance of learning to NEG is also increasingly recognized, particularly its value in facilitating adaptation to the continuing processes of change that are inevitably a feature of policy engagement with environmental problems (Orts, 1995, p1238).

Traditionally, accountability issues in public law and regulatory scholarship have been narrowly drawn. The focus was on formal, largely hierarchical principal-agent accountability relationships within which a legislature (the principal) confers on an administrative agency (the agent) responsibility for the performance of particular tasks – with a duty to explain, justify and be held accountable for their actions via legal or administrative mechanisms (e.g., judicial review) (Scott, 2000, pp39–40; Sabel and Simon, 2006, pp398–399; Bovens, 2007, p450).

In both NEG and broad regulatory reform scholarship, these traditional concepts have increasingly been supplemented and/or altered by 'new' understandings, formations and mechanisms of accountability (Freeman, 1997; Braithwaite, 1999, p91; Karkkainen et al, 2000).

One of the primary reasons for these developments has been the need to address accountability as part of an approach to governance in which non-government actors assume important roles (Freeman, 2000a; Fisher, 2004, p497). Indeed, a narrow assumption of a single principal with well-defined preferences is arguably too simplistic to capture the dynamic of multiple principals and preferences in a multi-agency, multi-stakeholder NEG collaboration. Further, rather than a solely hierarchical relationship, accountability in NEG may take on various horizontal forms (such as mutual accountability between collaborators who check each others' behaviour) as well as downward relationships (such as stakeholders being accountable to their respective sectors or groups) (Freeman and Farber, 2005, p904).

In addition, traditional administrative and legal mechanisms of accountability tend to constrain the discretion of agencies and other actors (e.g., rigid authorizing legislation coupled with judicial review). For this reason, conventional accountability mechanisms alone may lack the necessary flexibility to facilitate the incremental and provisional decision-making that is central to NEG's adaptive governance approach (discussed below) (Freeman, 2000a, p575; Fisher, 2004, p497). Indeed, traditional accountability approaches may prove counterproductive insofar as they constrain the contributions of non-governmental actors and multi-agency collaborations to environmental governance (Freeman, 2000a, p575; Scott, 2000, p39; Posner, 2002, pp524–528).

Accordingly, various authors have proposed the extensive modification of traditional political, administrative and legal forms of accountability. This chapter focuses on how these modifications play out within two broad levels of accountability common to legal regulation and governance. The first broadly relates to the accountability of those who make regulations and rules with respect to the content of these provisions, while the second relates broadly to the answerability and compliance of regulated entities in the implementation of rules and new governance provisions (May, 2003, p384; May, 2007).

At these two levels, a variety of 'new' mechanisms and approaches to accountability have been proposed in the NEG literature, typically under a rationale of providing *greater* deference to decision-making by agencies and stakeholders (Freeman, 1997, pp2 and 96). For instance, statutes that announce general goals without dictating the means of achieving them are often recommended as a means to afford agencies and stakeholders the latitude and discretion to devise more locally tailored and innovative solutions (Freeman, 1997, pp92–94; Wondolleck and Yaffee, 2000, p241; Karkkainen, 2003b, p963). Here, some authors would even relax judicial review, suggesting that courts grant a *presumptive deference* to agency and stakeholders' decisions (Freeman, 1997, p92). Others variously argue that traditional accountability approaches should coexist with (and would be enhanced by) 'new' accountability mechanisms in which private actors and institutions play active roles. Such new mechanisms include mutual accountability between multiple public and private collaborators who cooperatively negotiate rules and/or fulfil self-monitoring and reporting tasks (Weber, 1999, p453; Wondolleck and Yaffee, 2000, pp235–238; Freeman and Farber, 2005, pp905–908), 'professional' accountability of firms (May, 2007, p12), third-party certification and contractual agreements (Freeman, 2000b, pp198–201 and 207).

Within NEG, these new mechanisms tend to be located within two broad approaches, namely process and performance. The former specifies processes that must be adhered to in limiting harms (for example, undertaking a risk assessment) (May, 2007, p8). The latter, in contrast, focuses on outcomes (or outputs) and accord regulated actors process discretion as to how best to achieve prescribed results (May, 2007, p8).

Several authors have suggested that there is significant potential for unprincipled deal making, rent seeking and capture (i.e., economic or other interests benefiting from the NEG programme at the expense of the broader public interest) within NEG under both process- and performance-based approaches (Steinzor, 1998a, pp141–143; Farber, 2000, p74; Dana, 2000, pp52–57; Doremus, 2001, pp52 and 88; Fung and Wright, 2003b, pp21–22 and 36–37; Markell, 2005, pp56–57). Others, however, have argued that NEG offers new opportunities for enhanced accountability by replacing or supplementing traditional accountability controls through the development of 'new' innovative forms and mechanisms of accountability (Weber, 1999, p455; Freeman, 2000a, p665; Freeman, 2000b, p198). In this chapter we explore these competing perspectives of accountability through empirical enquiry. In particular, we evaluate the effectiveness of some specific mechanisms and approaches to accountability, most prominently: professional accountability in process-based regimes and mutual accountability; and agency and stakeholder decision-making within performance-orientated regimes (May, 2007, pp11–12).

We also consider the question of learning and adaptation, which is increasingly recognized as a vital feature of good NEG in its own right. Some NEG theories emphasize 'process-based' learning. Here the focus is on establishing management frameworks that guide and encourage industries to undertake self-reflective thinking, and learning, about their environmental impacts (see Orts, 1995, pp1253–1254; Fiorino, 2004, pp415–416; Holley and Gunningham, 2006). What has come to be termed 'passive adaptive' management is also common to NEG. This approach involves the monitoring of key indicators and adjustments to policies in light of what is learned through this monitoring (Karkkainen, 2005, pp62 and 70–72). However, some NEG initiatives have gone beyond this to utilize 'systemic' learning. This approach seeks to share information between collaborative groups and agencies to diffuse innovation and thereby facilitate a continual process of adaptation designed to enhance compliance with policy (Karkkainen et al, 2000, p691; Karkkainen, 2002/2003, p243).

As with accountability, there are a range of issues and debates associated with these different approaches to learning and in particular about their capacity to facilitate appropriate adaptation over time. Some authors, for example, argue that process-based learning will only be effective where enterprises have a commitment to improving environmental performance (Parker, 2002). Others point to a dearth of research on practical mechanisms that facilitate approaches to management (Paton et al, 2004; Allan and Curtis, 2005; Camacho, 2007; Lane et al, 2009; Lockwood et al, 2009), suggesting that insufficient attention has been paid to what happens 'on the ground'. Not least, it remains unclear whether, to what extent, and in what ways actors gather, analyse and act on information about their programme's effectiveness and shortcomings in practice (Thomas, 2003; Sturm, 2006, pp323 and 327–328). Similarly, beyond the architecture outlined by democratic experimentalists (Karkkainen et al, 2000) and studies of the Open Method of Coordination in the European Union (Sabel and Zeitlin, 2008), there have been few examples or investigations of NEG structures designed to achieve systemic learning in practice (Karkkainen, 2002/2003; Fung and Wright, 2003c).

Our analysis below seeks to respond to these gaps, but before we do so, it is necessary to understand why we have paired accountability with learning. At one level, the answer is that these two issues are broadly interrelated. As others have discussed, accountability can also be a tool to induce learning (Bovens, 2007, pp463–464). However, even where accountability is not designed to achieve such ends, accountability and learning processes will often depend on the same monitoring systems. These are commonly used to generate information capable of both holding actors to account *and* informing learning (Wondolleck and Yaffee, 2000, p141; Thomas, 2003, p153). They may also share a subtler interrelationship. The provisional decision-making associated with learning necessarily requires traditionally strict accountability controls to be relaxed in order to provide greater flexibility and room for revision as new information comes to hand. Hence the 'new' forms of and approaches to accountability we have just outlined seek to ensure sufficient flexibility for learning. As we will demonstrate, however, for accountability to be realized, flexibility must not come at the cost of relinquishing control (Karkkainen, 2003b, p963; Ruhl, 2005, p54).

While accountability and learning are important features of good NEG, surprisingly little research has been undertaken about them either independently or in terms of their relationship. Under-researched questions include: how effective are NEG initiatives in monitoring what happens (Steinzor, 2000, p15 of the pdf file; Gaines, 2002/2003, p16; Ewing, 2003, p408), and what impact does this have (Dovers, 2003a, pp522–523; Fung and Wright, 2003b, pp31–32; Thomas, 2003, p154; Head, 2005a, p145; Collaborative Democracy Network, 2006, p169; Sturm, 2006, pp328 and 333)? How effective are the 'new' approaches and forms of accountability, associated with NEG, at preventing perverse outcomes (Steinzor, 1998a, pp142–143; Steinzor, 2000, p17 of the pdf file; Fung and Wright, 2003b, pp36–37; Lane, 2006), and how is this balanced against the flexibility that successful learning requires (Wondolleck and Yaffee, 2000, pp235–237; Thomas, 2003, p156; Lawrence, 2004, pp13–14; Freeman, 2005, pp1871–1874; Sturm, 2006, p333)? How, and to what extent, can local initiatives be linked to monitoring processes so as to foster systemic learning (Karkkainen, 2002/2003, p243; Dovers, 2003a, pp522–523; Fung and Wright, 2003b, p32; Paton et al, 2004, p262; Head, 2005a, p146)?

This chapter provides insights into these and other questions through a description and analysis of our three programmes. First, we look at the legislation and guidelines to consider how each was designed to achieve accountability and learning. We then explore how effective both the accountability mechanisms and learning approaches were in practice, revealing significant shortcomings at a number of levels. We then analyse our findings to identify conditions for achieving effective learning and accountability. These conditions fall into five categories: (i) establishing effective monitoring processes; (ii) setting performance goals; (iii) fostering effective professional and mutual accountability; (iv) encouraging actors to implement accountability processes and adaptive learning approaches; and (v) designing systemic learning structures.

In order to facilitate an analysis of whether, and how, our programmes were able to foster accountability and learning we begin by considering their legal designs.

Legal Design: Accountability

Astute to the risks of capture and rent seeking, our programmes were designed in different ways to ensure accountability. All tended to relax rigid, traditional bureaucratic controls in favour of more flexible standards, discretion, and innovative forms of accountability (May, 2007, p23). These included mutual accountability between the collaborators, professional accountability of industry and different forms of government oversight.

These accountability mechanisms focused on relationships between different sets of actors. For example, professional accountability relationships (based on professional norms) were complemented by mutual or horizontal accountability between individual collaborators. Accountability mechanisms also focused on different aspects of conduct (Scott, 2000, p41; Bovens, 2007, pp454–455; May, 2007, p12), for example, holding actors accountable in terms of economic values (as when regional bodies were held accountable to the Joint Steering Committee for financial probity). Accountability also relates to social values, such as fairness and effectiveness (Posner, 2002, p524; Bovens, 2007, pp454–460) – as where the EIP programme facilitates industries to account to local residents for successfully reducing pollution impacts.

In this chapter, we have categorized accountability in terms of two broad categories (May, 2007, pp11–12). First, accountability to rules (with an emphasis on the appropriateness and fairness of the rules developed) and, second, the implementation of rules (with a focus on compliance) (May, 2007, pp11–12).

In order to analyse how these two broad categories of accountability relationships are applied in NEG, it is also important to note the relative emphasis on process- and performance-based standards in different regimes. While process- and performance-based approaches are not mutually exclusive (and the EIP regime includes elements of both), for heuristic purposes, it is helpful to treat them separately. Our discussion below first examines the process-based approach of the EIP, followed by an examination of the performance-based requirements of all three programmes.

The EIP's process regime prescribes minimal environmental management processes (e.g., audits and related assessments) that industries must adhere to (VEPA, 2004a, p2). For EIPs under Accredited Licenses, these processes are prescribed in legislation, while for other voluntary EIPs the content is established according to VEPA guidelines. In each case industry is to develop a management system in accordance with these processes (Manring, 2005, p61; May, 2007, pp10 and 13). Industry will also be subject to account upwards to the VEPA, whose role – in turn – is to ensure that the contents of the EIP plans are fair and appropriate (Scott, 2000, p43) and to review periodic reports and evaluations by industry regarding implementation (VEPA, 2002a, p10). Horizontal accountability relationships between industry and independent environmental auditors are used to evaluate the effectiveness of the industry's management system. Industry is to make necessary changes based on the auditor's report, but the VEPA has ultimate responsibility to ensure that the industry implements the plan (VEPA, 2002a, pp9–10).

As a number of authors have pointed out, the difficulty with focusing on process-based forms of accountability rather than on outcomes is that adherence to the process may not always guarantee the desired end results (Fiorino, 2004, p415). There is a danger that industries will simply go through the motions, set tokenistic goals and pay lip service to the process – ultimately failing to engender any real improvements in environmental performance (Gunningham and Sinclair, 2002, p180). However, in contrast to other process-based systems, such as ISO 14001, the EIP approach was expressly designed to combat this weakness by employing a complementary performance-based regime intended to ensure that environmental targets and outcomes were identified and achieved. The other two programmes also follow a performance-based approach, but in contrast to the EIP, without any process-based component. We turn now to the performance-based characteristics of all three programmes.

The first category of accountability mechanisms involved setting performance targets, which in the case of all programmes were measurable and intended to achieve minimum performance outcomes (Wondolleck and Yaffee, 2000, p240; Karkkainen, 2003b, pp993–997). Collaborators were horizontally accountable to each other, and vertically accountable to government agencies. Once targets had been developed, collaborative groups were expected to adhere to them and monitor, evaluate and report on their progress. This could involve monitoring the actual implementation of actions designed to achieve performance standards, as well as monitoring the impact of these actions and whether the programmes were achieving the intended outcomes. Again, collaborators were encouraged to hold each other to account for their performance – for example, through the use of shaming and peer pressure if compliance was not forthcoming. Collaborators were also accountable to government agencies, which were empowered to intervene to address non-compliance (May, 2007, pp10–11). Of course there are other forums to which actors may be held accountable (e.g., collaborators representing a non-government group may be accountable to the wider group members); however, for the purposes of our research, the two most important forums involved collaborators themselves and government agencies.

In the EIP programme, underperformance could lead to the VEPA threatening to amend an industry's licence and/or pursue other regulatory sanctions

(Gunningham and Sinclair, 2002, p180). In NEIP, the programme was designed to utilize a contractual mechanism that involved the NEIP's plan being gazetted by the VEPA, making the voluntary actions to which the partners signed on binding in law and thus subject to legal consequences if breached (although this remains untested in practice) (*Environment Protection Act 1970* (Vic), s19AI(4)). Finally, in the RNRM programme, non-compliance with regards to expenditure or a failure to achieve targets was to be addressed by the Joint Steering Committee, utilizing an administrative 'destabilization right' – a right to intervene and destabilize collaborative efforts that provide evidence of chronic underperformance and/or procedural defects (Chapter 2) (see Bilateral Agreement NHT, 2004, ss69, 71 and 94, Attachment J, cl 8.5; Bilateral Agreement NAP, 2001, ss8.1 and 14.1). While there are multiple government agencies and ministerial bodies that have a role in overseeing aspects of the programme, the Joint Steering Committee has the most direct accountability relationship to the regional body. Indeed, the JSC had the power to intervene on evidence of underperformance or financial impropriety – to conduct an evaluation, critique procedures and to assess skills and capacities of representatives. It was left to the regional body to respond to critiques and to improve its performance, subject to ongoing reports to the JSC on improvements (Karkkainen, 2006b, pp317–320).

While the features of performance accountability are broadly similar across the cases, the next section takes a closer look at the design of each case to illustrate some subtle (but important) differences that may have an impact on the effectiveness of performance-based accountability in each programme.

Designing accountability for performance

Setting performance targets

As indicated above, a performance approach, based on the setting of targets, was fundamental to all three programmes. In an attempt to protect the 'public interest' and to ensure the standards set by groups were fair and credible, legislatures sought to 'bind' the decision-space of collaborative groups and agencies by establishing targets that were to be consistent with relevant environmental quality standards (*Environment Protection Act 1970* (Vic) ss1K, 19AH(2), 19AI(2), 19AI(3)(b)(h)(i) and 26B; VEPA, 2002a, pp7 and 11; Bilateral Agreement NHT, 2004, ss80–81 and 89, Attachment E, p64). The difficulty legislatures faced in this process was striking the right balance between specificity and generality (Dana, 2000, pp53–54). Over-generalization with respect to outcomes would effectively allow them to be ignored and invite abuse, such as unprincipled deal making or capture by industry (see, for example McClosky, 1996; Freeman, 1997, pp92–95; Dana, 2000 p53; Farber, 2000, p74; Doremus, 2001, p82; Karkkainen, 2003b, p961; Koontz and Thomas, 2006, pp113; May, 2007). On the other hand, too much specificity might impede creativity, stymie flexibility and marginalize local context (Freeman, 1997, p93; Dana, 2000, p53).

A second difficulty in establishing appropriate performance targets has to do with the technical and financial challenges of monitoring. Some authors have suggested that the costs and technical skills needed to gather data on baseline environmental conditions can overwhelm the resources and capacities available, not least because establishing baseline conditions of the ambient environment and the implications of its contamination is often extremely demanding. This in turn can lead to crucial gaps in information needed to set targets, measure progress and hold groups accountable for achieving results (Steinzor, 1998b; Steinzor, 2000, pp15–16 of the pdf file; Gaines 2002/2003, p16; Ewing, 2003, p408).

Each of our programmes had been designed so as to overcome cost and technical deficiencies in these monitoring tasks. The EIP is the only programme that did not provide direct support for data collection. This is understandable given that the monitoring requirements established under industries' regulatory licences ensure extensive existing data records of point source pollution releases (VEPA, 2002a, pp7–9). In contrast to EIP programme, the NEIP and RNRM programmes have been designed to provide collaborators with more extensive support in the form of government data on environmental conditions (e.g., state agency monitoring, national resources audits) (Commonwealth and Queensland, 2004b, VEPA, 2002d, p9; Bilateral Agreement NHT, 2004, Attachment C, p113), as well as varying degrees of funding (RNRM providing comparatively more than NEIP) for additional monitoring and data collection (VEPA, 2002d, p9; Commonwealth and Queensland Interim Agreement, 2003, s51). Such support may prove vital given the significant costs and technical challenges associated with setting performance targets for these complex, multifaceted and dynamic environmental and natural resource issues. Significantly the RNRM programme was designed to allow for approval of regional plans without the establishment of baseline data and targets, provided there were commitments, as part of rigorous monitoring arrangements, to collect missing data (Bilateral Agreement, NHT, 2004, Attachment E, p65; Doremus, 2001, p72).

We turn now to a consideration of the effectiveness of these various support mechanisms.

Monitoring implementation

Beyond setting targets, achieving effective accountability for performance depended on collaborative groups conducting ongoing monitoring, evaluation and reporting on their progress against targets and their implementation of plans. The design of each programme imposed quite different monitoring, evaluation and reporting mechanisms.

The billions of Australian dollars invested in the RNRM programme encouraged policy designers to impose strict monitoring and reporting requirements on collaborative groups via state and national guidelines and partnership agreements (NRMMC, 2002a; NRMMC, 2002b; Commonwealth and Queensland, 2004b;

Corporations Act 2001 (Cth); Bilateral Agreement NHT, 2004, ss68, 69, 71, 94, 134 and 135; Bilateral Agreement NAP, 2001, ss7.1, 8.1, 14.1 and 30). Thus, regional bodies were to develop monitoring and evaluation strategies to gauge their performance, typically in accordance with established indicators and data collection and storage protocols (Bilateral Agreement NHT, 2004, Attachment E, p68). They received funding, and in-kind government support (e.g., state monitoring), to assist with monitoring, evaluation and upwards reporting to the JSC (Commonwealth and Queensland, 2004b, ss6.6.1 and 8.2.7). Reporting that related to funding and measured progress against milestones was required on a quarterly, six-monthly and an annual basis (Commonwealth and Queensland, 2004b, ss5.1.3–5.1.5; Bilateral Agreement NHT, 2004, ss94 and 146; Bilateral Agreement NAP, 2001, s14, 30.3 and 17.6). Data was aggregated at state and national levels for ministers. There were also state and national level evaluation processes (Commonwealth and Queensland, 2004b, s7; Bilateral Agreement NHT, 2004, s137; Bilateral Agreement NAP, 2001, s30). As some NEG scholars have suggested, such onerous requirements may in fact be counterproductive as they may hamper the intended flexible, community-orientated nature of regional bodies (Lawrence, 2004, pp13–14; Head, 2004, p31; Head, 2005a, p146).

In contrast, the NEIP and EIP programmes impose relatively few monitoring requirements – both programmes imposing only very general requirements while expecting collaborators and industry to develop their own processes and/or indicators for monitoring, evaluation (VEPA, 2002d, pp1 and 10; *Environmental Protection Act 1970* (Vic), s19AI(e)(f); VEPA, 2002a, p9) and reporting (VEPA, 2002d, pp1 and 10; *Environment Protection Act 1970* (Vic), ss19AI(3)(c)(e)(f) and 19AJ; VEPA, 2002a, p9), subject to the approval of the VEPA (*Environment Protection Act 1970* (Vic), ss19AI (e)(f) and 19AJ; VEPA, 2002a). Although neither NEIP nor EIP provided for funding or other assistance to promote accountability requirements, the EIP's arrangements sought to harness community and/or VEPA pressure to persuade industry to bear the ongoing monitoring and reporting costs. In contrast, the NEIP programme expected groups to meet their own costs or find external funding to assist with these costs.

To sum up, the programmes involve two broad sets of accountability relationships – accountability for setting standards and targets, and accountability for their implementation. While the EIP was the only programme to employ a process-based approach, all three programmes emphasized performance-based accountability. The design of each of the programmes raised questions about the effectiveness of its accountability mechanisms. Before we consider these issues in more detail we turn now to the legislative design of learning.

Legal design: learning and adaptation

Learning aspirations varied across passive adaptive management, reflexive process-based approaches and systemic learning. The passive adaptive management approach employed in each of our programmes involved collaborative groups developing processes to monitor and evaluate activities in ways that encouraged them to make ongoing adjustments in light of what they had learned (VEPA, 2002a, p10; VEPA, 2002d, p1; Bilateral Agreement NHT, 2004, Attachment E, p68; Commonwealth and Queensland, 2004b, s7.1; see also Karkkainen, 2005, pp70–72). Their designs encouraged this via a formal review process at the end of each plan's implementation (VEPA, 2002a, pp10–11; *Environment Protection Act 1970* (Vic), ss 19AI(e)(f) and 19AJ; Bilateral Agreement NHT, 2004, Attachment E, pp68–69; Commonwealth and Queensland, 2004b, s8.2.6). At the time of our research this had only happened as part of the older EIP programme. Nevertheless, all programmes encouraged ongoing adaptive management through the utilization of local knowledge of collaborators as well as through baseline data and ongoing monitoring and evaluation processes. Again, costs raised challenges.

Overlapping with these adaptive approaches were two other envisaged forms of learning. In the EIP programme, a process-based approach to learning was to be employed. Here an industry's design of, and adherence to, a minimum set of processes (e.g., identifying impacts and risks, setting of objectives and targets, and measurement techniques to ensure that they are reached) was intended to influence industry attitudes and create a framework for better environmental organization. It was hoped that these processes would stimulate industry to search for environmental impacts that fell outside of current regulation, encourage system self-correction and promote a commitment to continuous improvement (Gunningham and Sinclair, 2002, p180; Fiorino, 2004, p415).

A form of 'systemic learning' was envisaged in NEIP and RNRM. NEIP sought to promote the sharing of information and innovations to encourage effective and efficient collaborative problem solving (VEPA, 2002d, pp4 and 6; Fung and Wright, 2003b, p25). As the guidelines note: '[V]EPA is seeking to document and share ways different communities develop Neighbourhood EIP proposals and plans' (VEPA, 2002d, pp4, 6). Individual collaborations are also expected to embrace 'learning objectives' that involve 'developing and sharing Neighbourhood EIP models with other neighbourhoods' (VEPA, 2002d, pp4 and 6). Despite this aspiration, there appears to have been a significant gap between this vision and the legislative and policy processes designed to implement it. Indeed, beyond stating the above goal of sharing learning, the guidelines and legislation did not establish formal procedures or processes to facilitate the collaborative groups or VEPA to share learning across neighbourhoods (VEPA, 2002d).

Much greater detail was offered in RNRM's approach to systemic learning. Here the design provided for an assessment of the appropriateness, effectiveness and efficiency of the programme in achieving its objectives (Commonwealth and Queensland, 2004b, s7.1; NRMMC, 2002b). Regional bodies were also required to engage in ongoing monitoring, evaluation and reporting at 'key decision points' throughout the life of the programme (Commonwealth and Queensland, 2004b, s7.2.2).

Accountability and Learning in Practice – Findings

We turn now to an examination of whether, and to what extent, these approaches to accountability and learning were effective in practice, focusing on whether accountability mechanisms in fact prevented the abuse of authority, ensured that public resources were used appropriately and/or secured reasonable environmental performance expectations (May, 2007, p11). In terms of learning, we explore whether actors gathered and dispersed sufficient information, analysed it and then made relevant adjustments to their behaviour (Sturm, 2006, p327).

Environment Improvement Plan

Accountability – process and performance regimes

At the core of accountability in the EIP programme is the complementary interaction of novel and innovative accountability mechanisms in both process- and performance-based approaches. The findings indicated that agency oversight, as well as mutual and professional accountability employed in EIP, were effective in addressing some, but not all, risks of capture and tokenism. These findings, outlined below, focus first on accountability for process and then for performance. While these two approaches overlap, for heuristic purposes they are treated separately.

Process-based EIP accountability arrangements were reported to have been largely effective with regard to 'leading' and 'good' performers but more qualifiedly when it came to 'poor' performers. Most leading and good performers adequately discharged their professional accountability responsibilities to develop reportedly adequate management systems. As one VEPA officer explained, these industries often developed their management plan by drawing on their own accredited management systems (e.g., ISO 14001), which gave VEPA added 'satisfaction . . . [and] some comfort that the EIP [was] adequate' (Interview 132, VEPA). Auditors also monitored subsequent plan implementation, ensuring that industries followed adequate processes and that auditors' recommendations were implemented.

For all industries, these 'checks' on their management system, combined with their own professional judgement in designing them, ensured subsequent improvement in local impacts. Further, for good and leading firms, the process approach had assisted industry to achieve improvements in environmental performance on broader impacts, such as carbon emissions and natural gas usage.

However, when it came to poor performers, professional judgement 'went out the window' when designing processes to manage *broader* environmental issues. Indeed, deliberate subterfuge by industry saw both the VEPA and auditors reportedly struggle to address these management system shortcomings (May, 2007, p22). As one respondent described:

> . . . industry were trying very hard to have enough items on the EIP plan to make it look like a really good plan . . . they did some very minor things and . . . sort of passed it off as a plan . . . sometimes the form overcomes the substance.
>
> (Interview 15/62, Local Resident)

Such shams were apparently common (see Fiorino, 2004, pp413–416), notwithstanding that the EIP programme had expressly been designed to address this weakness through a complementary performance-based accountability regime. Accordingly, we now turn explicitly to performance-based accountability with two particular questions in mind. Why had some aspects of laggards' environmental performance sometimes slipped through the performance accountability net? And was the accountability regime able to sufficiently address other defects in performance?

At the core of a successful performance accountability approach is setting credible targets against which performance is judged. As expected, the costs and technical skills associated with collecting baseline data to set targets posed few problems in the EIP programme. Ample data was either available under existing licence monitoring requirements, or had been collected via hired consultants or newly installed monitoring devices as a result of their own initiative (for leading performers) or pressure on industry from VEPA and local residents (Interview 182, Local Resident; Interview 111, Industry).

The accountability arrangements had also been able to avoid industry dominating *local* performance targets. Certainly some local non-government interests that had an economic dependency on the industry, were potentially 'pro-industry' and vulnerable to capture (Interview 132, VEPA). However, this appeared to be more the exception than the rule. Indeed, even after long-term collaborative involvement, individual collaborators had reportedly maintained their independence from industry. As one respondent put it: '. . . we work with them so there's a friendly enough relationship, but they'll turn hostile like that [clicks fingers] if they've got good reason' (Interview 161, Industry). This independence ensured non-government collaborators were effective in a 'mutual accountability' role, and this enabled them to help secure appropriate and measurable local environmental targets. Through this approach, as one local resident put it:

> All the big problems for the community basically have been fixed. The smells, noises, things like that have basically been fixed . . . there hasn't been much that hasn't worked . . . you wouldn't know [industry] were here half the time now.
>
> (Interview 162, Local Resident)

Similar findings were made in the Living Streams Programme (LSP) demonstration programme where effective mutual accountability and successful monitoring had led to credible *local* targets being set (see Box 5.1 below). However, unlike LSP, EIP was also concerned with setting environmental performance targets relating to industry's impacts on the *wider* environment. Here the findings indicated much more mixed results. On the one hand, it appeared atypical for good and leading performers to try to 'capture' and distort the process. Indeed, even with a significant shortfall in both mutual accountability and VEPA oversight (on which more below), respondents reported that the performance targets, like those illustrated in Box 5.2 below, were set significantly beyond compliance for these industries (see also Gunningham and Sinclair, 2002, p168). This was due to industries' existing professional judgement and norms, including their commitment to environmental performance, identified costs/reputation benefits, and a drive for continuous improvement fostered by the process-based approach to learning (see below).

BOX 5.1 NEW ZEALAND DEMONSTRATION CASE: LIVING STREAMS PROGRAMME (LSP)

LSP adopted a performance-based approach involving localized targets and actions designed to maintain and improve the health of waterways (ECan, 2009b, p2). Central to achieving accountability in LSP were two mechanisms – mutual accountability between collaborators, and upwards accountability of collaborators to the regulator, ECan. These mechanisms applied with regard to developing credible and fair targets, as well as to implementation.

In terms of the former, respondents reported that these accountability mechanisms had been effective in ensuring the group reached credible, appropriate and quantifiable targets. The establishment of tangible targets (e.g., clear flowing water; water that is safe to recreate in; and stable banks), clear performance indicators (e.g., sediment, faecal coliform and nitrogen levels) and verifiable standards to be met (e.g., minimum regulatory standards relating to environment or health) (ECan, 2009b, p19) ensured that collaborators and ECan officers had a clear understanding of the issues to be measured and the magnitude of targets expected.

Another important aspect of accountability was the existence of sufficient baseline data to inform the setting of robust targets against which subsequent performance could be judged. Indeed, ECan already had significant existing monitoring data on stream conditions, and where gaps were identified, the limited number of polluters (20 or less farmers) enabled new monitoring sites and costs to be kept to a minimum. As one respondent generalized: 'there's nothing hugely difficult to understand about . . . water

continued . . .

BOX 5.1 *. . . continued*

and . . . effluent and the farmer situation . . . You don't need a scientist or an army of folk collecting figures to tell you this doesn't work and that doesn't work' (Interview NZ312, Farmer). The fact that local impacts from pollution were tangible and visible led to significant peer pressure on polluting farmers and ensured effective mutual accountability to secure credible targets.

In terms of accountability for implementation and delivery of targets, questions were raised about the extent to which groups would be held to account for achieving some of their longer-term targets, given that LSP groups found it difficult to maintain their collaborative enterprise over lengthy periods (see Chapter 6). Nevertheless, the large majority of the short- to medium-term targets, such as achieving a clear flowing stream, were apparently achieved with a recalcitrant minority being successfully held accountable for non-compliance.

The ever looming threat of regulatory enforcement (see Chapter 3), coupled with mutual accountability between collaborators, largely accounted for this success, with stakeholders utilizing their own visual observations of farm and stream conditions, as well as information provided by ECan's ongoing monitoring of the stream, to verify implementation. Any identification of unfulfilled responsibilities in this regard led quickly to concentrated pressure from peers.

However, neither such mutual accountability nor the shadow cast by ECan's regulatory powers were effective on all farmers, with around 10 per cent or more 'recalcitrant' collaborators falling through the cracks of the mutual accountability function exercised by time-strapped volunteers. Upwards accountability to ECan was accordingly vital, and occasionally required more traditional recourse to the direct force of law:

> Well, we had one individual there who was steadfastly ignoring . . . and had all his cattle in the bloody creek there . . . we'd already written him about two or three warning letters . . . so we issued an abatement notice. So he's been forced to do some fencing . . . he still comes along to the meetings and he's taken it like a man [laughs].
>
> (Interview NZ331, ECan)

Overall this combination of traditional oversight and mutual accountability translated into the group implementing nearly all their actions and ultimately achieving the majority of their medium-term targets.

BOX 5.2 EXAMPLE OF OBJECTIVES THAT GO BEYOND COMPLIANCE

In EIP cases involving leading and good performers, industries set the following objectives relating to issues not covered by their licence or that went beyond licence standards:

- keep stack SO_2 emissions at levels 10 per cent lower than licensed requirements
- over five years reduce gas, electricity and water usage each by 10 per cent with achievement to target reviewed and if targets are exceeded, a further 2 per cent reduction is applied to maintain continuous improvement
- retain secondary effluent treated during storms that occur less than once in 50 years (as opposed to licence requirements of once every 10 to 20 years' storms)
- reduce benzene and butadiene emissions by 10 per cent and 25 per cent respectively over three years
- achieve 50 per cent reduction of landfill use by 2003 compared to 1997
- achieve 20 per cent water recycling of its total effluent production
- reduce our greenhouse gas emissions by 35 per cent by 2006.

However, unlike either leading or good performers, poor performers typically lacked commitment to environmental management and had little interest in improving overall environmental performance under the process-based approach (Interview 174, Industry). This meant that effectiveness depended largely on the credibility of broader environmental performance targets. But we found much evidence that these targets were largely tokenistic and rarely went significantly beyond compliance. As one VEPA respondent explained: '. . . the company gives a long list of EIP items . . . but it is very weak in terms of environmental improvements, most are just housekeeping items' (Interview 181, VEPA).

Although the VEPA and collaborators had sometimes identified these weaknesses, their motivation or capacity to take action to resolve such defects was severely limited (see, for example May, 2007, p17). Indeed, as we saw in Chapter 4, nearly all non-government collaborators had either a noted indifference to broader environmental issues or lacked technical knowledge to play an effective mutual accountability role to push industry to set higher targets on these issues. As one VEPA respondent put it:

> . . . there's no one really who's got the strategic big picture . . . from that point of view I didn't think anybody in the [collaboration] has really made much of an impact . . . [industry] stayed very much in control over the process.
> (Interview 123, VEPA)

The VEPA also reportedly had 'underplayed their accountability hand' and failed to address tokenism by poor performers (May, 2007, p17; Doremus, 2001, p61). The problem did not appear to be one of agency 'capture'. As a number of respondents pointed out, VEPA officers undertook their role with a sincere intention to protect the environment and there was almost always a 'regulator–industry tension' in the EIP process (Interview 121, Industry; see, for example Doremus, 2001, p61). Rather, the real difficulty appeared to arise from the overly general performance requirement that had afforded very broad discretion to VEPA officers to assess the matters for targets and the extent they should go beyond compliance.

The most direct legislated requirements arise under EIPs pursuant to Accredited Licences, which must 'maintain and improve environmental performance' and must set targets that comply or go beyond compliance with licences and regulations (*Environment Protection Act 1970* (Vic), s 26B(1)(b)). However, in the case of purely voluntary EIPs, there is no formal legislated goal per se. Instead, the agency is free to experiment within the bounds of its enforcement discretion, which requires that it conduct enforcement of environmental requirements for the goal of 'better protecting the environment and its economic and social uses' (*Environment Protection Act 1970* (Vic), s 1K). This broad discretion has allowed VEPA to develop its own guidelines that set out a similar desired outcome to that stated in legislation, namely setting targets that improve environmental performance of industry and that comply with or go beyond legislative requirements (VEPA, 2002a, pp2, 7 and 9).

Within these bounds, the VEPA did not appear to have the capacity to exercise this discretion effectively. Certainly VEPA officers had tried to ensure that, where there were obvious opportunities for improvement, industry implemented them (Interview 142, Industry). However, officers lacked detailed knowledge of the many technical issues associated with each individual industry operation (Doremus, 2001, p82). This made it difficult to direct each industry meaningfully on relevant target setting. Instead, officers tended to stick to their 'traditional role' of enforcing minimum legislative standards and typically took a 'backseat' (Interview 181, VEPA), 'caretaker' (Interview 113, VEPA) and 'passive' (Interview 131, Industry) role when it came to setting beyond-compliance targets on broader environmental issues.

Apart from these difficulties with regard to poor industry performers and broad-based environmental goals, our findings indicated that the programme's 'new' forms of accountability were generally successful in ensuring all industries achieved targets and were held accountable for non-compliance (May, 2007, p12).

There are a number of explanations for this relative success. Of particular importance was the fact that all industries had reportedly carried out effective monitoring and reporting processes in a 'very open' manner (Interview 133,

Resident/Environmental Group) and provided 'quite detailed' information on their performance against targets (Interview 132, VEPA; Interview 133, Local Resident/Environmental Group; Wondolleck and Yaffee, 2000, p241). While these responsibilities added costs to industry, they had been able to reduce these burdens by drawing on pre-existing monitoring and reporting processes. According to respondents, the reason industry had credibly and willingly discharged its monitoring responsibilities was because the validity of its data was potentially subject to scrutiny by the VEPA and/or local collaborators. If industry could not show whether and for what reasons targets were or were not being achieved, subsequent pressure would be forthcoming.

Both VEPA and non-government collaborators were reportedly effective in holding industry to account in the event of non-compliance. As one industry respondent reflected, in the event of default, local collaborators could bring significant pressure to bear on industry: '. . . the consequences of not achieving that target . . . you know you are audited very, very heavily by the community . . . so there is an accountability' (Interview 141, Industry).

VEPA supervision was also vital to ensuring overall compliance with targets, particularly in cases involving poor performers, where community pressure had less of an impact on these typically less reputation-conscious companies. In these cases, ensuring even basic compliance with minimal targets required the VEPA to 'keep a close eye' on industry (Interview 181, VEPA), threatening or carrying out licence changes or other enforcement. As one VEPA respondent noted regarding a poor performer:

> They were in denial . . . They've committed [Australian] $5 million plus [over two EIPs] . . . and it hasn't worked . . . The community meanwhile is trying to be patient . . . so we've actually changed the licence, amended the licence and had severe discussions with them.
>
> (Interview 121, VEPA)

To sum up with regard to EIPs, novel forms and mechanisms of NEG accountability had some significant success but also some limitations. Industry's professional judgement often accorded with established norms of environmental management, such as ISO 14001, and auditor and VEPA oversight were largely successful in ensuring accountability for processes. A combination of mutual accountability and VEPA oversight ensured industry set adequate targets on local issues and were held accountable for overall performance. Real or implied community and VEPA pressure had also been vital to industry successfully meeting the costs and technical challenges of gathering baseline data and carrying out ongoing monitoring.

This success, however, was limited by significant shortfalls in accountability mechanisms – which gave rise to opportunities for poor performers to manipulate performance targets on broader environmental issues. The findings suggested this was attributable in part to highly general legislated goals and extensive VEPA discretion, as well as shortfalls in professional accountability (May, 2007, p21) and oversight of the process-based approach by the VEPA (even with advice from auditors). Mutual accountability was also ineffective in ensuring that adequate performance targets were set due to a mismatch between environmental issues and the knowledge and interests of non-government participants.

Learning – process-based learning and adaptive management

The EIP case was designed to employ two forms of learning – a process-based approach and a 'passive' style of adaptive management. The findings indicated that both of these have value, but that they also have limitations.

When it came to good performers, the findings indicated that a process-based approach had provided a structure that had improved industries' capacity to detect and develop solutions to environmental problems in a more strategic and reflexive manner (Gunningham and Sinclair, 2002, p177). In particular, respondents suggested the EIP processes had allowed industry to become more sensitized to their environmental impact, and to the risks to their social and regulatory licences. This in turn impressed upon them the 'business case' for continual learning about their impacts and subsequent environmental improvement (Gunningham and Sinclair, 2002, p177). As one respondent put it:

> . . . it helps [industry] think about how they can improve by focusing on process rather than outcomes . . . and once companies start on the path of improvement they realize there are business benefits . . . from an environmental perspective but also from a financial perspective.
>
> (Interview 181, VEPA)

In addition, their long-term participation in the EIP process – with the requisite search for environmental aspects, target setting, planning, priority setting and risk analysis that this entailed – had reportedly served to improve their self-regulatory capacities (Holley and Gunningham, 2006). This enabled them to better learn about the effectiveness of their environmental management systems and refine and adapt internal approaches (Holley and Gunningham, 2006). According to one industry representative:

> . . . internally within the industry [EIPs] just make you think so laterally and so broad about the way your business needs to be performing in the future from a social and environmental point of view . . . I am thinking about things that are going to bite us in 6 or 7 years' time if we don't start acting on them now.
>
> (Interview 141, Industry)

These EIP achievements appeared to be far more limited in cases involving leaders. This was, however, not because of some inherent failure in process-based learning, but because these industries were already following existing 'reflexive' environmental management systems, and had 'slotted' their EIP into them (Interview 131, Industry).

Significantly, the process-based approach to learning was reportedly ineffective when it came to poor performers. Certainly, some of these industries recognized the benefits of the management system (Interview 174, Industry). However, their general lack of commitment to environmental improvement reportedly translated into a strong reluctance to embrace a goal of learning and continuous environmental improvement. As one poor performer put it: '. . . environment was not such an important aspect of the business . . . I don't think there was the commitment to improve the situation' (Interview 174, Industry; Interview 184, Industry).

To some extent, industry's commitment to a process-based framework and environmental improvement appeared to have been influenced through external VEPA or community pressure. As we saw above, such pressure had motivated all industries to follow processes to identify local environmental impacts, develop credible performance targets and implement new management response to these local impacts. However, when it came to looking at broader environmental impacts, the absence of any meaningful pressure from VEPA or local residents meant these already reluctant industries simply went through the motions to meet the process requirements – basically remaining unchanged by the experience (Gunningham and Sinclair, 2002, p166). Consistent with findings in other contexts (Fiorino, 2004, pp415–416), process-based regulation appears to be a valuable learning tool only when it is placed in the 'right hands' (Holley and Gunningham, 2006) or there is sufficient pressure or incentive to ensure commitment to its precepts (Parker, 2002, pp275–288; Holley and Gunningham, 2006).

Turning to the overlapping approach of adaptive management, informal monitoring by local residents reportedly assisted industry to re-evaluate the actions taken to reduce local impacts (Interview 173, Local Community). Certainly there were reports that feedback from the local community provided insights and led to action that would not otherwise have been taken. In addition to using local knowledge of residents, the collaborative group also drew on industry's monitoring data to collectively evaluate the success of strategies and develop new plans of action where they were failing. This included a detailed review at the completion of each plan where groups 'looked at the bigger picture' to determine whether the EIP is achieving what the group wanted it to achieve and subsequently redrafting a new plan (Interview 151, Industry). In between such formal evaluations the groups also conducted a variety of successful collaborative evaluations and adaptations. Some illustrations of adaptive management in practice are detailed in Box 5.3 below.

Despite these successes, there was little evidence of the collaborative group engaging in 'adaptive management' processes beyond local issues. This is arguably unsurprising given that the groups were predominantly composed of local stakeholders who tended to lack the capacity or willingness to engage with broader issues.

BOX 5.3 ILLUSTRATIONS OF GROUP REVIEW AND ADAPTATION IN THE EIP PROGRAMME

Illustration 1

> Two years ago we were having a number of incidents . . . So our environmental impact had hardly changed, but we were having a string of these little things and they just got on the radar and the EIP group just said 'we're concerned with the number of these things and as it goes, the more incidents you have sooner or later you have a big one, so ideally you want to have none'. So they raised this with us, 'we're really concerned and we want to know what's going to be done'. So out of that we volunteered to do a full review of all the incidents we'd had on this site, going back over a number of years and out of that . . . we identified some specific trends and it looks like we're having more of this particular type of thing, so it helped us to identify where we needed to focus . . . two or three of the group were involved and sat in on all the discussions and part of the feedback to the whole group and everything . . . there were a number of improvement opportunities which were identified and implemented as a result of that . . . there was about 14 items on that list. Some were soft culture stuff and some were real field items, but there were a number of new items that were identified and that actually added some re-emphasis to some existing ones and they've been implemented and they've resulted in less impact and less incidents. So it's a real example of them raising their concern, getting involved in a process that leads to some outcomes which then reduced the impact – it closes the loop.
>
> (Interview 161, Industry)

Illustration 2

One respondent described the ongoing learning process of one industry who had significant impacts of odour on the local area:

> Industry invested heavily in concrete batts, plastic conduits out of odour sources into these biofilters and found that they can't get the bits to join properly so odour vapour's leaking out and now putting stainless steel pipes in . . . they had tried to solve some of the problem and they invested in what they called an RTO, which was 'something or other Thermal Oxidise'. It was a new incinerator that they had sent some people to America to look at. It was a gas fired thing and it was going

continued . . .

BOX 5.3 *... continued*

to solve the problem – collect as many odour's gases as they could and wack it into this thing. And they described that to us. Do you think this will ever work? ... Turned out after a year or two of trying that the gas burners were clogged up by the fat so the damn thing never worked ... They had consultants and thing to try and make it work and it took a long time to work out that this wasn't going to be the solution ... And after a couple of years of trying with this thing they found it didn't work ... the EPA's solution when they got me involved in it was what we need to do is put a big shed around all this, suck up the air and burn it or treat it and that was what they were trying to do so they agreed that they would try and enclose much of their operations – which they did spent a bit of money on it too – but there is a lot of hydrogen sulphide in there apparently, gets up the top with a bit of moisture and causes corrosion so just recently they have had to replace the roof of this relatively new thing ... So they are now doing that so they are learning a lot through the process.

(Interview 182, Local Resident)

Overall, the EIP programme achieved some success in fostering effective learning. Industry and local residents' monitoring had informed an effective adaptive management process for local impacts of industry. Process-based strategies had also successfully provided a framework for many enterprises to identify and think through new solutions to environmental problems, stimulating reflective management, and continual processes of adaptation and environmental improvement. However, it was less clear that a process-based approach was effective in circumstances where industry had little commitment to achieving environmental improvement – as with poor performers. While external pressure helped foster such commitment for local issues (see Parker, 2002, pp275–288), weaknesses in collaborator and VEPA oversight (coupled with VEPA lack of knowledge and community lack of interest in broader environmental impacts) meant laggards lacked the incentive to engage.

Neighbourhood Environment Improvement Plan

Accountability

Despite some limitations, the novel accountability mechanisms used in EIP programme were able to achieve a considerable degree of success in securing effective performance. In contrast, the experience of the NEIP evidenced imprecise target setting and inept monitoring that undermined effective accountability for performance.

As we will see, these weaknesses did not appear to arise from malevolence, per se, but rather were attributable to a shortfall in VEPA oversight and insufficient support and resources for monitoring and collecting data. The discussion below explores these flaws by first considering accountability for setting targets, before turning to consider accountability for implementation. The analysis draws primarily on our Sustainable Township and Degraded Creek cases as, at the time of research, they were the only cases that had progressed substantially in terms of implementation.

The primary task in any performance-based accountability regime is setting targets. As with the EIP programme, NEIP faced risks that powerful economic or other interests would capture agendas. However, this was less of a problem in NEIP than EIP because most NEIP collaborators did not have specific 'industry' interests. Furthermore, respondents suggested that the participation of multiple government agencies with responsibilities for the environment, including the VEPA, had ensured that targets set by the group respected 'broader regional-wide context' (Interview 214, Government Agency) and accounted for wider environment priorities, planning schemes and other existing laws (Dana, 2000, p54; Thomas, 2003, p163).

Despite avoiding any evident distortion by industry interests, the environmental performance targets set by collaborators, and approved by the VEPA, were extremely vague. As illustrated in Box 5.4 below, many targets aimed to achieve an 'improvement' in a stated environmental quality variable, but few provide any direct quantifiable measures regarding the *level of improvement* to be realized.

A sympathetic reading of these targets would suggest the collaborators were striving to achieve as much 'improvement' in the given environmental conditions as humanly possible but were precluded from greater precision by a lack of relevant data and a break down in VEPA's accountability responsibilities. However, a more critical stance raises the possibility of 'unprincipled deal making' among collaborators to avoid any significant improvements through setting vague and tokenistic targets (Doremus, 2001; Karkkainen, 2003b, p963). While it is too early to know which of these two readings is correct, the significant scope for tokenism and negligible environmental improvements remains a serious concern.

As with the EIP programme, sweeping legislative statements regarding expected outcomes for NEIP had left significant discretion to VEPA officers regarding the nature and magnitude of performance targets. While NEIPs are required to be consistent with relevant environmental quality standards, planning schemes and laws, the legislation leaves much of the details about a NEIP's goals, targets, form and manner to the VEPA (*Environmental Protection Act 1970* (Vic), ss 4(1), 19AE, 19AF, 19AG, 19AH(2), 19AI(2), 19AI(3)(b), (h), (i), 19AH; VEPA, 2002c). While this was not inherently a problem, the findings suggested the VEPA lacked direction and/or technical capacity to exercise their discretion effectively with respect to what targets should contain and the improvements expected. In part, this may be

BOX 5.4 NEIP VISION, TARGETS AND OBJECTIVES (MARIBYRNONG CITY COUNCIL AND STONY CREEK NEIP PARTNERS, 2004; SURF COAST SHIRE COUNCIL AND ANGLESEA NEIP PARTNERS, 2004; TOWONG SHIRE COUNCIL AND PARTNERS OF LITTLE SNOWY CREEK NEIP, 2006)

NEIP 1

Vision: A clean Creek corridor that is the pride of all our community

- Improve water quality
- A reduction of the number of pollution incidents
- Improvement in baseline water quality defined by an index of Stream Condition tool

NEIP 2

Vision: A proud and connected community creating a prosperous and sustainable future in a healthy and beautiful environment

- Protect natural ecological values
- Reduce ecological footprint defined by baseline of a cross section of households and businesses then estimating the towns footprint

NEIP 3

Vision: A healthy Creek that supports a range of uses and is managed in a cooperative and considerate manner for the benefit of all

- To improve the stream health of Creek and consequently improve water quality
- Reduction in the level of nutrients entering the Creek from farming practices in 2004 levels in 5 years
- Improve water quality within three years by reducing sediment load from 2004 levels using turbidity as a measure
- Reduce the amount of greywater entering the stormwater system without treatment to 10% of properties or less within 5 years
- To provide clean, drinkable water.

a reflection of the fact that our two cases were pilots and VEPA was still learning about the NEIP. However, similar problems have persisted in later NEIPs, such as the Water Supply case where targets (although showing slightly greater specificity) still evidenced a high level of generality and lacked quantifiable improvements. As one VEPA officer reported: '. . . there weren't really detailed guidelines of what you needed to include. . . . [so] you want to improve water quality, but how are we going to measure that? That in itself posed certain problems' (Interview 211, VEPA).

An overlapping cause of imprecision in performance targets were gaps in baseline data. As discussed in Box 5.5 (further below), this was a problem in the CCM case as much as it was in the NEIP programme. Certainly in NEIP the VEPA, along with other well-resourced agency collaborators, had tried to assist collaborative groups by providing limited monitoring data and/or facilitating modest short-term grants to support further monitoring. This ranged from resources to complete baseline water quality monitoring (Degraded Creek case), support for a water monitoring kit and training for local non-government volunteers (Water Supply case) and funding, and in-kind support, for 'VEPA ecofootprint calculators' (Sustainable Township case).

Respondents reported that this support and funding was insufficient. For example, because of underfunding, the eco-footprint calculators contained underdeveloped 'metrics' (Surf Coast Shire Council, 2002, p14). This led the group to shelve the tool and fall back on extremely imprecise estimates of the town's ecological impact (Interview 224, VEPA). Similarly a lack of technical skills of volunteer monitors and inadequate funding in the Degraded Creek and Water Supply case lead to scientifically questionable measurements and significant gaps in water quality data. As one respondent put it:

> . . . we were doing some base line monitoring [but] there was a bit of a stuff-up on that . . . we need[ed] some more sophisticated systems . . . the issue was the cost of collecting that data and how we're going to do that.
>
> (Interview 215, Local Government)

Without the existence of credible or complete baseline data, it was virtually impossible to achieve accountability for performance and judge whether progress toward even vague targets had been made (Doremus, 2001, p62). Surprisingly, even some years after having their plan approved, our cases had neither taken steps to try and improve baseline data, nor set up or conducted any monitoring of environmental indicators to try and judge whether progress was being made against what limited baseline data had been generated.

Certainly all three cases had developed monitoring frameworks. However, these processes appeared to fall short at the implementation stage due to a lack of funding and technical capacity – a damning finding for a programme premised on accountability for performance. As one respondent explained:

> I don't think that we've come up yet with a system that we think is sustainable in terms of the cost of getting that data with the access and measurability and us being able to interpret and use it . . . I would accept that as a bit of a criticism.
>
> (Interview 215, Local Government)

Until more effective monitoring mechanisms are developed, outputs will remain the primary 'indicator' of performance in NEIP (Interview 237, VEPA; Markell, 2005, p62). However, even monitoring outputs and implementation appeared to face significant difficulties in the Degraded Creek and Sustainable Township cases (the Water Supply case having only just begun implementation). While key collaborators, such as NEIP 'sponsors', provided in-kind administrative support and had obtained a few short-term grants, in general the groups relied on their own resources to monitor implementation.

Respondents argued that these resources were insufficient to implement formal monitoring and reporting on implementation. Indeed, collaborators' 'monitoring' and reporting of compliance was generally verbal and informal (Interview 214, Government Agency) or conducted 'behind the scenes' (Interview 227, Local Resident; Interview 228, Local Government). For example, as one respondent noted: '. . . there's a kind of a policing/monitoring role that is important, that's part of the nature of the NEIP, but that slipped without funding' (Interview 215, Local Government).

Not surprisingly, with little formal monitoring, holding collaborators and the collaborative group accountable for implementation and outputs was difficult at best (Interview 215, Local Government; Interview 228, Local Government; Bovens, 2007, p450, Karkkainen, 2006b, p317). The result was that many collaborators in the Degraded Creek case failed to deliver actions and outputs 'on time'. As one respondent explained: '. . . some of the targets were pretty far in the future, but a lot were supposed to be done in the first couple of years after NEIP and they weren't really actually done' (Interview 218, Environmental Interest Group). Similarly, in the Sustainable Township case, accountabilities for implementing the plan had reportedly 'got a bit lost' (Interview 228, Local Government), and the collaborators themselves were beginning to drift away from some of the formal actions and objectives of the plan: '. . . they're supposed to be implementing their plan now but it's like they haven't even looked at the plan' (Interview 241, VEPA).

There was no evidence of deliberate collusion to hide this underperformance – many, in fact, expressed a desire for a better monitoring and reporting system (Interview 214, Government Agency). Rather, the problem was that the verbal and informal process of monitoring each other's behaviour was insufficient to 'catch out' collaborators who were skilled at 'hiding' behind their words. This can be contrasted to the CCM demonstration programme discussed in Box 5.5 (below), where sufficient funding was used to a hire a coordinator and ensure good monitoring support for accountability regarding most (but not all) outputs.

One may wonder why the VEPA had not tried to take a more active role in encouraging partners to remain accountable to their commitments. In part, the VEPA officers appeared to want to avoid too much control over the group in the first few years of implementing the five-year and three-year plan of the Degraded Creek case and Sustainable Township case, respectively. Furthermore, the VEPA may well have held back from trying to persuade parties to keep to the commitments because they were aware that the NEIP had been designed so that specific parties could ultimately be held accountable for performing their actions at the end of the plan under the contractual NEIP mechanism (Interview 214, Government Agency).

Notably, recent short-term grants to both cases appeared likely to turn around abysmal monitoring of implementation and reduce the likelihood that such enforcement would be needed. While the Sustainable Township case had only just received the grant at time of research, the Degraded Creek case had applied their grant to hire a coordinator, who had implemented a new monitoring protocol, developed and distributed a formal register of actions and produced a report for the VEPA. This appeared to provide partners with the information they needed to shame and exert pressure on under-performers. As one respondent described: 'Things are starting to happen now . . . the coordinator has spent the last six months now just chasing up what previously hadn't been done and what each partner was supposed to do . . . they have re-initiated that process' (Interview 218, Environment Group).

To summarize, while the NEIP programme is still in its infancy, the findings suggest it has laid ineffective and unstable foundations for enabling the programme to hold collaborations accountable for performance in the future. Although risks of capture evident in the EIP programme were avoided, NEIP faced a raft of other challenges attributable to two broad weaknesses. As with the EIP programme, the first weakness arose from broad and imprecise performance requirements, and the fact that the VEPA lacked the guidance or knowledge to ensure appropriate targets. Second, in contrast to the EIP programme, the findings revealed that complex second-generation problems posed significant and costly monitoring demands as well as weaknesses in baseline data collection and monitoring indicators. Without these resources it was difficult for collaborators to fulfil mutual accountability roles or for agencies to ensure even basic accountability for implementation, let alone hold groups accountable for environmental results.

BOX 5.5 NEW ZEALAND DEMONSTRATION CASE: COLLABORATIVE CATCHMENT MANAGEMENT (CCM)

As with most of our new governance programmes, the CCM programme employed a performance-based accountability regime. As a purely voluntary programme, it placed a heavy reliance on mutual accountability between multiple public and private collaborators, both for setting targets and for their implementation.

continued . . .

BOX 5.5 *. . . continued*

The fundamental step in the CCM's approach to accountability was developing 'the vision, goals, targets and actions for the ongoing management of the [water resource]' against which collaborators would be held to account (Waihora Ellesmere Trust, 2004, p1). As with the other programmes, the target-setting process itself was tasked to collaborators, who benefitted from the monitoring data available from ECan and other government agencies, as well as from funding, which was in part used to collect data to inform and underpin various targets. However, even with such support, significant gaps in data understandably remained, particularly with regard to complex environmental and ecosystem issues and the impacts of diffuse sources of pollution.

Facing such gaps in data, the CCM groups fell back upon their personal knowledge and observations. As one respondent explained: 'I don't think it's done from a strong science guiding process. It was really done by people that had interest in the [water resource] and what was happening, mostly from their own observations and their own knowledge' (Interview NZ226, Non-government Collaborator). Lacking credible data, the groups produced relatively nebulous goals and targets that did not enable credible measurement of environmental outcomes. Indeed, much like the Australian NEIP programme, broad targets such as 'water quality in the Estuary and its rivers supports healthy aquatic ecosystems' left significant scope for tokenism (Avon-Heathcote Estuary Ihutai Trust, 2004, p9). As one respondent explained, such targets were 'not really acting as an accountability mechanism . . . it just leaves things to float a little bit' (Interview NZ227, Government Body).

Subsequently, external funding enabled groups to put into place significant ongoing monitoring to better inform targets and judge progress (e.g., develop indicators and better understand baseline conditions). A coordinator was also employed, which ensured good administration and monitoring of outputs.

However, even with improved environmental monitoring and the capacity to track who was implementing what, there were two significant weaknesses in these accountability mechanisms. First, respondents reported that although a large majority of collaborators had implemented their actions, when it came to holding key reluctant performers to account for delivery, volunteers lacked the time or skill to ensure mutual accountability, and proved unable to 'persuade' District Councils to take positive action and subsequently hold them to account. According to respondents, without such action it was highly unlikely that the group as a whole would achieve their environmental performance targets: 'the fundamental questions are the big water quantity questions . . . it's these people that actually have to do something, the [District Councils]

continued . . .

BOX 5.5 *... continued*

... but to be honest the District Councils that can make that happen don't want that to happen' (Interview NZ226, Non-government Collaborator).

The second weakness in the CCM accountability arrangements was that the ongoing monitoring of implementation and environmental conditions was still insufficient to inform judgements as to whether the actions that were being implemented were delivering on targets and goals. As one respondent explained:

> ... its problematic in the work that we do to evaluate whether what we do is successful ... whether or not achieving the actions are actually resulting in achieving any outcomes or vision for the plan, that is very difficult to measure ... as an organisation we are still working through it ... we're really struggling with how to quantify it.
>
> (Interview NZ213, Government Body)

To the extent such problems remain in the medium to longer term, it appeared unlikely that the CCM programme would be effective in holding collaborations accountable for achievement of their environmental targets.

Learning – adaptive management and systematic learning

Learning in the NEIP programme took two forms, a passive form of adaptive management and an overlapping form of 'systemic learning' that aspired to spread learning and information between different NEIP collaborations. While it is still early days, the findings suggest that neither learning approach had been successful, nor were they likely to be successful in the future without significant changes to the NEIP programme.

Regarding adaptive management, there had been at best very modest attempts at learning, which had relied on partners' perceptions of what had or had not been working, whether improvements to the local environment were occurring and whether behaviour should be adapted in response (Interview 225, VEPA; Karkkainen, 2003b, pp952–953). As one respondent expressed it: '... issues that come up as part of the meetings ... we've noticed that there's a problem here; how about you go check it out or what other things can we do' (Interview 213, Local Government).

Moreover, a lack of funding had produced ineffective monitoring processes (particularly regarding baseline environmental conditions and ongoing progress against targets), and this in turn had effectively prevented the generation of detailed and meaningful data on which to base robust attempts to learn from and adapt behaviour (Ewing, 2003, pp407–408).

A further constraint on the adaptive capacities of groups related to the nature of their external funding. Respondents suggested that the monitoring requirements for short-term government grants were typically focused on the requirements of the funding body, and provided little opportunity for the groups themselves to monitor, test by results, and learn adaptively from their experience. As one respondent explained:

> . . . there isn't a single funding opportunity at the moment where they go, 'Here is [Australian]$20K to roll out a project and here is [Australian]$5K more to do monitoring and evaluation for it after you finish' . . . there's no monitoring and evaluation cycle.
>
> (Interview 222, Local Government)

Turning to systemic learning, there was no evidence that even the most basic learning and experiences of collaborators had been diffused among NEIP groups. Certainly, early NEIPs had been encouraged by VEPA to adopt 'sharing learning' as a primary objective. A common statement of this goal was as follows: '[The NEIP] is to use what has been learnt from the process to develop the potential for other Neighbourhood EIPs to assist in the management of other urban waterway corridors' (Maribyrnong City Council, 2004, p25; Surf Coast Shire Council, 2004, p14).

However, respondents reported that VEPA officers had not provided any direct guidance or support to the group to assist them in meeting such goals. As the following comment from one respondent explains, the result was predictable:

> . . . there's never been any sort of communication between groups or between any of us with other groups . . . I don't think the [V]EPA actually knew how to support these groups in terms of building the capacity of these groups or providing strategies for these groups to fulfil their needs.
>
> (Interview 225, VEPA)

Like the collaborative groups, the VEPA had also failed to hold up its end of the systemic learning bargain, sidestepping any 'information pooling' role, and making no attempt to monitor or feed lessons back to collaboratives. As one VEPA respondent put it: '[Learning] is not going on at the moment' (Interview 237, VEPA). Another noted: '[The VEPA] sort of left us to our own devices. They haven't run a monitoring and evaluation programme to see how we went and what works and what didn't' (Interview 222, Local Government).

The above weaknesses were arguably attributable to the 'gap' between the vision of sharing learning and the lack of mechanisms to implement it in practice. According to respondents, one source of this gap between vision and practice was that policy designers and VEPA officers, who were charged with developing institutional mechanisms and carrying them out in practice, were embedded in an old culture – of being a 'regulator' – and they were unsure how to step into a new role that involved facilitating learning. As one VEPA respondent explained:

> [V]EPA is so confused about its role in NEIPs . . . traditionally we were a regulator, a stick waving role and now we're much more touchy feely, but when it comes down to it I think we're plain scared to leave that regulation role behind because that's what we see as giving us strength.
>
> (Interview 241, VEPA)

As the above quote suggests, the VEPA were 'self aware' and acknowledged the challenges it faced in changing its culture to better support NEIP aspirations, such as systemic learning. Indeed, at the time of research the VEPA had begun to try and change its culture and better support NEIPs through retraining staff, hiring 'community development' officers and providing greater funding to groups to assist with implementation and sharing lessons between NEIPs.

To summarize: the experience of the early years of the NEIP suggests that both systemic learning and adaptive management have produced little success. Anaemic learning processes are likely to arise where there is insufficient funding specifically designated to support groups in data collection and monitoring and evaluation processes. Our analysis of systemic learning adds support to these claims and points to the very real challenges that policymakers and regulatory agencies face in implementing new approaches to learning.

Regional NRM

Accountability – performance-based accountability

Unlike either the NEIP or EIP programmes, the RNRM programme emphasizes financial accountability, as well as accountability for performance. We found that these mechanisms were effective, at least compared to the experience of EIP or NEIP. As discussed below, performance targets appeared to avoid distortions arising from the domination of economic interests. Furthermore, although the collection of baseline data and ongoing monitoring of environmental indicators evidenced some shortcomings, the programme had taken more significant steps towards establishing effective monitoring than NEIP and had resolved evident 'rent seeking'. Notwithstanding this success, accountability for RNRM came at a price. Monitoring and reporting obligations were onerous and threatened to turn the supposedly flexible, community-based regional bodies into bureaucracies.

The setting of resource condition and management action targets in RNRM was guided by a regional body that was weighted in favour of primary producer interests. While this created significant risks for distortion, government oversight appeared to have largely addressed these defects. Certainly, having scientific interests on regional bodies and the wider community consultation process had improved the robustness of the targets (Interview 323, Government Agency). But more important, as one Joint Steering Committee respondent explained, was how government oversight had been repeatedly used to veto targets set by the regional body (see Table 5.1 below) and ensure that they were consistent with existing laws and maintained credible environmental standards: 'The plan would say . . . "change the Vegetation Management Act," and we'd say "why did you waste the ink [as] that is not a decision that is appropriate to this group"' (Interview 323, Government Agency).

Most of our respondents also suggested the Joint Steering Committee had ensured that targets were appropriate, measurable and quantifiable. As was the case in LSP (see Box 5.1 above), this success in RNRM was partly attributable to the specificity in the overarching frameworks regarding expected outcomes and matters for

TABLE 5.1 Illustration of Resource Condition and Management Action Targets in RNRM

Illustration of resource condition targets	*Illustration of management action targets*
• By 2024, achieve a 10 per cent improvement in soil health in extensive and intensive agricultural areas. • By 2024, the conservation of naturally occurring aquatic organisms and ecological values of 80 per cent of priority, permanent, natural waterholes will be ensured. • By 2012, the health and diversity of 75 per cent of the mapped key groundwater dependent ecosystems (e.g., springs, wetlands, wonky holes) is stable. • By 2020, 40 per cent of landscapes in poor biodiversity condition, focusing on endangered and of concern regional ecosystems and riparian areas are rehabilitated to a good biodiversity condition. • By 2015, ensure 90 per cent of all threatened flora and fauna species in the region will be represented in conservation reserves or under voluntary conservation agreements. • By 2020, CO_2 and other greenhouse gas emissions in the regional airshed are reduced by 5 per cent from 1990 levels.	• By 2010, 75 per cent of landholders in cropping areas are implementing farm management systems. • By 2010, facilitate the development of a regional (surface and ground) water management organization. • By 2010 1 million ha of land are managed for nature conservation purposes under voluntary management agreements • By 2010, complete state agency pest management planning. • By 2008, assess the impact of climate change on the region. • By 2008, a strategic plan for the removal of impediments (either by complete removal or modification to structures) between marine and freshwater environments will be completed for the BDT regions.

Source: Burdekin Dry Tropics Natural Resource Management (2005a).

target, which ensured the Committee had a relatively clear picture of the issues to be measured and the magnitude of targets expected: '. . . the regional bodies planning is largely operational . . . all the decision making will be taken in the government framework, veg[etation] management, water planning, for example: there's no discretion' (Interview 321, Government Agency).

Successful target setting was also attributable to quite significant baseline data and monitoring mechanisms established by the RNRM programme. Vital here was existing environmental monitoring data from state government agencies (Interview 3211, Government Advisor), as well as quite extensive funding made available to the regional body to seek scientific advice via a technical advisory panel (BDTNRM, 2005a, p32) and conduct multiple studies on regional resource, social and economic conditions (BDTNRM, 2005a). This is not to suggest that all technical constraints and scientific uncertainties, characteristic of such a complex ecosystem management system, had been overcome (Interview 323, Government Agency). Like many NEG experiments, RNRM operated on 'best available science' (Interview 341, Regional Body), a fact that led some to question the scientific appropriateness of some targets (e.g., causal links between management actions and outcomes, and 'hydrological models' associated with load-based end-of-river targets) (Interview 311, 'Peak' Industry Body; Interview 341, Regional Body; Watts, 2004, pp36–37).

A number of other problems were also apparent. These included insufficiencies in funding for monitoring. State agencies also reportedly prevented access to some of its data. As one respondent pointed out: '. . . the agencies had done a lot of work . . . but you know they were keeping it . . . so it wasn't going out to bodies' (Interview 315, Peak Industry Body). These problems contributed to a number of gaps in baseline data. This prevented targets being set for issues such as dry land salinity, terrestrial weeds, acidity, biodiversity in flora and fauna, wetlands and hydraulic links, ground water and water bodies, coastal condition and water quality (BDTNRM, 2005a, pp81–82; see also RM Consulting Group, 2006, pp15–16; Bellamy et al, 2005, ppvii and viii; Keogh et al, 2006, p7). As one government respondent put it: 'the reality is that in NRM there are huge information gaps' (Interview 323, Government Agency).

Of course, the RNRM programme had anticipated gaps in data. Much will accordingly depend upon whether commitments to fill these gaps are funded by the government and successfully implemented by the regional body over the next few years. In addition to filling baseline gaps, an equally important task for delivering accountability in RNRM will be ongoing environmental monitoring of indicators to enable progress to be judged against resource condition targets (BDTNRM, 2005a, p146).

Our findings suggest that the regional body and state agencies had made significant progress in developing long-term data capture processes, including obtaining satellite imagery of the region, implementing drilling programmes and building monitoring components into projects (Interview 334, Regional Body; Interview 341, Regional Body). However, such ongoing monitoring is likely to face two key difficulties. First, respondents suggested there was a lack of coordination in ongoing monitoring by agencies. As one respondent explained regarding water monitoring: '. . . one of the problems I suppose is there are so many different agencies doing so many different things. There is no commonality, or no communication you know bringing them together' (Interview 342, Sub-regional Body).

The second challenge related to funding. Available funding was seen by many as simply too small and too 'short term' for regional bodies to sustain long-term monitoring and implementation responsibilities to ultimately achieve their targets (Interview 3210, Science). Without further funding or improved coordination, these monitoring barriers may reduce the capacity of government and the public to judge whether they are getting good value for expenditure and whether progress is being made toward national outcomes (Interview 3215, Government Agency).

In contrast, the RNRM programme appeared to face fewer problems in monitoring financial activity, outputs and adherence to management action milestones. The effectiveness of this monitoring process is perhaps best illustrated by exploring how it enabled the Joint Steering Committee to step in and rectify emerging rent-seeking behaviour at the regional body level.

Two unique factors appeared to have given rise to problems of rent seeking. The first was the regional body's 'nested' structure. As we saw in Chapter 3, this nested structure involved giving majority membership to five sub-regional groups. While this structure was useful for planning, when it came to the regional body managing the roll out of government investment to implement the plan, it gave rise to potential conflicts of interests. As one respondent explained, this was because the sub-regional bodies were potential recipients of the funding that their representatives on the regional body controlled:

> . . . when it came to actually roll out and receiving the money and making the decision you all of a sudden had a structure that was full of conflict of interest . . . [because] the board of directors consists of 99 per cent of potential providers of services to the organization.
>
> (Interview, 341, Regional Body; Paton et al, 2004, p265)

Compounding this problem was the fact that many of the sub-regional representatives lacked the knowledge or training for managing an incorporated body. As one respondent explained, 'the 5 sub-regional bodies and other organizations [had] nominate[d] people on the board regardless of qualifications or their background, their ability to govern' (Interview 341, Regional Body). This stymied mutual accountability between partners and reportedly created 'incompetence at a board level' (Interview 3210, Science).

The result was governance and management problems regarding the use of public funds, sparking concerns of 'rent seeking' behaviour. As one respondent explained: '. . . out of the funding available they decided to fund a [capacity building project] for each of their organizations . . . but that was the funding that was supposed to be used for setting up the roll out of the plan' (Interview 341, Regional Body).

Fortunately, the regional body had received sufficient funding to complete administration tasks and hire staff to meet monitoring and reporting expectations on finances and implementation. Further, the government-based Regional Coordinating Group and Regional Body Advisors had reportedly kept the Joint Steering Committee informed on whether 'projects were being implemented, conducted successfully/not successful and whether there were problems' (Interview 3211, Government Agency). These processes alerted the Joint Steering Committee to the above problems and it exercised its 'destabilization right' to initiate a review of governance and operational arrangements. This was followed by a second Business Improvement Review of all regional bodies some months later. These two review processes involved government officers working with regional body directors and staff to identify a range of potential improvements (e.g., change the focus, structure and composition of the board, develop new corporate policies) (BDTNRM, 2005b, pp7 and 9; BDTNRM, 2007, p3).

The precise details of the recommended improvements were largely left to the regional body. However, the Joint Steering Committee retained the ongoing right to review the changes over time (Karkkainen, 2005, p68). At the time of writing, the regional body has successfully responded to many of the recommendations (e.g., appointing a new CEO, staff and membership of the board, corporate governance training, commitments to rewrite the constitution and develop various governance and business plans) (BDTNRM, 2005b, pp7 and 9; Interview 341, Regional Body; BDTNRM, 2007, pp3 and 15).

Despite successfully preventing rent seeking, there was at least one downside to RNRM's accountability arrangements (see Paton et al, 2004, p261; Keogh et al, 2006, p60; Posner, 2002, p529). Some respondents suggested accountability requirements were 'smothering' regional bodies (Interview 349, Regional Groups Collective), imposing excessive 'red tape' and onerous obligations both for the programme as a whole and individual projects (Interview 344, Sub-regional Body). This had negative impacts upon adaptive management processes. As one respondent put it: '. . . it's just quite a burden, you're just sticking that bureaucratic stuff into a really small organization that doesn't have the capacity' (Interview 349, Regional Groups Collective).

Many respondents suggested such bureaucratic monitoring and reporting, combined with tight government controls over investment decisions, had left regional bodies 'over governed' by government (Interview 313, Peak Industry Body). The risk here was that too much government control was beginning to 'morph' regional bodies into the very government bureaucracies that these supposedly flexible and participatory organizations were designed to replace (Lawrence, 2004, p13; Lawrence and Cheshire, 2004, p9; May, 2007, p23). As one respondent summed it up: 'It's getting to the stage now where the board was starting to look as if it's just another state department and if that is going to be the case we may as well not have wasted all our money' (Interview 342, Sub-regional Body).

To conclude, accountability mechanisms in RNRM appeared to avoid many of the problems that plagued the other case studies. The RNRM programme appeared to secure credible, measurable targets free from blatant industry dominance. This was achieved in part because of the greater level of specificity in performance expectation and outcomes that had assisted the Joint Steering Committee to effectively exercise its discretion. Furthermore, dedicated funding and state government monitoring ensured that regional bodies had greater success than NEIP in seeking scientific advice, collecting baseline data and conducting ongoing monitoring of indicators, milestones, finances and outputs. Moreover, the RNRM programme had been able to intervene successfully to ensure that regional bodies complied with their responsibilities and were held accountable via destabilization rights for rent seeking behaviour.

Such success must, however, be weighed against the challenges faced by RNRM. Uncertainties remain about the scientific basis of targets. Indeed, bodies accountable for delivery of results are likely to face difficulties in the future if evident gaps in baseline data and uncoordinated or inadequately funded long-term monitoring processes are not resolved in the immediate future. Shortfalls in mutual accountability were also evident, in part because of mutual interests of regional body members and a lack of necessary knowledge and skills to check rent seeking tendencies. Moreover, distinct from both NEIP and EIP programmes, the RNRM programme appeared to be obsessed with tight accountability controls, which our findings suggested may undermine the unique contribution of regional bodies and marginalize their learning processes (Lawrence and Cheshire, 2004, p9).

Learning – adaptive management and systemic learning

The learning aspirations of the RNRM programme were twofold: 'passive' adaptive management at regional body level, which is overlaid with a form of systemic learning at the programme level. As we will see, adaptive management at the regional body level confronted greater obstacles in terms both of getting off the ground and being carried out effectively than systemic learning. However, systemic learning in RNRM itself could have been improved if the programme had aspired to share experiences between regional bodies.

At an early stage, the RNRM programme appeared to have laid some important foundations for implementing an adaptive management process, at least compared to the NEIP programme. As discussed above, significant levels of funding provided to the regional body, along with government monitoring, had ensured that at least some baseline data had been collected and some longer-term monitoring infrastructure had been put into place. These elements should have assisted the regional bodies to gather data on ongoing implementation, conduct evaluations regarding the suitability and achievement of regional targets, and thus facilitate adaptations as needed (Commonwealth and Queensland, 2004b).

However, regional bodies faced a number of hurdles that limited the achievement of effective adaptive management. Some of these have already been noted regarding RNRM monitoring processes. A second hurdle was that many of the environmental monitoring processes were designed to monitor environmental conditions at a *regional* level for resource condition targets. This meant that the data being produced was not always suitable to effective adaptive management regarding more *localized* environmental changes. As one respondent put it:

> . . . the plans put in monitoring points that are well down stream of farms, they are [regional] catchment scale . . . if we are going to get continuous improvement we need something that is giving us feedback . . . because all this catchment planning, basin planning is too broad scale.
>
> (Interview 314, Peak Industry Body)

A third and final hurdle to achieving adaptive management related to the capacity of regional bodies to actually act as effective adaptive managers. Certainly, the RNRM programme had taken important steps to ensure that bodies were equipped with skills and data – including training regional body staff in monitoring processes and developing a database to provide a central source of knowledge. However, the regional body has made slow progress in implementing procedures necessary for it to follow an adaptive approach. Not least, they were well over a year behind in developing (let alone implementing) a formal monitoring and evaluation strategy that was to guide learning and adaptation.

The capacity of the body to perform adaptive management was also constrained by an overemphasis on financial accountability and management action milestones. These requirements appeared to be well beyond the resources and capacity of regional groups and skewed time and effort in these directions, reducing opportunities to operate as effective and adaptive natural resource management organizations. Indeed, respondents routinely complained of disproportionate amounts of time being spent on 'monitoring and evaluation in the form of quarterly performance and financial reports' (Interview 342, Regional Body; BDTNRM, 2005b, pp7 and 9).

Turning to systemic learning, insights can be gained from the results of the first scheduled programme evaluation (see www.nrm.gov.au/me/evaluation/national.html). Following procedures laid out in overarching frameworks, government bodies had engaged consultants and set the scope, objectives and terms of reference for six comprehensive national evaluations (Commonwealth and Queensland, 2004b, ss7.1–7.3). These evaluations brought to light a number of successes, but also identified areas for improvement, including issues regarding baseline data gaps, and overly onerous accountability requirements. It remains to be seen whether, having identified these weaknesses, the government will agree to improve programme delivery (Farrelly, 2005, p403).

The government has committed to a 'new phase' of the programme for 2008–2013, known as Caring for Our Country (see generally http://nrm.gov.au). This programme aims to address weaknesses of NHT/NAP by offering 'an integrated package with one clear goal, a business approach to investment, clearly articulated outcomes and priorities and improved accountability' (Commonwealth of Australia, 2008, p1). However, at least according to one review, such promises have not been fulfilled:

> . . . the government's intention was to build on the legacy of three decades of investment in natural resource management while addressing weaknesses identified in previous programmes. In the committee's opinion, in its current form Caring for our Country falls well short of achieving this.
>
> (RRAT References Committee, 2009, p67)

As such, this report raises doubts about the capacity of government agencies to fulfil an effective systemic learning approach. Nevertheless, even in its earlier incarnations, at the very least, RNRM has far exceeded the NEIP programme's approach to systemic learning by reviewing the programme and establishing and following procedures for future reviews.

Despite this modest success, many respondents were critical of the RNRM programme's failure to share (or even aspire to sharing) learning and experiences between regional bodies. While there had been some national seminars and other events organized that allowed regional bodies to share information, there were very few formal systems put in place (Head, 2005a, p146; see also NRM Toolbar at www.nrmnavigator.net.au). This is problematic given that there were 56 regions across Australia with bodies that varied in age and experience, providing rich opportunities for sharing experiences of success and failure under different approaches and for pooling knowledge of lessons learned so as to improve the overall effectiveness of the programme (Paton et al, 2004, p262). But instead, as one respondent explained: 'a lot of these kind of groups are just working in a vacuum' (Interview 349, Regional Group Collective).

With no formal information sharing, the Regional Groups Collective (RGC) in Queensland had taken matters into their own hands. The RGC was composed of representatives of each regional body in Queensland and was underpinned by government funding directed by regional bodies to hire staff and an office for the RGC. Utilizing these resources, the body provided a forum at the state level for 'regional bodies to share what they're doing', and learn and build capacities to face their many similar challenges (Interview 349, Regional Group Collective). This initiative has been warmly received. As one respondent explained: 'the groups are so diverse and the regions so diverse, so you get a lot of good ideas' (Interview 341, Regional Body). However, these ideas, and the wider information sharing facilitated by RGC was largely practical and far more limited than a democratic experimentalist vision of sharing of standards, targets and measures to achieve them (Karkkainen et al, 2000). However, at a minimum, the RGC embodies at least a nascent form of information sharing that appeared more effective than relying on government agency efforts such as in NEIPs.

To summarize, adaptive management and systemic learning are both underpinned by solid foundations. In contrast to the NEIP programme, RNRM funding and government support have positioned regional groups with greater access to necessary information capable of facilitating learning processes. Further, the form of systemic learning in RNRM involving policy review and adaptation was also implemented more successfully than NEIP's attempts to share learning among collaboratives, in part because of the presence of formal procedures to guide agencies in these tasks (Ewing, 2003, p407).

Yet notwithstanding its successes, RNRM confronted a number of obstacles to achieving effective adaptive management. These included gaps in baseline data due to insufficient funding, inadequacies in monitoring at multiple scales, and lack of capacity at regional body level to conduct adaptive management tasks. The findings also suggested that systemic learning aspirations lacked what many respondents suggested were vital information-sharing goals. To fill this void the RGC structure appears to offer some promise, at least compared to the attempts by VEPA in the NEIP programme.

Conclusions

We have investigated the conditions that fostered novel forms of accountability and learning in practice. For the most part our findings focused on approaches and mechanisms appropriate to each programme. For example, the findings in EIP touched on accountability and learning in process- and performance-based approaches, pointing to the risk of laggards paying 'lip service' to processes and pursuing tokenistic targets (Fiorino, 2004). The NEIP findings reflected on systemic learning, revealing what we termed a 'vision deficit'. Insufficiencies in funding and support for NEIP collaborative groups were also identified and found to have undermined effective monitoring of performance. Our findings for RNRM provided evidence of more effective monitoring and accountability mechanisms. However, this success came at the price of onerous controls that threatened flexibility and learning.

Beyond programme specific issues, a number of cross-cutting themes can be identified, many of which connect with issues explored in the wider NEG literature. Not least, we found that the emergence of novel forms and approaches to accountability created significant risks of agency capture, unprincipled deal making and rent seeking (Steinzor, 2000; Doremus, 2001; Posner, 2002, p529; Karkkainen, 2003b, p961). These risks arose in all three of our programmes. While no level of 'perfect accountability' was identified (Freeman, 2005, p908), it was clear that in each programme there were one or more shortfalls in accountability that had made it vulnerable to such risks. Overly broad performance standards, weaknesses in agency oversight and in mutual and/or professional accountability with EIP and NEIP were all found to have left the door open to risks of capture and unprincipled deal making – undermining environmental performance. Similarly, our findings for RNRM pointed to a failure in mutual accountability that saw regional bodies pursue rent seeking behaviour. However, RNRM was able to successfully address this weakness through an accountability regime that had provided greater specificity in expected performance outcomes and imposed stricter monitoring and reporting requirements.

Generally our findings support claims that NEG is prone to capture or unscrupulous behaviour by private interests (McCloskey, 1996; Karkkainen, 2003b, p961; Posner, 2002, p529; Steinzor, 2000) and suggest that more, rather than less formal accountability safeguards are needed, including heightened scrutiny such as in RNRM, less deference to discretion and more precise statutes to guarantee accountability (Freeman, 1997, p34). Yet as our RNRM findings caution, the risk is that stricter controls may undermine the creativity and flexibility that is essential to address diverse localized problems successfully (Freeman, 1997, p93; Steinzor, 2000, p15; Wondolleck and Yaffee, 2000, p241; Taylor, 2003, p229; Head, 2005b, p58). Accordingly, our findings are consistent with those parts of the NEG literature that emphasize the need to balance accountability controls (to ensure consistency) with sufficient discretion (to promote flexibility and innovation) (Freeman, 1997, p96; Wondolleck and Yaffee, 2000, pp235–237; Freeman, 2005, pp1871–1872; Head, 2005a, p31; May, 2007, p23). More concretely, our findings suggest the importance of designing accountability mechanisms to address risks of capture and other distortions in NEG, but of doing so with an awareness of the trade-off between accountability and arriving at and implementing creative agreements in a provisional and adaptive manner (Freeman, 2005, p1871). Finally, although the breadth of our data collection on accountability in New Zealand was too narrow to give us confidence in terms of testing such theoretical propositions, there were some interesting lessons regarding design conditions, which we will return to below.

In terms of learning, we found that each of the approaches we reviewed achieved only limited success. Process-based learning in EIP was effective only when it was placed in the hands of industries with a commitment to environmental outcomes. The passive adaptive management approach pursued across the cases appeared effective in some circumstances, with collaborators using their local knowledge and/or available monitoring data to identify shortcomings and assess alternatives to reach feasible approaches that worked (Sturm, 2006, p326). However, this approach fell short of complete success where there was either (i) a lack of capacity by collaborators, such as local resident in EIP who failed to engage with broader environmental issues, and/or (ii) insufficient funding and support for data collection and ongoing monitoring, such as in NEIP and RNRM.

Finally, systemic learning approaches appeared effective in RNRM, while NEIP evidenced a complete failure by government and collaborations to pool and share information.

These three approaches to learning all failed because those charged with learning lacked the capacity or incentives to gather, analyse and act on information about practice (Sturm, 2006, p327). The lesson for scholars and practitioners is that the capacity for learning is not a given, and that NEG accordingly must ensure that appropriate incentives, capacity building and support is built into programmes to ensure that effective learning is achieved (Sturm, 2006, p327).

On the basis of this analysis, several lessons can be identified. The first of these relates to both learning and accountability, namely the importance of designing effective monitoring processes. With respect to accountability specifically, two primary themes emerged: (i) the need to set overarching legislative goals; and (ii) the need to achieve effective professional and mutual accountability (May, 2007, pp23–24). Similarly, two themes emerged in relation to learning: (i) the need to assist or encourage actors to effectively implement process and adaptive learning approaches; and (ii) the need to design systemic learning structures. For each of these themes our findings suggest several empirical-based lessons for NEG theory and for policymakers.

First, with respect to monitoring, the NEG literature has raised many questions about the conditions under which collaborative groups best conduct monitoring vital to both learning (Dovers, 2003a, pp522–523; Fung and Wright, 2003b, pp31–32; Thomas, 2003, p154; Head, 2005a, p145; Collaborative Democracy Network, 2006, p169; Sturm, 2006, p328) and performance-based accountability (Fung and Wright, 2003b, p521; Gaines, 2002/2003, p16; Sturm, 2006, p333). Based on our findings, it appears that NEG programmes like EIP, which focus on point source pollution emissions (as opposed to their ambient impact), or LSP, which involved a very small number of polluters and a limited set of easily measurable pollutants, were likely to face fewer direct monitoring challenges. This was not least because the environmental problems are 'simpler' and industries or government will often have well established monitoring processes under traditional regulatory regimes (Dovers, 2003a, p522).

In contrast, the challenges of monitoring are much greater in programmes like NEIP and RNRM in Australia or CCM in New Zealand, which were focused on complex and diffuse environmental issues. Even with varying degrees of support, these programmes evidenced significant gaps in baseline monitoring, ineffective or limited ongoing monitoring of environment conditions, and in the NEIP case, weak monitoring of outputs. These findings are generally consistent with other NEG research, which suggests that, in similar ecosystem-focused experiments, monitoring is often weak and can have a negative impact on securing effective accountability and learning (Steinzor, 2000, pp15 and 21; Wondolleck and Yaffee, 2000, pp136–137; Ewing, 2003, pp407–408; Karkkainen, 2003a, p218; Thomas, 2003, pp153–156).

Based on this analysis several conditions can be identified that are likely to improve the chances of successful monitoring. At the broadest level, there is a need to improve the extent and effectiveness of basic environmental monitoring in order to better support NEG experiments (Dovers, 2003a, p522). Certainly there have been significant improvements in government data gathering (e.g., in Australia State of the Environment reporting, National Land and Water Resources Audit, and recent Bureau of Meteorology water data responsibilities). However, it is clear that governments continue to ignore the breadth of basic monitoring that needs to be conducted to inform effective learning and accountability processes at decentralized levels. Further, even when relevant information is available, governments have often failed to marshal the systems necessary for ensuring that data is accessible to NEG participants (Dovers, 2003a, pp521–522). Indeed, as the difficulties in coordination, relevancy and access to monitoring data in RNRM revealed, it is vital that there is clarity on why data is collected, who will and is collecting it, and who must have access to it (Karkkainen, 2006a, pp230–231; Dovers, 2003a, p521).

A second insight into conditions supportive of effective monitoring was identified in our analysis of the EIP programme. The programme's capacity to harness community and VEPA pressure on industry proved to be a powerful means of encouraging effective monitoring. This resonates with suggestions in the literature that negative incentives such as 'the shadow of the law' can be used to great effect to ensure appropriate monitoring (Karkkainen, 2003b, p996).

Third, in the absence of specific incentives, support and funding is important if collaborative groups are to fulfil their monitoring requirements (Thomas, 2003, pp167–169; Ewing, 2003, p408). Without sufficient funding, NEG experiments risk severe breakdowns in monitoring processes as evidenced in the NEIP programme, or at best are left with significant gaps to fill as evidenced in RNRM and CCM.

Turning to the second set of lessons, the findings shed light on the challenges of securing accountability in performance-based initiatives. Many in the literature suggest that legislating the outcomes to be achieved by collaborative groups can protect the public interest, while also preserving the discretion needed to develop innovative and tailored solutions to environmental problems (Freeman, 1997, p93; Wondolleck and Yaffee, 2000, p241; Dana, 2000, pp53–54). However – consistent with the concerns of other authors – the findings in EIP and NEIP demonstrated that specifying overly general performance outcomes creates very real risks of 'abuse' by collaborators, industry and overworked or inexperienced government officers (Freeman, 1997, p94; Dana, 2000, pp53–54; Wondolleck and Yaffee, 2000, p241). A rule of thumb for overcoming this problem would be for legislatures to avoid broad sweeping statements, such as evidenced in EIP and NEIP, and instead specify as clearly as possible the outcomes expected – an approach that contributed to successful target setting in LSP and RNRM (Wondolleck and Yaffee, 2000, p241).

A more extensive reform suggested in the literature for improving outcome specificity, while retaining sufficient flexibility, would be for NEG experiments to adopt a form of systemic learning structure. This would involve various collaborators functioning as information-gathering mechanisms to inform processes of benchmarking, coupled with the periodic overhaul of acceptable outcomes and targets (Freeman, 1997, p93; Karkkainen, 2003b). For example, instances of tokenism in the EIP programme would arguably have been minimized if targets set by comparable industries had been pooled and benchmarked, leading the VEPA to periodically refine and specify minimal 'beyond compliance' targets (Cohen and Sabel, 1997, p313). Indeed, such a process would likely have provided greater guidance and information for VEPA officers who otherwise appeared to lack the time, knowledge or skills to know what level of environmental improvement was capable of achievement by industries. Such an approach would have then enabled poorer performers to be brought into line with others. A difficulty, however, with this approach is that such information-gathering structures may pose significant problems for agencies (see below).

Beyond setting overarching performance goals, the findings also provide some insights into conditions for effective professional and mutual accountability. Of course, few NEG experiments are likely to rely exclusively on either professional or mutual accountability, nor should they. Even so, given their increasingly central role in NEG, and the weaknesses revealed in our findings, it is useful to explore some of the conditions that may be supportive of these forms of accountability.

Professional accountability was most prominent in industries' management frameworks in the EIP programme (May, 2007, p13). Here, the professional expertise of most industries appeared capable of successfully designing and implementing adequate management systems. However, shortfalls in professional accountability were identified with poor performers, who appeared to deceive others purposefully and often flouted their responsibilities (May, 2007, p24). The implication here is the need for NEG programmes to compensate for such 'bad apples' by enhancing a sense of 'professional accountability' (May, 2007, p24). While some authors have suggested this could involve education programmes, a more plausible route to enhance professional accountability would be to increase the economic or regulatory consequences for failing to meet particular norms or codes of practice (May, 2007, p24). To some extent, the latter approach was evident in the EIP case where process and performance-based systems operated in unison. Here, social and regulatory consequences for failing to deliver improvements in local environment outcomes were effective in ensuring industry designed and implemented systems to improve their management of local environmental impacts. However, without effective pressure from local residents or government on broader environmental issues, the professional accountability of poor performers slipped into tokenism.

Turning to mutual accountability, many authors suggest that between multiple actors, this form of accountability can ensure environmental considerations are not neglected in target setting and that actors achieve effective implementation (Braithwaite, 1999, p92; Wondolleck and Yaffee, 2000, p238; Freeman and Farber, 2005, p908). This was confirmed in the EIP, and to a lesser degree in the LSP, at least to the extent that local residents and townspeople appeared capable of ensuring that local environmental considerations were not neglected in industry and farmer targets, and ensuring that industry and most (but as discussed below not all) farmers were accountable for their achievement. It was, however, more common for the findings to reveal significant shortfalls in mutual accountability, with public and private actors failing to enforce compliance or ensure apposite targets were set.

As we saw in EIP, local resident and local environmental interest groups appeared to lack the technical knowledge and capacity to engage with the full range of broader environmental issues, leaving target setting open to industry manipulation. In NEIP, inadequate technical skills and inadequacies in funding for monitoring and administrative assistance effectively blunted mutual accountability and allowed some partners to fall behind in implementation (Acar and Robertson, 2004, pp336–337). In RNRM, problems of mutual interest and a lack of technical skills and training on corporate governance served to reduce the capacity of regional body members to prevent rent seeking behaviour. Similarly in both the LSP and CCM demonstration programmes, collaborators lacked the time or capacity to hold the most reluctant farmers and government actors to account for their performance.

The implication here is that effective mutual accountability is only likely to be achieved where self interest can be subverted and monitoring and technical capacities secured (see Harlow and Rawlings, 2007, p545; Freeman and Farber, 2005, p908). One way of achieving this may be to ensure collaborations contain representation from non-local environmental interests, who may be more likely to question the kind of self interested behaviour evident in RNRM and/or bring greater skills and capacities to the table to input into non-local issues in programmes such as EIP (Fung and Wright, 2003a, p271; Karkkainen, 2003b, pp961–962). However, as discussed in Chapter 6, securing such NGO representation may be a difficult task in itself. Alternatively, training and information provision may help to improve the capacity of local stakeholders to deal with complex issues. Basic core funding to support effective monitoring and reporting is also required to impart basic capacities and avoid weaknesses in mutual accountability such as those experienced in NEIP (Acar and Robertson, 2004, pp336–341).

Turning to the issue of learning, the findings suggested the importance of assisting and encouraging actors without which the aspirations of either process-based learning or adaptive management are unlikely to be achieved (Thomas, 2003, pp153–154; Sturm, 2006, pp327 and 328). With regard to the former, the key implication raised by our findings was that success could not be achieved in the absence of industry commitment to environmental improvements (Fiorino, 2004, pp413–416). Accordingly, inevitable 'bad apples' – like the poor performers in EIP – will not 'buy into' such initiatives in the absence of incentives to ensure their commitment to using and following the process (as we discussed above) (Fiorino, 2004, pp413–416).

Turning to passive adaptive management, our analysis suggests that effectiveness will depend upon a number of conditions being satisfied. Data gaps and limited or partial monitoring mechanisms evidenced in NEIP and RNRM, for example, suggest that adaptive approaches are unlikely to be effective without relevant funding for and effective coordination of monitoring (Thomas, 2003, pp167–169; Freeman and Farber, 2005, p889). The findings in the EIP case also suggest the importance of ensuring training of citizens and other local non-government actors or sufficient representation from actors capable of engaging with broader environmental issues to foster more complete processes of adaptive management. Further, as we saw in RNRM, NEG experiments may need to reduce onerous accountability obligations so as not to divert the group's time and capacity away from acting as adaptive managers.

Finally, our analysis provided insights into forms of systemic learning. At present, the implementation of systemic learning aspirations have remained largely unexplored in NEG (Fung and Wright, 2003b, pp31–32; Head, 2005a, p145;

Collaborative Democracy Network, 2006, p169; Sturm, 2006, p328). The few experiments that have been examined have largely been disappointments in practice and our findings in the NEIP case were no exception (Dovers, 2003a, pp522–523; Karkkainen, 2003b, p243; Paton et al, 2004, p262; Camacho, 2007). Indeed, NEIP evidences what we can think of as a 'vision gap' that has occurred in the translation process from a vision of sharing, learning and adaptive programmes through institutional mechanisms to practice (Gunningham et al, 2007, p125). An important source of this gap is that those who are charged with developing implementation mechanisms are often embedded in a culture of how things were done that arose out of an older set of understanding and visions (similar arguments are made in Trubek and Trubek, 2005; Camacho, 2007, p331). This led to NEIP legislation that lacked formal procedures for fostering its vision and VEPA officers who lacked the skills to develop and implement it further.

Countering this vision gap will require changing implementation mechanisms and experimenting with new mechanisms for information sharing. This is an important call to arms to those concerned with systemic learning and adaptation, where so far much has been said about the vision but little about the mechanisms. One potential step towards developing an institutional structure for sharing learning was demonstrated in RNRM cases, where the RGC achieved considerable success in sharing information between groups. This approach avoided relying on agencies, per se, and instead used government funding to set up a state level forum composed of representatives from each collaborative group. While questions remain about the extent of information-sharing capable of being achieved through the RGC structure, it may offer a novel avenue for NEG approaches to fostering a form of systemic learning.

The RNRM case also demonstrates that government agencies, with properly designed procedures for conducting periodic evaluations, can successfully evaluate and potentially adapt government policy prescriptions (as opposed to sharing information among collaborative groups themselves). The more formal system of evaluations and requirements for evaluations at stated periods made some important progress toward ensuring this form of systemic learning was possible.

Given the scope of our analysis, and our focus on specific instances and relationships of accountability (Freeman and Farber, 2005, p908), some of our conclusions are necessarily suggestive rather than conclusive. This is particularly the case with regard to our findings on learning, which offered no more than a snapshot of evolving processes that may or may not improve over time. Time is, of course, a vital issue from the perspective of successful learning approaches (Dovers, 2003b, p6). It is to this issue that we now turn in the following chapter.

6

SUSTAINING COLLABORATION

Introduction

The previous three chapters examined the extent to which programmes designed to realize a new form of environmental governance have fared in the crucible of practice. We compared the track record of these programmes in realizing NEG ideals of collaboration, participatory engagement as well as accountability and adaptive learning, with the record of NEG initiatives elsewhere. On the basis of this analysis we extracted lessons, in the form of design principles, for realizing these ideals. In this chapter, we revisit the foundational ideal of collaboration and examine it from another angle. We have already examined how this foundation can be laid. We now turn to the equally important issue of how it can best be maintained.

As we saw in Chapter 3, NEG initiatives find themselves faced with many collaboration challenges, especially during the initial stages of their development. Yet, even after a group coalesces, these challenges do not disappear (Lubell et al, 2005, p287). Collaborative groups must still seek to sustain their efficacy, maintain the interest of volunteer collaborators (Bonnell and Koontz, 2007, p154) and continue to operate as an organization, including administrating ongoing meetings, hiring staff, fundraising and financial management (Taylor, 2003, p153; Bonnell and Koontz, 2007, p720). Of course the survival of a particular collaborative organization over the long term may not always be a good thing (Bonnell and Koontz, 2007, p154). However, in most cases success in discharging the above tasks *over time* is critical if aspirations are to be carried through to their successful realization, learning to be incorporated through adaptive management and the collaborative enterprise is to create an enduring niche in the governance landscape (Varughese and Ostrom, 2001, p752; Karkkainen, 2002/2003, p240; Head, 2005a, p148; Sabatier et al, 2005a, p11). This chapter examines the challenges of maintaining and sustaining collaboration.

Surprisingly, there is a significant 'gap' in the NEG literature regarding the challenges of sustaining collaboration in practice. Although interest in this issue is increasing (see e.g. Parker et al, 2010; Bonnell and Koontz, 2007), a number of under-researched questions remain, including: Under what conditions and to what extent can the engagement of volunteer collaborators be sustained? What forms of government assistance might address organizational challenges? How long do collaborative institutions typically survive and how long do they need to survive to be useful? What happens to the participants when a collaborative initiative has achieved its goals (Bonnell and Koontz, 2007, pp154–155; Lubell et al, 2005, pp294–295; Koontz et al, 2004, p27; see also Head, 2005a, pp145–146; Head, 2008, pp735 and 740; Hornstein, 2005, pp946 and 959–960; Menkel-Meadow, 2008, p847; Emerson, 2008, pp832–833)? While these questions could be explored from multiple angles, our focus in this chapter will be on the crucial conditions of institutional and legal design (Trachtenberg and Focht, 2005, p53).

Designing Sustainable Collaboration

In contrast to NEG experiments that involve short-term voluntary cooperation around a specific task, our three programmes all sought to establish effective collaborative groups with long-term roles in implementation, monitoring and 'adaptive management' in response to hitherto intractable and complex environmental issues (Head, 2005b, p57). In order to examine how our programme designers sought to accomplish this, we turn to the legal structure of our initiatives. To do so we will begin with an overview of these design features, before exploring some of these features in greater depth.

Overview of Design Features that Support Survival

The architects of our programmes developed a variety of strategies to support the emergence of successful collaboration, including: harnessing community and regulatory pressure (Selin and Chavez, 1995, p191; Gunningham and Sinclair, 2002); funding and assistance to reduce initial transaction costs; building trust; and pursuing 'consensus' decision-making among parties to ensure some form of commitment to targets and actions. Many of these strategies can also contribute to the maintenance and survival of collaboration (Sabatier et al, 2005b, p184). For example, it is arguable that trust shares a reciprocal relationship with collaborative success over time (Leach and Sabatier, 2005, p234). That is, after building trust to reach an agreement through negotiation, the group's subsequent successful implementation of a project spawns trust because it demonstrates that stakeholders honour their commitments and work competently. Such trust may serve to increase the ability of collaborators to work together and carry out the next project, and so on (Leach and Sabatier, 2005, p234).

There is, however, more to sustaining successful collaboration than these supporting strategies. For example, as the literature on 'common pool resources' suggests, enduring institutional structures are likely to succeed when they contain a number of additional design features, including: (i) affected interests can participate in decision-making and modifying rules; (ii) there are efficient and low-cost conflict resolution mechanisms available; (iii) government authorities do not significantly challenge the collaborators' decisions and actions; and (iv) the benefits individuals receive from the collaborative process are commensurate with the contributions they make toward managing the resource (Ostrom, 2000, pp149–150; Schlager, 2004, pp154–162; Sabatier et al, 2005b, p184).

The architects of the EIP, NEIP and RNRM programmes were mindful of these sorts of principles, at least in broad terms. All three programmes sought to embed a variety of these conditions, including requiring ongoing cooperative, negotiated-style decision-making and sanctioning the work of the collaborative endeavour as a government-based programme (Nickelsburg, 1998). The programmes also require collaborators to continue to welcome interested stakeholders and include affected interest in reviewing and updating plans (VEPA, 2002a; *Environment Protection Act 1970* (Vic), s 19AI(3); Bilateral Agreement NHT, 2004, Attachment E, p68). There is evidence that such openness and participation can enhance stakeholders' perceptions of fairness and contribute to wider acceptance and legitimacy of the collaboration, something that is important for sustainability (Lubell et al, 2005, pp287–288).

It is design principle (iv), above, that is perhaps the most relevant and challenging issue for successfully sustaining collaboration. This is because the majority of *volunteer* collaborators are unlikely to be willing to bear the many ongoing costs of actively collaborating if they do not receive some benefit in return, be it the protection of resources they value, personal satisfaction from focusing on 'their' physical place and community (John, 2004, pp237–238; Sabatier et al, 2005b, p184), or additional benefits provided through the NEG programme such as access to grant money, new knowledge or new social and professional networks (Sabatier et al, 2005b, p184).

Our programmes were, accordingly, designed to impart support and resources to offset the burdens imposed on collaborators and, in so doing, increase the likelihood of maintaining voluntary involvement. In addition, such support was intended to contribute to the efficacy of collaborations by bolstering their capacity to sustain the sort of active and effective organization (e.g., maintain communication between partners and recruit support staff) that is necessary to successfully provide for ongoing implementation (Isaac and Heller, 2003, pp93 and 101; John, 2004, p239; Lubell et al, 2005, p288).

The costs and benefits of collaborating: EIP and NEIP

The design of EIP and NEIP programmes share a major similarity insofar as both place almost exclusive reliance on the contributions of collaborators to support the organization and their activities. Collaborators in both cases must contribute their own time and resources to support a range of organizational actions and projects over the life of the collaboration (Margerum, 2007, p141; John, 2004, p239). These actions include basic administrative tasks, such as facilitating communication between collaborators, calling and attending regular meetings, taking minutes and managing budgets. Collaborators must also use their own resources or identify external funding to maintain the momentum of the group to conduct ongoing projects, carry out monitoring and adaptation processes, review and update plans and fulfil ongoing communication and reporting to the wider public about activities (VEPA, 1996; VEPA, 2002a, p6; VEPA, 2004a, p5; *Environment Protection Act 1970* (Vic), s 19AI (3)(c)).

Both programmes, however, include design features intended to lessen the magnitude of many of these burdens for volunteers, such as local residents and community groups. Ongoing VEPA assistance (e.g., provision of technical information) is to be provided across both programmes (VEPA, 2002c, pp6–9; VEPA, 2004a). In addition, many of the more expensive administrative and organizational tasks are imposed on those with greater resources and capacities.

For example, in the EIP programme the industry partner is expected to fund and/or perform the majority of administrative (e.g., circulate agenda and minutes) and implementation tasks (VEPA, 2001a, p5; VEPA, 2002c, p9). To ensure this occurs, the EIP has been designed to incorporate mechanisms that change industry's cost-benefit equation, providing reputation incentives to leading industries (VEPA, 2002c, p1; *Environment Protection Act 1970* (Vic), s 26B(2)(c)), and/or utilizing regulatory, social or economic threats (even the direct application of law) to ensure that 'good' and poorer performing industries see benefits as outweighing the costs of collaborating (see Chapter 5; VEPA, 2002c, p2). Beyond this, the guidelines suggest that industry may also be motivated to support the collaboration because ongoing benefits from collaborating, including improved environmental performance, can lead to better relationships with the local community, reduce environmental impacts and liabilities, and improve financial performance (VEPA, 2002c, p1).

In the NEIP programme, the intention is to harness and lock in the resources and capacities of a governmental partner – a 'NEIP sponsor' – who is responsible for obtaining approval of the plan. The guidelines provide very little information on benefits government bodies may receive from collaborating – simply suggesting they will have and maintain 'an interest' in the issue (e.g., statutory powers regarding protecting the environment). As we have seen, this sponsoring agency or government body must volunteer to take on this role and is encouraged to provide leadership and support to the group, and is granted relative autonomy as to how it does so (VEPA, 2002d, p7). Whether these organizations are willing and capable of committing sufficient *long-term* resources and information to support the maintenance of the collaborative process is an important issue to examine (John, 2004, p239).

If these sponsors decide not to directly support the collaborating group, the design of the NEIP does not contemplate any alternative sponsorship mechanism (VEPA, 2002d, p9). Surprisingly, this is contrary to the NEIP's approach when it came to supporting the initial emergence of collaboration, where both the time and skill of government officers and 'seed' funding were provided to reduce transaction costs. However, upon the approval of the NEIP plan by the VEPA, such seed funding ceases and the resource burden of continuing collaborative momentum and organization falls to the partners. This approach is common to other NEG experiments where short-term funding for coordinators is used to 'kick start' the collaboration, with the expectation that over time the group will become independent of funding and support themselves (Curtis, 2003).

Whether the NEIP groups will rise to this challenge over time remains unclear. Certainly it is likely that the NEIP partners will implement actions they committed to in the plan by virtue of NEIP's contractual accountability mechanisms, which make failure to complete actions a breach of law. However, this does little to ensure the collaborators will pool sufficient resources together to maintain the groups' organization, or indeed recommit to the effort after the initial plan has been implemented (Bonnell and Koontz, 2007, pp154–155).

Of course, both NEIP and EIP collaborators may well be more than compensated for such organizational burdens by the long-term benefits of collaboration (Fung and Wright, 2003a, p27). Such benefits, however, are unlikely to include continuing access to grant money, which is not contemplated in either case (Fung and Wright, 2003a). Instead, the two programmes assume that continuing collaboration will be sustained by the possibility of beneficial programme outcomes. For example, local residents in the EIP programme may gain benefits from reducing industry's deleterious impacts on their day-to-day life (VEPA, 2002d, p2; VEPA, 2002c, p1). The NEIP programme may provide local resident and community groups with benefits by addressing environmental issues of importance to the community at the local scale (VEPA, 2002d, p1).

The VEPA has recognized that the benefits may be insufficient or that the practical demands may be too great to sustain participation of all volunteer collaborators. As one guideline notes, a 'common occurrence' is 'membership reduction over time', particularly by less well-resourced local residents (see VEPA, 2002c, p3). For this reason, the guidelines encourage the collaboration to seek out additional collaborators over the longer term to prevent the collaboration from collapsing and ensure it remains effective and legitimate by reflecting the range of different community interests and perspectives (VEPA, 2002c, pp3 and 6; VEPA, 2002d; Lubell et al, 2005, p287).

It is unclear how long these efforts to renew collaborative participation can continue, not least because the guidelines remain silent on the precise length of any specific EIP or NEIP collaboration. This lack of clarity raises a number of questions. For example, in what circumstance and for how long are these collaborations capable of being sustained in this manner? Indeed, if a collaborative initiative achieves many of its goals over the longer term, will the collaboration dissolve or will collaborators or others in the community still identify sufficient benefits in collaborating (Lubell et al, 2005, p294; Bonnell and Koontz, 2007, p154)? As the NEIP programme is only a few years old it is still too early to consider many of these issues. However, the EIP programme, with a 15-year history is capable of providing insights into many of these questions (Fung and Wright, 2003a, p38). We will have more to say about this below. Before we do so, we turn to the RNRM.

The costs and benefits of collaborating: RNRM programme

The RNRM programme presents a far more complex and onerous set of ongoing responsibilities for collaborative bodies than either the EIP or NEIP frameworks. However, RNRM also provides far more direct governmental support and 'benefits' for collaborators, such as access to grant money.

In terms of the tasks and costs associated with collaborating, volunteers are required to manage their regional body as an incorporated body, as well as carry out administration tasks such as hiring and managing staff, balancing budgets of many millions of Australian dollars and managing and implementing projects. In addition, regional collaborations are required to conduct ongoing monitoring and evaluation and multiple reporting processes (Bilateral Agreement NHT, 2004, ss 69, 83 and 94, Attachment E pp65, 68 and 70), as well as communication and reporting to the wider public about their activities and spending (Bilateral Agreement NHT, 2004, s 68; Bilateral Agreement NAP, 2001, s 7.1). These tasks are likely to be a significant burden for even the most committed and skilled volunteers, particularly if, as some NEG scholars assert, rural Australia is fast approaching the limits of volunteerism (Curtis, 2003; Lawrence and Cheshire, 2004, p9).

To mitigate this potential problem, the RNRM programme has been designed to offset many of the ongoing costs of collaborating. Indeed, the nested structure of RNRM acts to enhance sustainability of lower-level collaborative bodies by providing greater access to pooled resources of governments and support services (Karkkainen, 2006a, pp235–236; Margerum, 2007, p141). This includes governments providing a small ongoing remuneration to collaborators (e.g., funding to cover travel costs), as well as providing funding for regional organizations' core operations (Interview 323, Government Agency). Core operations comprise activities such as plan evaluation, integrated monitoring and reporting, communication, board functions and meeting requirements, employing staff (e.g., Executive Officer, Finance Officer, Administrative Assistant) and paying rent (BDTNRM, 2005d, pp8–9 and 57). Regional communities are, however, expected to seek investment from other external sources (and their capacity to do so may be vital to sustaining RNRM if dedicated government funding were to cease sometime in the future) (Bilateral Agreement NHT, 2004, ss 71, 117, 118, 119, Attachment A, p40).

Regardless of the funding source, the regional body must not only maintain its own collaborative structure, but it must also liaise, engage, work with and oversee timely implementation of government-funded projects by other regional stakeholders (such as farmers or other stakeholders who were involved in the development of the plan and committed to its targets, actions and priorities) (Bilateral Agreement

NHT, 2004, Attachment E, pp62–63). Depending on the arrangements developed by a given regional community, the body's relationships with these lower-level implementers may take on a number of different forms. For example, some may be characterized by close collaboration between regional bodies and 'sub-regional' groups, while others may involve a service-provider style of relationship, where projects are subcontracted out by the regional body to individuals. Other bodies may employ a mix of these or other strategies. Despite such variation, all these relationships are central to the success of RNRM in the long term and for the purposes of this discussion they are all considered to fall under RNRM's broad idea of 'cooperative partnerships'.

The RNRM programme may succeed in sustaining such broader collaboration because access to and use of government funding is likely to act as a key benefit in return for collaborators' efforts. As we have seen, securing funding was a strong motivator for sub-regional groups. Notably, rewards are in addition to any personal benefits participants receive from collaborating, such as protecting a natural resource they value (Sabatier et al, 2005b, pp182–185). Of course, even with rewards, such as government funding, it is possible that personal benefits may change over time, or the costs of collaborating may become too much and participants on the regional body may seek to disengage. The RNRM programme is accordingly designed to maintain numbers and stakeholders on the body to ensure effectiveness and legitimacy, and thus its survival. This is done through each regional body's mandated ongoing commitment to government that its membership remains 'appropriate' and the body remains designated (Bilateral Agreement, NAP, 2001, ss 7.1(f) and 7.1(g); Bilateral Agreement NHT, 2004, ss 67 and 68).

Despite the extensive support and benefits RNRM may provide to collaborators, the literature suggests that the programme's arrangements may still face a number of challenges in sustaining broad collaboration. Among other things, the nested structure may be weakened by conflict and unwillingness of governments and agencies to share power at 'higher levels' in nested arrangements (a problem that also beset the emergence of successful collaboration in RNRM as discussed in Chapter 5) (Margerum, 2007, p141). Inadequacies in the magnitude of government support may also undermine the chances of sustaining successful collaborative organization.

In summary, our programmes employed a number of strategies to sustain their respective collaborative approaches. All three sought to make the benefits that individuals receive from the collaborative process commensurate with the contributions they make toward managing the resource (Ostrom, 2000, p149; Schlager, 2004, pp154–162; Sabatier et al, 2005b, p184). To do this, our programmes were designed to reduce costs of collaborating and increase its efficacy in implementation through the provision of funding and/or designing support structures.

EIP and NEIP were designed to depend heavily on industry and sponsors' support and encourage groups to renew participation if drop-off occurs. Comparatively, RNRM may be more successful over the long term (John, 2004, p239; Sabatier et al, 2005b, p184; Margerum, 2007, p141), not least because of its nested support and funding arrangements and the provision of additional 'benefits', such as access to grants for stakeholders.

Given their design and structure, to what extent were our programmes able to sustain collaboration in practice? It is to this question that we now turn.

EIPs – the 'Lifecycle' of Collaboration

One of our cases was one of the oldest collaborations within the EIP programme. Four others had sustained their collaboration over second and third iterations of plans and ranged in age between four to ten years. The remaining three cases – each implementing their first plan – had been operating as a collaborative group for over three years. Across these cases, the findings indicated that all had achieved substantial success in maintaining an effective collaborative organization during the implementation and monitoring of their initial plans. This success is attributable to a number of factors, including securing sufficient commitment and support from industry, stability in local residents' numbers and efficiency in implementing actions to reduce industries' impact on the local environment. However, having achieved success in the early stages, long-standing EIP collaborations sometimes produced diminishing returns and suffered from other problems

A central strategy in sustaining collaborations in the EIP programme was securing industry resources and support to facilitate the collaborative group's organization and administration. Leading, good and poor performing industries had all provided or paid for an appropriate space to conduct regular collaborative meetings (Interview 161, Industry). They also facilitated (sometimes along with local governments) the administration of meetings, including minute-taking and paying for a negotiator (who often resolved ongoing conflicts), as well as funding internal communications between group members by circulating agendas and supporting data monitoring (Interview 133, Resident/Environmental Group). Industry funding and support also ensured the group was effective in conducting monitoring and implementation.

Certainly respondents recognized that providing support for these activities and tasks had imposed significant costs on industry (Interview 151, Industry; Interview 184, Industry). Industries in better financial positions were accordingly often better placed to fund both the collaborative group's implementation activities and administration (Interview 181, VEPA; Interview 173, Local Resident). However, even financially constrained industries had, for the most part, reportedly done the best they could with available resources to support the collaborative organization (Interview 184, Local Industry; Interview 132, VEPA). As one local resident put it: 'you've got to work within budgets' (Interview 162, Local Resident).

Aside from the most recalcitrant performers that had been threatened or directly compelled to conduct an EIP under their licence, most industries were motivated to make these resource contributions to support the group because they saw the benefits of collaborating in the EIP programme as outweighing the costs.

All industries pointed to gains that had materialized from ongoing collaboration with local residents, including accessing local and 'outside' knowledge of non-government collaborators, which had helped industry to identify its impacts on the surrounding community and encouraged innovation. As one respondent explained:

> I'm talking about walking away from an EIP meeting and saying 'hey there's something to think about, maybe we should consider that, isn't that a good idea'. If you are getting that constant feedback and ideas from outside it almost encourages innovation in the organization and innovation will encourage continuous improvement.
>
> (Interview 141, Industry)

Other benefits that motivated industries' continued commitment and support for their collaborative groups tended to vary across industry types. For leading and good performers it was, respectively, the ongoing 'reputation bonus' (Interview 151, Industry) from having an EIP and Accredited Licence, and the protection of industry's public and commercial profile, achieved through ongoing engagements with otherwise aggrieved local communities (Gunningham and Sinclair, 2002, p164; Interview 141, Industry).

Most poor performers, however, were motivated primarily by VEPA threats of prosecution or the imposition of harsh licensing conditions if they did not participate (Interview 174, Industry). Such leverage (or in rare cases the inclusion of EIP conditions in their licence) reportedly allowed VEPA to ensure that poorer performing industries provided appropriate support for the collaborative group (Interview 182, Local Resident). Direct community involvement and pressure also provided motivation for poorer performing industries to sustain their funding commitment and involvement in the EIP. As one respondent explained: '. . . if there weren't the [local stakeholders on the EIP] then there would [be] no second EIP, the company wouldn't do it, it costs a lot of money' (Interview 184, Industry).

In addition to commitments from industry, VEPA officers also provided ongoing support to the group, including attending all meetings, assisting in negotiation to resolve periodic conflicts and renegotiating many targets and reviewing the plans. With such VEPA assistance and industry support, few non-government respondents reported that the time and costs of collaborating were too onerous, or outweighed the benefits of progressive environmental improvements (Sabatier et al, 2005b). As a result, local resident and non-government membership remained relatively stable during the early stages of implementation.

Despite these members lacking representativeness, the wider legitimacy and acceptance of the collaborative group may have been enhanced by the fact that the collaborations had remained open to new participants and the wider local community during these stages. For example, collaborative groups held annual general meetings that were advertised and open to all who wished to attend, or published meeting times on public websites allowing interested individuals to show up, while others required individuals to express interest in attending meetings.

The above features ensured that the EIP groups operated undisturbed, comfortably and relatively successfully through their youth and into middle age. During this period the groups were able to implement nearly all the actions in their plans. As a result, respondents were able to point to a range of outputs, such as broad plant upgrades (Interview 184, Industry), staff training (Interview 112, Local Resident), replacing specific equipment (Interview 161, Industry), operation changes (Interview 174, Industry) – including community complaint procedures (Interview 111, Industry) – as well as the conduct of monitoring studies to guide actions (Interview 174, Industry). These outputs progressively led to a range of reported environmental improvements. These improvements often included achievements on broader environmental issues (e.g., reductions in 10,000 cubic metres of natural gas per day; 33 per cent reduction in freshwater usage; substantial rehabilitation of industrial and mining sites through developing wetlands and native plant species; and 80 per cent reduction in site incidents over five years), but it was more common for industries to achieve significant reductions in their impact on the local area. The following comment was a common refrain across the programmes, sometimes even after the completion of only one plan: 'All the big problems for the community basically have been fixed . . . there hasn't been much that hasn't worked . . . you wouldn't know [industry] were here half the time now' (Interview 162, Local Resident). Yet it was this progressive success of the collaborative group at resolving local environmental issues that resulted in perhaps the most significant challenge to sustaining an effective collaboration over the longer term: maintaining the interest and involvement of local residents.

As was the case in one of our New Zealand demonstration programmes (see Box 6.1 below), the experience of the five oldest EIP collaborations revealed that as the local impacts of industry were gradually solved, many local residents saw very little reason to continue this time-consuming engagement. Rather than evolving in their environmental interests from local to broader environmental issues or in their expectations of the company's environmental performance, many local residents simply disengaged once the problems that affected them personally had been resolved. As one respondent explained:

> One of our neighbours down there. He has issues with noise at a certain frequency. When he told them about his noise issues and they eventually fixed it, his issue was pacified. He's not going to get up every third Thursday to go to the meeting.
>
> (Interview 112, Local Resident)

Various respondents recounted the decline in interest and participation, particularly those from good and poor performers where local impacts of industry had been one of the strongest motivations for the initial involvement. For example, one local resident told a story of how 'a core membership of around a dozen . . . [had] dropped off because the community . . . concerns have been addressed and it's no longer a big deal' (Interview 123, VEPA). Other industry participants reported

BOX 6.1 NEW ZEALAND DEMONSTRATION CASE: LIVING STREAMS PROGRAMME (LSP)

In its initial stages, our LSP demonstration case fostered very successful collaboration. The small communities involved and the programme's capacity to harness regulatory pressure and the in-kind assistance from ECan had ensured that all farming stakeholders had come to the table and agreed to a plan of action to improve the condition of polluted streams.

This initial success was largely maintained during the subsequent implementation stages. Indeed, over a four-year period the group successfully implemented actions to reduce sediment, phosphorus and faecal coliforms and improved riparian vegetation in small streams. This success was attributable to a number of key factors, including stakeholder buy-in fostered by the collaborative process; small government grants (e.g., NZ$5,000, which at the time of writing was approximately US$3,700) for on-farm actions, such as fencing; and, as we saw in Chapter 5, the ongoing threat of regulatory or peer pressure. Reported outcomes were very positive, and included changes in farm management (e.g., improved irrigation practices), and demonstrable improvements in environmental outcomes. Indeed, all respondents reported visual improvements in stream conditions. ECan monitoring in each LSP stream also showed increased spawning places for fish (as compared to similar non-LSP streams), and significant decreases in key pollutants such as E. coli, phosphate and sediment below pre-LSP collaboration levels.

Despite these impressive achievements, the one significant weakness of LSP was that it lacked the capacity to extend the above 'episodic' successes into vital long-term monitoring and management of the stream. Certainly LSP outputs, such as changes in farming practice, may have lasting effects in terms of ongoing management. However, at the time of research the collaborative groups were showing strong signs of formal shut down. Respondents pointed to the increasing 'difficulty in getting the collaboration to take the next step' and insufficient numbers of participants to sustain meetings (Interview NZ313, Farmer).

With most of the initial environmental problems having been resolved, there were few incentives (peer pressure or regulatory action) left to motivate farmers to bear the ongoing time and resource costs of collaborating. Indeed, volunteers were reportedly already fatigued. LSP collaborators received in-kind support from ECan officers but *no funding* to hire coordinators or other compensation for the ongoing organizational costs of volunteers. The unsurprising result was that the time and effort of these volunteers over the four years had taken its toll. As one person put it simply: 'we're worn out' (Interview NZ332, Farmer).

continued . . .

BOX 6.1 *. . . continued*

The unfortunate result for the LSP programme was that weary collaborators would likely disband and environmental problems would reoccur. Indeed, without ongoing collaborative engagement to monitor behaviour, provide peer pressure to avoid regression and to respond to changing land uses, long-term adaptive management and environmental achievements appeared unlikely. As one respondent put it: 'things will spring up along the banks of the creeks and someone is going to have to control them and it will cost an enormous amount of money . . . I can see that in the future it will become a mess again' (Interview NZ323, Farmer).

that participation of local residents had declined to very small or occasionally zero attendance at meetings (Interview 111, Industry).

The drop off in participation from local residents was, as we have seen, anticipated by the designers of EIPs who required collaborators to try and renew participation. However, respondents characterized efforts to generate new participants as unsuccessful and often futile (Interview 15/62, Community; Interview 131, Industry). In rare situations when an industry committed a localized pollution incident, local resident participation would certainly mushroom, but it would quickly plummet as soon as the issue was resolved (Interview 162, Local Resident). Even extensive efforts to generate new membership, such as public notices in local papers and newsletters, and holding public meetings to find new members, met with little success (Interview 15/62, Resident).

The reason such efforts failed was largely attributable to the collaboration's success in resolving local environmental problems. That is, there were no longer sufficient preconditions for collaboration, such as urgent pressing problems, to galvanize concern. It also appeared that efforts to renew participation were hampered by the usual cost barriers and the tendency of some local residents to 'free ride' on the labours of others (Ostrom, 1990, p6). As one respondent pointed out: 'We still can't get members to join . . . People haven't got time, I can understand that . . . Providing things are running well they say you're doing a good job, we're not interested' (Interview 162, Local Residents). Yet, despite the decline in participation and a failure to engage new collaborators, all five mature cases continued to address remaining local issues as well as industry's wider environmental performance. This is of significant interest because it provides an opportunity to reflect on the challenges of maintaining collaborative momentum once some of the initial objectives of collaboration have been substantially achieved (Lubell et al, 2005, p295; Dovers, 2003a, p518).

Who, then, bucked the wider trends of decline and what motivated them to continue to collaborate to address industries' wider environmental performance?

Non-government groups, such as the local environmental interest groups in EIPs were the most stable participants, with only one reportedly disengaging. In part, their ability to sustain their involvement may have arisen because these groups had a wider and more experienced membership upon which to draw (Interview 131, Industry; Fung and Wright, 2003a, p264). In addition, they maintained a genuine interest in wider environmental issues (e.g., biodiversity, wetlands, and the condition of the marine environment) that were longer term and thus remained unresolved. While these issues had yet to be solved, the collaboration had nevertheless achieved sufficient success to encourage environmental groups to continue to collaborate to try and achieve more: '. . . the [groups'] interest . . . is ensuring that we are going the next step, not just creating a wetland but looking to see where the improvements are occurring' (Interview 131, Industry).

In addition to environmental groups, a number of local residents maintained their participation because they had identified longer-term benefits that were seen to outweigh ongoing costs of collaborating. Without interviewing all collaborators it is difficult to identify all benefits that local residents pursued. Even so, a number of themes emerged from the interviews. Some residents were concerned to fulfil personal interests in industry operations (Interview 132, EPA), while others were reportedly motivated by more altruistic returns (Interview 161, Industry). However, the most interesting, and one of the most commonly mentioned motivations for local residents continuing to collaborate, was *a lack of trust*. While a few industries did suggest they had built trust with particular participants, as opposed to all the members of the collaborative group (Interview 111, Industry), continuing mistrust was reported as a motivation, driving ongoing participation in many mature cases that had involved good and poor performers. Here a high degree of mistrust had characterized the initial stages of the collaboration. While local residents confirmed that they had developed 'friendships' (Interview 15/62, Local Resident) and 'mature relationships' with industry representatives (Interview 111, Industry), they were quick to add that this had not mitigated or replaced a continuing feeling of mistrust for industry itself – a feeling that had sustained their ongoing involvement (Interview 112, Community; Interview 15/62, Local Resident). As one local resident and one industry respondent from different cases explained:

> We still go there [to the meetings] even when nothing's wrong . . . If we didn't go some of the guys might revert.
>
> (Interview 112, Local Resident)

> . . . there's still this element of 'hang on, it's not right to trust you completely' . . . It's a funny thing . . . So it might not be trusting, but certainly they are more accepting that we're here and that we're doing what we can and we're doing our best.
>
> (Interview 161, Industry)

The irony is that although trust is often seen in the literature as a factor in successful collaborations, these findings suggest that, in at least some circumstances, collaboration may actually achieve quite significant improvement in environmental problems and sustain ongoing involvement with very little or no trust at all and, indeed, because of a level of mistrust (Interview 161, Industry).

Regardless of the motivation for collaborators sustaining their involvement, respondents suggested the collection of 'die hard' stakeholders that remained were unlikely to contribute to *successful* collaboration in the future. There were two main reasons why this was so. First, in some of the most mature cases, some residents who continued to collaborate had moved well outside of the local area, reducing their capacity to bring in local knowledge and contribute to adaptive management processes: '. . . they've been around for a while and they're moving away . . . Outside of our influence zone . . . That's an issue for us . . . they're not going to be in a position to tell us what the current most important issue is' (Interview 161, Industry). Second, even in cases where local residents had tended to stay in the local area, the reduction in numbers and attendance at meetings, combined with lack of technical knowledge and/or interest in broader environmental issues (discussed in Chapter 4) led some respondents to suggest that the collaboration was 'losing its punch'.

Participating industries, even many of those with wider input from environmental group representation, were no longer subject to significant wide-ranging pressure to improve environmental performance nor exposed to many novel ideas that can fuel innovation. Notwithstanding the initial success of many EIPs in resolving community concerns, the corollary was a substantial dropping off in environmental achievement. While this problem of diminishing returns is hardly unique to collaborative approaches, it was – in the case of many mature EIPs – a fundamental limitation. One long-term industry participant summed up a common situation as follows:

> . . . for somebody who's getting to the mature point in the EIP process, we've been at it for a while. Like I said before all the low hanging fruit has gone. Our first EIP had two or three hundred action items . . . but now we're at the point we've come down the curve and we're sort of plateauing . . . now it's about what can we do to get the next little step change?
>
> (Interview 161, Industry)

This lifecycle from a dynamic youth to a moribund old age raises the obvious question of whether it is desirable to continue to sustain the collaboration. Some may argue that there are inherent democratic values in sustaining collaborative institutions, which give citizens an additional channel to express their environmental preferences to government (Lubell et al, 2005, p287). Furthermore, in complex natural resource management contexts, like the Living Streams Programme detailed in Box 6.1 above, there is arguably significant benefit in sustaining groups to carry out long-term adaptive management. In a similar vein, some EIP respondents suggested that sustaining the collaborative group had the benefit of creating an experienced network that could respond to potential new industry projects, such as an expansion of a plant (Interview 111, Industry).

Even so, with environmental improvements beginning to plateau, community concerns largely having been addressed and minimal local stakeholder collaboration, it appeared the VEPA was no longer getting the 'bang for its buck' in continuing to service collaborations (e.g., significant attendance at regular meetings and reviews of industry progress against the plan). Furthermore, as some VEPA officers acknowledged, attending meetings of mature EIP collaborations diverted their time away from enterprises with worse environmental records, who were not participating in an EIP:

> . . . there is not too many companies out there that would see an [V]EPA officer every three months . . . the thought has crossed my mind that time [spent on EIPs] would be better spent ploughing into things that are actually burning issues at the time.
>
> (Interview 113, VEPA)

In short, so long as VEPA continues to support mature collaborations there appears to be a risk that the 'over-regulation' of some mature EIP collaborations may be producing the 'under-regulation' of other environmental problems (Dovers, 2003a, p581). Of course much depends on individual circumstances. For example, in collaborations involving more recalcitrant or locally hazardous facilities, continuing resource input from VEPA may be more justified than in EIPs involving mature non-hazardous or well performing EIP enterprises. Even so, the implication of the findings is that in at least some cases, collaborations can outlive their usefulness and their continued survival can become an imposition (at least in cost-benefit terms) (Dovers, 2003a, p518).

The above analysis suggests a 'life cycle' of collaboration (Fung and Wright, 2003a, p38; Lubell et al, 2005, p295), which, after an active youth, lapses into a comfortable middle age before finally succumbing to senility. As the findings indicated, for much of its early life the EIP programme was able to sustain a successful collaborative process. Particularly vital to its success was a capacity to secure sufficient funding and in-kind support from industry by using community and regulatory pressure and/or providing benefits to industry.

The gradual success in implementing actions to improve local environmental conditions ensured that stakeholders identified benefits for continuing participation (Isaac and Heller, 2003, pp93 and 101; John, 2004; Lubell et al, 2005, p288). However, once the specific local environmental issues that had originally motivated local residents to collaborate were resolved, many disengaged because they saw little benefit in continuing to bear the practical demands of collaborative institutions (Fung and Wright, 2003a, p38; Margerum, 2007, p141). Part of the issue here was that many of the local residents appeared to have their own interests and agendas, which were sometimes at odds with overall improvement in industry environmental performance or wider public concerns. This did not prevent them from making a valuable contribution to the broader public interest, but it did appear to constrain the overall effectiveness of the EIP programme.

With reduced collaborator numbers – residents moving out of the local area and a lack of technical knowledge – the collaborations' adaptive management capabilities appeared weakened and environmental improvements began to plateau. While there are many viewpoints on the benefits of sustaining such collaborations, from a cost-benefit perspective of the government regulator, it is hard to avoid the conclusion that in some cases euthanasia was preferable to life support (Lubell et al, 2005, pp286 and 295).

NEIPs – Breakdowns, Stoppages and Malfunctions

As we have seen, EIP achieved considerable success in sustaining an effective collaborative organization in its early stages of implementation. In contrast, the experience of the two oldest NEIP cases – the Degraded Creek case and the Sustainable Township case – was characterized by breakdowns, stoppages and malfunctions. Indeed, the findings indicated that these cases had been unable to sustain a functioning and collaborative organization. As a consequence, they had not been able to fully capitalize on the collaborative momentum that government seed funding, negotiation, consultation and trust-building had set in motion. The Water Supply case is not discussed here because it had only just commenced implementation at the time of research.

The collaborative groups' struggle, in the two cases under examination, coalesced around four interrelated challenges: (i) gaining sufficient support from a 'sponsor'; (ii) formalizing and managing an organizational structure; (iii) accessing external funding to provide support to the groups' operations and actions; and (iv) maintaining stakeholder interest and motivation.

A key feature of the NEIP's design for sustaining collaborations was gaining the support of a sponsor. Around the time plans were finalized and the initial short-term seed funding commitments had ceased (including direct monetary contributions from the sponsor), the local government sponsors were expected to 'facilitate funding applications' to maintain the collaborative process and its implementation into the future (Interview 222, Local Government; Interview 215, Local Government). While none committed ongoing financial resources to the groups, sponsors did provide in-kind support in the form of an administrative role (filing, organizing meetings and recording information) (Interview 215, Local Government; Interview 222, Local Government; Interview 234, Local Government). However, unlike the elected official or top agency manager who NEG scholar, Dewitt John, envisages as playing a key sponsor role in collaborative approaches to environmental governance (John, 1994; John, 2004), these local government sponsors reported that they lacked the capacity to meet such ongoing responsibilities fully. This is not surprising given that local governments are notoriously under-resourced. Indeed, resources and time were already substantially stretched by support to a range of other community groups and by the many statutory (and thus higher priority) obligations relating to 'rates, roads and rubbish'. As a consequence, local government sponsors typically viewed their sponsorship responsibilities under the NEIP as an add-on to an already overloaded schedule:

> I don't see the NEIP as a sustainable, long-term project . . . [because] if you leave it up to local government it's going to be one of the many projects we have to manage . . . and we can't continue to support them all.
>
> (Interview 222, Local Government)

After voicing these issues to VEPA, these sponsors were quickly encouraged to submit applications to a VEPA grant programme to obtain funding for a project and an associated coordinator who could dedicate time to supporting the NEIP. While they were successful in obtaining the grants, almost three years passed between submitting the application and ultimately receiving the funding. During this time the collaborations faced three further key challenges.

The first of these related to collaborators' efforts to maintain effective operation and organization of the collaboration with little of the expected assistance from the sponsor and only very limited in-kind support from the VEPA. As a consequence the collaborators largely lacked the necessary time, resources and capacities to complete core administration and organizational tasks and make significant progress on implementing actions. As one respondent put it: 'I think the lack of support to the core function of the NEIP has made it difficult to sustain' (Interview 226, Peak Local Government Body).

Indeed, in the Degraded Creek case the group struggled to hold formal meetings, actively coordinate collaborator activities, circulate minutes and undertake public communication (Interview 215, Local Government). With little coordination to speak of, the group was unable to effectively pool its resources to implement actions. Progress was accordingly significantly 'slower' than expected (Interview 215, Local Government), with many actions not being implemented at all (Interview 218, Environmental Group). As one respondent explained:

> . . . it fell into a bit of a hole . . . It seems to be dependent on what funds each group can scrounge together, but they haven't really got around to doing that . . . that has probably been the biggest drawback, they can't follow through these ideas.
>
> (Interview 218, Environmental Group)

In the Sustainable Township case the collaborators had more success in supporting their operation for a short period and were able to implement a project by virtue of a grant they had originally received during the planning stages. But, on the whole, collaborators struggled to maintain effective organization and momentum (Surf Coast Shire Council, 2004). Indeed, as one respondent explained, the time-strapped, and sometimes inexperienced, volunteers often lacked a clear sense of how to conduct meetings and coordinate the group to implement actions: '. . . not everyone has a professional background where they have sat on committees that have to perform a task . . . the meetings become a bit of talk fest . . . it needs someone pushing the thought into action' (Interview 223, Industry).

With clear limits to the capacity and resources of groups to sustain an effective collaboration, obtaining external funding might have assisted them in better sustaining the NEIP and ensuring implementation of more actions. However, this was a 'catch-22' situation, as the weak organization and administration capacities meant collaborators struggled to obtain the necessary information about potential funding opportunities, or meeting the extensive demands of writing applications (Interview 231, CMA; Interview 215, Local Government). As a number of respondents saw it, there were simply too many 'barriers that volunteer groups have in accessing funding' (Interview 211, Coordinator).

Even so, both collaborations had early success in identifying and obtaining external government funding (e.g., to address storm water issues, reduce household greenhouse gas emissions) while they had been supported with a coordinator paid for by initial seed funding (Maribyrnong City Council, 2004, p25; Surf Coast Shire Council, 2004, p23). This external funding had constraints. In particular, most funding was short term, and focused on a specific project. This resulted in fluctuating motivational cycles on the part of the collaborative group (Interview 215, Local Government). That is, when a project grant was utilized, the collaboration moved from a lull into action, sometimes using a small amount of grant funding for a project officer to support the collaboration. However, it would again drift towards inertia as soon as the grant ended.

This cycle was aptly illustrated in the Sustainable Township case. During the period of study, they had successfully implemented a 'plastic bag free' campaign funded through short-term grants and some partners' resources, where a resource project officer assisted the group in coordinating the project and implementing action. However, upon completion the group immediately fell into a lull. While the collaborators had multiple ideas about possible directions for the group, as we saw above, they lacked the basic capacity or resources themselves to coordinate and move forward to identify a new project. As one respondent pointed out: '. . . we spent at least a year of just having meetings and just going round in circles and getting nowhere and in fact we've stopped having meetings altogether and we've only just picked up again' (Interview 227, Local Resident).

Both cases reported a gradual decline in stakeholder interest and involvement between completing the plan and implementing it. For example, in the Sustainable Township case, non-governmental stakeholders went from over 15 to '4 to 6' people who were interested in the plastic bag campaign (Interview 228, Local Government), while the Degraded Creek case had similar problems with declining attendance, including industry, business and non-sponsor local government partners (Interview 214, Government Agency; Interview 215, Local Government; Interview 218, Environmental Group). Organizational and implementation deficits appeared to be the primary cause of these drop offs. The failure of the group to maintain effective communication structures and links between the partners meant some lost enthusiasm and motivation (Interview 222, Local Government). Similarly, when there were few improvements for periods, participants lost interest. For some individuals and community groups there simply was not enough likely return to justify bearing the ongoing costs of participation (Interview 222, Local Government; Interview 228, Local Government). As one local resident explained: '. . . it's hard for people to get home from work and then go "I've got a NEIP meeting at seven o'clock." It's like for what?' (Interview 224, VEPA). An unfortunate side effect of this decline in active stakeholders was that it reduced the groups' capacities to conduct effective organizational and implementation tasks.

These interrelated challenges plagued the NEIP groups for nearly three years. However, near the end of this time both sponsors obtained a small, short-term grant from the VEPA (discussed in Chapter 5). In the Sustainable Township case, the collaboration made a strategic decision to fund community events (e.g., movie nights) and initiatives to re-connect with the wider community and look for new resources, capacities and ideas to reinvigorate and sustain the group into the future (Interview 228, Local Government; Interview 227, Local Resident; see Taylor et al, 2007, p76).

In the Degraded Creek case, a part-time coordinator was employed for two years. On all accounts, even after the lengthy period of inaction, the momentum and implementation had improved dramatically. The new coordinator provided administration and organizational support, went back and reviewed where partner organizations were in terms of implementation and did some significant 'chasing . . . to re-initiate that process' (Interview 213, Local Government). Despite this improvement in the Degraded Creek case and the potential in the Sustainable Township case, the VEPA grant was, by definition, a short-term 'fix' for the collaboration. While such support may assist groups to identify new or more stable sources of funding, respondents were doubtful and suggested that once the grant had ceased the group would drift back towards the struggles of ineffective coordination, slow implementation and missed opportunities for funding (Interview 215, Local Government). As one respondent pointed out: 'Yeah I think it will probably be cycles . . . we would hate to be constantly dependent upon those kind of [short-term] funds' (Interview 215, Local Government).

Ultimately, respondents believed that sustaining an effective NEIP collaboration required sufficient and secure long-term funding (Interview 213, Local Government). As one respondent summed up: 'I don't believe a group like ours is sustainable without funding and without someone to co-ordinate us some more' (Interview 221, Coordinator).

While NEIP was still in its infancy at the time of our research, it appears that, in the longer term, it is unlikely to sustain effective collaborative organizations. Indeed, it is clear that the core strategy of kick-starting a group and then leaving it to its own devices is flawed (Curtis, 2003, p453). Without sufficient provision of resourcing, sustaining successful collaboration appears unlikely (Margerum, 2007, p141; John, 2004, p239).

The importance of such resourcing was certainly confirmed by the different experiences of our two demonstration programmes from New Zealand, detailed in Box 6.1 above and Box 6.2 below. Further, it is clear from the NEIP programme that, while small amounts of funding can shift the group from inaction to action, the nature of such support is important. Grants that are difficult to obtain, and short term in nature, do little for sustaining collaborative momentum (John, 2004, pp239 and 241; Freeman and Farber, 2005, p870; Bonnell and Koontz, 2007, p159; Margerum, 2007, pp149–150).

Finally, unlike the EIP programme, where gradual improvements in local environmental conditions maintained stakeholder interest (at least for early periods), NEIP faced significant difficulty in maintaining stakeholder interest. In part, this related to the inability to maintain links between partners, but it is also attributable to the fact that the collaborations' slowed or limited progress in implementing actions failed to produce significant improvements and returns to outweigh the stakeholders costs required to obtain them (Isaac and Heller, 2003, pp93 and 101; John, 2004, pp239 and 241–242; Lubell et al, 2005, p288).

BOX 6.2 NEW ZEALAND DEMONSTRATION CASE: COLLABORATIVE CATCHMENT MANAGEMENT (CCM)

As we saw in Chapter 3, the CCM programme achieved some significant success in terms of fostering collaboration. Although its purely voluntary nature left gaps in industry engagement, CCM had successfully brought together a diverse mix of public and community stakeholders to agree to a plan of action to improve estuaries and lakes.

Following this agreement, we found that CCM achieved significant success in maintaining the engagement of its collaborators and implementing the plan. Indeed, around 80 per cent of the actions specified in the plan had been implemented over a four-year period (the remainder of the actions were not yet achieved or planned for future action).

The result was a number of important outputs, including (i) raising community awareness about the water resources via public events (e.g., bus trips around the lake, information days and seminars); (ii) better integrating and coordinating government agency programmes, by updating long-term plans to reflect new objectives and jointly delivered actions; (iii) improving the monitoring of the water resources via research projects; and (iv) achieving *minor* improvements to environmental conditions, via planting days, weed removal, fish population restoration and fencing.

continued . . .

BOX 6.2 *... continued*

As we saw in Chapter 5, major environmental improvements arising from CCM actions were stymied by a lack of regulatory or economic leverage to 'persuade' free-riding Council partners to live up to their commitments. Nevertheless, a major success of CCM was that its collaborative groups had operated smoothly and effectively during the implementation stage and showed no signs of disbanding or succumbing to lethargy. Indeed, the two CCM groups we examined had both reviewed and redrafted their management plans and targets with a view to ongoing action.

Such findings stand in stark contrast to the NEIP and LSP, where regular lulls and the dissolution of groups were familiar occurrences, respectively. The stability of the CCM collaborative enterprise was in part attributable to the trust and relationships that had developed between the participants during the initial collaborative process (which ensured the actors could effectively and smoothly cooperate together). However, more fundamental to this success was the sustained provision of a small amount of funding (NZ$30,000 – approximately US$22,000) by ECan and council partners to the collaborative groups. As was the case in the RNRM programme, the sustained nature of this funding ensured the CCM groups could hire coordinators to assist volunteers and generally compensate for the high costs of communication, information exchange and organization. Further, the coordinator was also vital in assisting the CCM groups to successfully obtain a number of external funding grants.

Overall, our respondents were adamant that without this funding (or indeed its continuance into the future), the CCM groups would suffer significant periods of inaction – a problem that was similarly raised in our Australian NEIP programme. As one respondent put it: 'we are very dependent on funding . . . once the [councils] say "oh not this year we've got to fund so and so", we're in trouble' (Interview NZ224, Local Resident).

RNRM – the Benefits and Limitations of Funding Support

RNRM, like the NEIP programme, was still in the early stages of implementation at the time of our research, having obtained a government commitment to support the programme until at least 2013 (see www.nrm.gov.au). This means the RNRM will, at minimum, probably have a 13-year life. Our case study involved a regional body that is approximately six years old. While a longer history would have been helpful, nevertheless a number of insights can be gained from its experience to date.

RNRM was relatively successful in sustaining a broad collaboration. The regional body moved fairly smoothly from planning to implementation, maintaining an active regional organization and engaging and involving local-level stakeholders in implementation. However, the overall effectiveness of the collaborative process appeared to be hindered by a number of inadequacies in funding arrangements for the administration of the regional body and its projects.

On all accounts, the regional body avoided the significant periods of inaction and lulls that plagued the NEIP groups. For the most part, stakeholder groups, such as sub-regional bodies, remained engaged as collaborators throughout. This was in part because their membership numbers allowed them to replace individual representatives as needed. However, the groups were also motivated to maintain their involvement because of benefits they received from collaborating, including improvements to natural resources through implementation and the potential to control and obtain grant money (BDTNRM, 2007, p3).

With relatively stable stakeholder involvement, the regional body maintained an active collaborative organization, conducting regular board meetings and hiring new staff (Interview 341, Regional Body). As was the case in the Collaborative Catchment Management demonstration programme, detailed in Box 6.2 above, this success was due directly to the core government funding the body received to organize and carry out actions (Interview 342, Regional Body).

Even though RNRM appears unlikely to succumb to the type of inaction and lulls that characterized the NEIP, it had nevertheless faced a number of challenges that reduced the likely overall success of the collaboration. These included inadequacies in support funding for the regional body, difficulties obtaining external private funding, uncertainties in long-term support from state and federal governments, and limited funding to implement actions and deliver improvements.

A crucial requirement in maintaining an effective and robust regional collaborative body (particularly one responsible for managing multimillion Australian dollar budgets) is ensuring sustained volunteer engagement and staff retention (Interview 344, Sub-regional Group; BDTNRM, 2007, p5). Yet, this was a major problem, with ongoing turnover in both representatives from stakeholders groups on the body and the body's support staff (BDTNRM, 2007, p3; Interview 345, Sub-regional Group). This led to the regional body reportedly facing risks of loss of corporate knowledge, difficulties developing and refining its day-to-day operations and experiencing periods that were 'a real shemozzle' (Interview 344, Sub-regional Group; BDTNRM, 2007, p5).

The turnover in regional body support staff was seen to arise primarily from two serious inadequacies in funding arrangements (BDTNRM, 2007, p16). First, the level of remuneration needed to attract and then retain staff was often insufficient compared to opportunities in the wider labour market (Interview 3210, Science; BDTNRM, 2007, p20). Second, respondents pointed to the short-term nature of funded projects, which reportedly created undesirable job instability:

> . . . the way the projects are run at the moment, for only 12 months at a time, and only months into that project, the officer will already be looking for the next job because they know it's going to run out . . . [it] creates a very unstable environment.
>
> (Interview 345, Sub-regional Group)

Further inadequacies in funding and support arrangements with regard to individual volunteers contributed to their high turnover (Interview 342, Sub-regional Group). While regional-body volunteers received a small remuneration for time and travel costs, this did little to compensate many stakeholders who were already suffering burnout from long histories of involvement in volunteer NRM programmes (Curtis, 2003): '. . . when people have been involved in the Landcare groups and what not for years and some have been secretary and chairs, they just get tired and they have had enough' (Interview 345, Sub-regional Group).

Even for collaborators who were not suffering such fatigue, the positions were still seen to be 'not very well paid', given the numerous and onerous responsibilities expected of collaborators (Interview 3210, Science; Interview 349, Regional Group Collective). Indeed, the accountability and money-management responsibilities were themselves seen to be onerous and challenging, particularly for the many volunteers who were unskilled or untrained. As one respondent simply explained: '. . . the administrative burden in itself is sufficient to roll the whole process over and to give everyone the shits' (Interview 3210, Science).

Given these burdens, regional bodies often sought to obtain additional external funding to supplement government support and to help them meet their responsibilities (Paton et al, 2004, p263). By all accounts, the regional body had experienced some success in acquiring funds (most often for projects) from a local industry organization, state departments, and the Sugar Research and Development Corporation (BDTNRM, 2005d, pp29–30). However, such investment was minimal compared to government investment, and unlikely to replace government funds as the primary source of support over the longer term (Interview 361, Regional Group Collective; Keogh et al, 2006, p28). Indeed, according to documentation from the regional body, its capacity to attract significant external investment from the private sector was still severely constrained by perceptions of conflict of interest that threatened the general legitimacy and probity of the group (Lawrence and Cheshire, 2004, p9; BDTNRM, 2007, pp15, 16 and 22).

Further threats to the long-term sustainability of successful collaboration arose from uncertainties about governments' commitment to funding the programme at both the federal and state levels. At the federal level, there was significant uncertainty associated with continued government backing and investment in RNRM. Prior to the announcement, late in 2006, that the federal government would extend investment for a further five years, many respondents were unsure whether government funding would continue past its scheduled completion date in 2007–2008. Such uncertainty did little to create an environment of stability, with regional bodies and staff reportedly speculating that they may have to 'close their doors' (Interview 361, Regional Group Collective). Even the announcement of a further five years of funding arguably does little to overcome this underlying uncertainty if regional bodies are unable to successfully wean themselves from government investment. As one respondent summed it up: '. . . the biggest problem with RNRM is they don't have surety of funding. People come and people go . . . who wants to live on soft money you know . . .' (Interview 313, Industry).

At the state level there were different tensions and uncertainties created about the level of long-term support from the state government (Interview 323, Government Agency). As with the 'turf warfare' among administrative departments that has undermined sustainability of other earlier NEG experiments (Ewing, 2003, p406), state agencies jockeyed for position and reportedly struggled to find agreement regarding their collective approach to RNRM. While some agencies with direct responsibility for NRM reportedly wished to pursue a collaborative and 'whole-of-government' approach, others were more resistant to sharing their power, leading to a reportedly 'disintegrated government system' (Interview 334, Regional Body).

With 'government solidarity' at a low point, a number of independent reviews of the RNRM system were conducted during its planning stages (Interview 334, Regional Body). Around the time of transitioning from planning to implementation, an options paper was published on the future of RNRM for the state (Department of Natural Resource Management, 2005, p7). Although there was overwhelming support for the current system, the review did little to contribute to a stable and sustainable collaborative approach, creating significant uncertainty about the future of the programme for staff, regional stakeholders and regional bodies:

> Queensland government has just reviewed arrangements . . . that's added to the cynicism of 'well shit what are we trying to do here if we are putting all this effort into getting partnerships' . . . it makes it very difficult . . . to actually get on and commit to something.
>
> (Interview 311, Industry Body)

The final weakness and challenge to sustainability relates to the ability of the regional body to deliver results. As suggested in both EIP and NEIP, central to maintaining stakeholders' involvement and ensuring a sustainable collaboration was the capacity to deliver environmental improvements. However, many respondents questioned the capacity of RNRM to actually achieve its goals to improve resource conditions, not least because there were major inadequacies in funding for implementation. As one respondent put it: 'there is, quite frankly, sweet fuck all money' (Interview 334, Regional Body). Respondents saw government funding as not commensurate with the responsibilities and outcomes to be delivered by regional bodies. As one respondent pointed out:

> . . . our budget is a few million a year. Now what we are expected to do with a few million dollars is make sustainable land use, protect all the biodiversity and fix the water quality out to the reef, all within 10 years. That's a pretty big ask.
>
> (Interview 337, Local Government)

A further consequence of this lack of funding was the constraints it imposed on the capacity of RNRM to engage a wider range of local stakeholders in environmental and natural resource issues. Indeed, while a 'win-win' strategy may be a superficially attractive means towards engaging many farmers, the reality is that 'win-win' opportunities are limited (Interview 313, Industry Body). In the common situation where private benefits of farmers have disappeared and outcomes become 'win-lose', then respondents suggested it was unlikely that regional bodies with limited funding had much to offer: 'It will probably need more of the cash element to really work . . . where there is a high level of public benefit and no private benefit that's obviously where you are going to need incentives, compensation' (Interview 331, Science).

To summarize, RNRM has been able to achieve some success in sustaining collaborative momentum of the regional body, implementing actions and engaging and maintaining involvement of a range of farmers and other stakeholders. Compared to the NEIP programme, these are impressive results and like the early success in EIP, are attributable largely to the competent arrangements for resourcing and supporting organization and implementation.

However, this success must be weighed against the challenges faced by RNRM. Conflict among state government agencies and overall uncertainty about long-term funding arrangements weakened stakeholder commitment and the stability of the programme. It is also clear that the likelihood of sustaining *successful* collaboration will be threatened by insufficient funding, a failure to match support to responsibilities (both for staff and volunteers) and, as with the NEIP experience, a tendency to provide short-term rather than long-term funding. These problems have undermined corporate knowledge, the effective operation of the regional body and potentially contribute to the marginalization of local stakeholders. Indeed, if more resources are not forthcoming over the longer term, improvements on the ground may decline or disappear, RNRM's substantive legitimacy may dissipate and with it the willingness of stakeholders to remain engaged. This leaves a large question mark hanging over the future of the programme in the long term, if government decides to scale down or withdraw support.

Conclusions

The conclusion that reliable long-term funding (and in-kind support) is crucial to NEG sustainability has been common to our analysis of each of the programmes. However, simply suggesting that more government investment and support is needed begs the question: how much more? Do the findings allow us to draw out some specific guiding principles? Certainly our analysis suggests that governments' contribution to supporting NEG need not be large. Indeed, consistent with the findings of Taylor and others in different collaborative governance contexts, the resources that appear to make the difference between stasis and a connected, organized and active group may be relatively modest (Taylor, 2003, pp153–154). As we saw in the NEIP programme, quite significant shifts from lulls into action occurred with the injection of a very limited resource input that facilitated the hiring of a single, part-time staff member whose brief was to keep the group in contact with each other, and maintain momentum. So, too, in the Collaborative Catchment Management programme in New Zealand, where the importance of sustained funding, of even small amounts, to the survival of successful collaboration was confirmed.

However, at a time of increasing resource constraints on government, and government agency load shedding, it may be unrealistic to expect even small contributions to support collaboration over the long term (Crawford, 1997, pp165–168). In this context, it becomes important to explore how to design and create *new* institutional mechanisms and ways of redirecting funding to provide more sustained longer-term resourcing commensurate to the tasks and responsibilities (Steinzor, 1998a).

Our findings provide insights into a range of possible design conditions for better resourcing and supporting sustained collaboration. First, the findings in EIP suggest that focusing community or regulatory pressure on the most well-resourced parties (in this case, industry) can prove a relatively successful way to resource a collaborative group. This resonates with suggestions in the literature that harsh default rules (rules that alter the incentives of actors by making the transaction costs of collaboration preferable to bearing the costs imposed by the default rule itself – see Karkkainen, 2006b) can contribute to the survival and success of collaboration (Selin and Chavez, 1995, p191; Gunningham and Sinclair, 2002, p149). Such pressure may be used simply to compel the party to commence collaboration, subsequently trusting that benefits delivered by the collaborative process itself (e.g., improved public and commercial profile) will provide sufficient motivation for continued resource contribution (as was the case with good performers). Alternatively, for reluctant collaborators, such as poorer performing industries, sustained pressure (direct or implied) may be vital (Freeman and Farber, 2005, pp870 and 903).

While the support and resources provided from industry in EIP were not sufficient to offset the costs of many local resident collaborators, this is arguably not attributable to the mechanism of resourcing itself, but to how it was applied in practice. Indeed, one could imagine a more appropriate application of pressure by VEPA to encourage industry to provide financial reimbursement for citizens and other local non-government stakeholders for the costs associated with their participation in the EIP programme. Robust accountability mechanisms would of course be needed to avoid enhanced risks of capture (Johnston and Shearing, 2003, p154).

A second insight into designing support arrangements arose in the NEIP programme. Contrary to claims that outside 'sponsors' – such as agency managers or elected officials – might facilitate funding and information to support the collaborative process and implement agreements (John, 2004, pp239 and 241–242), the translation of a similar strategy met with very limited success. Overstretched and under-resourced local governments were largely ineffective as long-term sponsors had failed to provide long-term funding support for the group. Clearly, not all actors can be apposite sponsors for the purposes of sustaining collaboration, and attention must be paid to selecting the right 'sponsor' and using effective incentives to harness their support.

The findings also shed some light on designing nested structures to support organizational sustainability. Some authors have suggested that nested arrangements provide an important avenue to obtain more apposite funding for local collaborations, not least because they allow pooling of agency resources for special projects and greater access to support services (Karkkainen, 2006a, pp235–266; Margerum, 2007, p141). However, as the same authors hypothesize, various parts of this structure may impose additional challenges, such as achieving power-sharing between agencies/governments at higher regional or state scales (Margerum, 2007, pp144–146; Bonnell and Koontz, 2007, pp161 and 163). While such challenges did not debilitate the RNRM collaboration, the evident tensions between state government agencies and their impact on programme stability suggests that such challenges are likely to pose a very real threat to the effectiveness of nested arrangements to support sustained collaboration successfully (Margerum, 2007).

The issue of how to support and resource collaborations also raises the important policy question: is it necessarily *desirable* for governments to support NEG collaborations indefinitely (Lubell et al, 2005, p295; Dovers, 2003a, p518)? Speaking to questions raised in the literature about whether the survival of collaborations will always be a worthwhile goal (Dovers, 2003a, p518; Lubell et al, 2005), our findings on EIP suggest that sustaining collaboration in the long term is not necessarily desirable. After local problems had been resolved and participants disengaged, many of the collaborations that remained were a shadow of their former selves. Arguably, they had come to the end of their lifecycle and outlived their effectiveness to generate innovative proposals and conduct robust adaptive management monitoring. Moreover, at least some were becoming an imposition on government resources.

As we have seen, there are different positions one can take on the importance of sustaining collaboration indefinitely: from a simple cost-benefit view, to seeing the institution as enhancing democracy and social capital and facilitating vital ongoing adaptive management. Much will depend on individual circumstances, as well as how effective collaborations are in addressing the sorts of weaknesses that brought about EIP decline, including maintaining volunteer involvement, and generating new participants. Even so, the importance of the EIP finding is its empirical confirmation that not all situations may justify the survival of collaboration per se.

To conclude, our findings suggest that appropriately resourcing collaborative organizations and maintaining volunteer involvement are two challenges that NEG must overcome to sustain successful collaboration. In considering these challenges we have pointed to a number of conditions and mechanisms that might contribute to the survival of NEG institutions over the longer term, and contribute to good NEG.

7
CONCLUSION

Introduction

As an empirical project, this book has provided a series of 'snapshots' of various innovative NEG programmes over a limited period of time. Even in the short period since our fieldwork was completed, events have moved on. While the relatively successful EIP programme continues to command respect, the VEPA is nevertheless contemplating streamlining it (VEPA, 2010), while the far less successful NEIP has been put on hold while an evaluation and review is conducted. The RNRM programme has also undergone a transition, in part brought about by a change in government, but also as a result of deficiencies highlighted by a number of government reviews, including concerns as to whether it and similar programmes are providing value for investment. Nevertheless, there was no suggestion that this most ambitious of the NEG experiments should be abandoned. Rather, existing programmes have been integrated into a new programme known as Caring for Our Country, an initiative that involves an investment of approximately Australian $2 billion (about US $2.05 billion) over five years (for a recent overview of Caring for Our Country, see Rural and Regional Affairs and Transport References Committee, 2009).

Progress is equally evident in our New Zealand demonstration programmes, with an ongoing governance reform process currently underway in Canterbury (see e.g. *Environment Canterbury Temporary Commissioners and Improved Water Management Act 2010* (NZ)). ECan continues to consolidate the successful Living Streams Programme (LSP) (see e.g. ECan, 2009a); the Canterbury Water Management Strategy (CWMS) is now being implemented via local and regional multi-stakeholder collaborative committees (www.canterburywater.org.nz); and two new collaborative groups (a statutory agencies group and a local zone committee) have been set up to better coordinate, monitor and improve implementation of the Collaborative Catchment Management programme (CCM).

The value of studies such as our own lies not in understanding the specifics of individual programmes – which almost invariably shift over time – but rather in identifying the wider lessons that can be taken from them. Such lessons are both empirical and theoretical. In terms of the former, we explore a number of broad themes relating to the future of NEG by returning to the central question that has underpinned our research: under what conditions can 'good' NEG be achieved? At least some of these conditions, we argue, can be encapsulated in a series of design principles for NEG, which are set out below. In terms of theoretical lessons, we seek to distil our insights by revisiting the theme with which we started this book: the role of the state in NEG.

Design Principles for Successful NEG

At one level, NEG is a continuing social experiment. However, NEG is also maturing – transitioning from a period of testing by trial and error to one of consolidation and refinement. But the success of this new stage depends principally upon heeding the lessons of earlier successes and failures and drawing broader lessons from them. While we made a number of observations about the practical implications of our findings in each of the preceding chapters, a broader statement of the conditions (or at least *some* of the conditions) necessary to realize good NEG, is also important. We provide such a statement through a set of 'design principles' (Ostrom, 1990). Such principles are intended to offer guidance to decision-makers, but given the extent to which complex dynamics, chaos and path dependency, among other variables, will ultimately shape policy outcomes, they should not be taken as prescriptions (Young et al, 2008).

Design principle 1 – successful NEG requires significant investment

The costs of NEG and the importance of resources to cover these costs were evident across all of our programmes. More often than not, we found it was inadequacies in funding that caused some of the most fundamental weaknesses in NEG. In particular, inadequate funding from government in both NEIP and RNRM (see for example Farrelly, 2009) not only undermined successful collaboration (Bonnell and Koontz, 2007, p165), but stymied the effective monitoring required to fulfil accountability and learning aspirations, and constrained the commitments and actions necessary to improve environmental conditions on the ground. This was also the case in our New Zealand programmes, where limited funding undermined sustained collaboration (LSP) and contributed to gaps in engagement (CCM). Moreover, the adverse consequences of inadequate resourcing were evident across *all* of our Australian programmes, particularly in terms of constraining the contribution of time- and cash-strapped volunteers.

The adverse effects of inadequate funding expose a crucial contradiction that is evident in many NEG programmes. Governments find NEG and similar collaborative governance approaches attractive in part because of its perceived promise to reduce state expenditure by engaging other actors and their resources (Crawford, 1997, pp165–168). But governments' preoccupation with minimizing expenditure often results in such programmes being denied the very resources that are essential to their success. There could be no starker illustration of this than the resource starvation that resulted in NEIP failing to fulfil the large majority of its NEG aspirations.

Of course, pleas for 'more funding' are hardly new in environmental law and governance. Government funds are invariably in short supply and there will always be difficult trade-offs to be made in their deployment. Nevertheless, the harsh reality is that NEG can rarely work effectively without resources to cover core costs, especially transaction costs. Certainly, NEG may attract investments from other stakeholders that can be added to government investments, but they can rarely, if ever, replace them. To imagine that NEG programmes will relieve governments of funding pressures is not only mistaken, but counterproductive. If governments see advantages in NEG programmes and want them to work, they must also fund them adequately.

Design principle 2 – NEG is best used in situations where environmental challenges are severe (or perceived to be severe)

Flowing directly from design principle 1, NEG is unlikely to be an appropriate (and certainly not a cost-effective) form of governance when the issues to be addressed are of only modest social or environmental importance (Lubell et al, 2002, p290). Put simply, since NEG is unlikely to be successful in the absence of considerable expenditure, the likely results must be sufficiently beneficial so as to justify such expenditure. This proved to be the case, for example, in the EIP. In cost-benefit terms, there was no justification for engaging with leading environmental performers who achieved little more as a result of the EIP than they would have without it. This truly was 'collaboration with little cause'.

There are further reasons to believe that NEG is best used in situations where environmental challenges are severe. As we saw across our programmes, the presence of severe and urgent environmental problems (or at least problems perceived to be so by stakeholders, see Ostrom, 1990; Heikkila and Gerlak, 2005, p586) created high personal stakes and strong motivation for non-government actors to actively collaborate and participate in efforts to solve them. This is not to suggest that NEG need be confined to environmental crises – to do so would deny NEG's contribution as a proactive approach to looming environmental problems (Menkel-Meadow, 2008). However, based on our findings, governments and other social groups who wish to harness NEG in the latter circumstances would be well advised to educate stakeholders as to the severe risks and impacts of emerging environmental threats *prior* to developing such initiatives. Put differently, they must manufacture, as it were, the preconditions for stakeholder motivation and engagement in order to maximize the chances of NEG success.

Design principle 3 – carefully designed incentives are crucial to the success of NEG

Negative incentives, such as 'penalty default' rules (Karkkainen, 2006b), and positive incentives, such as funding, can do much to encourage action and change behaviour in situations where the self-interest of those causing environmental harm and the public interest in protecting the environment do not coincide (Gunningham and Rees, 1997, p36). Certainly in the absence of such incentives, the gap between public and private interests often proves insurmountable, and NEG is rendered ineffective.

A powerful illustration of the importance of effective incentives to good NEG is provided by the EIP. Here, negative incentives (the threat of penalties invoked under the traditional regulatory regime) were successfully harnessed to ensure that unwilling industries engaged in collaboration, divulged information, negotiated on local issues, and invested in monitoring, implementation and sustained collaboration. This approach was equally evident in LSP, which relied heavily on the regulatory framework of the *Resource Management Act 1991* (NZ) to deliver accountability and compel reluctant farmers to collaborate.

Conversely, as the experience of other programmes, such as the NEIP and CCM, reveals, in the absence of incentives, organizational barriers such as a lack of involvement and commitment from key industry stakeholders, will severely undermine NEG initiatives.

We are of course hardly the first to claim that regulatory or other spurs are vital to cooperation and effective self-regulatory behaviour (Ayres and Braithwaite, 1992; Karkkainen, 2003b). However, in the collective rush to experiment with NEG (and perhaps because it is commonly seen as an alternative rather than a complement to other regulatory approaches) these lessons have often been overlooked, almost invariably with adverse consequences in terms of effectiveness.

Design principle 4 – NEG requires the identification, creation, nurturing and maintenance of governance capacities

The importance of this design principle was evident by its neglect. For example, asymmetries in knowledge and skills undermined deliberation in both NEIP and EIP, where government officers and industry officials, respectively, used their experience and technical knowledge to dominate untrained and ill-informed citizens, and to drive the decision-making agenda (Fung and Wright, 2003a, p259; Fung and Wright, 2003b, p23). So too a failure to nurture the capacities of non-government actors was an issue when it came to the participation of marginalized interests and ordinary citizens. Unskilled volunteers, for example, were often ineffective at a range of tasks, including fulfilling mutual accountability functions, monitoring and maintaining a successful collaborative endeavour.

This tendency of NEG to undervalue and overlook the creation, nurturing and maintenance of governance capacities was a fundamental issue when it came to non-government actors, but it was similarly evident when it came to government officers. As we saw with the VEPA, officers reportedly lacked the skills necessary to perform a range of NEG functions, including knowing what should or should not be monitored at local levels and how to facilitate information sharing and learning.

Accordingly, it is essential to the success of NEG that all of the abovementioned capacities are created and nurtured (Freeman, 1997, pp31–32). This will not only require additional funding, but also the development of institutional mechanisms crafted to build capacities, such as mechanisms to educate participants with respect to NEG (e.g., how to identify and obtain external funding; how to conduct scientific monitoring and use or interpret data), impart deliberative and management skills (Cohen and Rogers, 2003, p246) and provide language or other support (particularly for those who are already marginalized within society). In particular, policymakers need to ensure they assess what roles and responsibilities they expect non-government actors to fulfil, and to provide the corresponding support.

Design principle 5 – design NEG mindful of size and scale

Our comparative findings suggest that it was easier to achieve successful NEG in 'small-scale' settings, such as the NEIP Water Supply case, the LSP demonstration study and arguably the EIP programme's local context, than in those addressing larger catchment and regional-scale resources.

In particular, because the local scale provides greater possibilities of repeated interactions and restricts the number of exchange actors in the network, NEG approaches at the local level appear less costly, to have greater access to 'social coordination and control features', such as peer pressure and networks of representation and participation, and a greater store of social capital that can make negotiation easier (Duit and Galaz, 2008, p311 and 324; Gaines, 2002/2003). It is also the case, as many others have pointed out, that 'collective action problems' (Olson, 1965; Cannon, 2000, p408), such as free riding, are likely to be minimized where numbers are small.

This is not to suggest that size alone will determine NEG outcomes (see also Schlager, 2004, pp162–163; John, 2004, pp236–237). Other variables (not least the presence of regulatory incentives and government funding) will also be important. But what can be said is that the chances of achieving successful outcomes are higher (all other things being equal) in smaller settings and communities.

Nevertheless, the chances of success with larger scale NEG initiatives can be enhanced, so our comparative research suggests, by operating across multiple scales to the extent practicable. This is contrary to the conventional wisdom within much of the NEG literature that governance should be devolved to the 'local' level. Rather, employing nested collaborative arrangements that operate at different scales or organizational levels can do much to mitigate the challenges confronting larger-scale NEG initiatives.

For example, as we saw in RNRM, large *regional* collaboration was relatively successful because it had worked simultaneously at comparatively 'easier' smaller scales. It did so by dividing the large region into small areas, at which level collaborative processes faced fewer transaction costs and were more closely connected to local actors. Yet important benefits also arose from RNRM operating at the higher regional and state levels as well. While this can create power-sharing problems, collaborating at high scales may help reduce *overall* transaction costs of interactions between local collaborators, help pool resources (Karkkainen, 2006a, pp235–236; Margerum, 2007, p141), and foster information sharing.

Design principle 6 – develop innovative mechanisms to engage environmental groups in NEG

Environmental groups have traditionally played important roles in ensuring accountability and improved environmental and regulatory outcomes (see e.g. Gormley, 1981; Farber, 1992). Yet there are substantial obstacles to environmental groups participating in NEG. National- and state-level interest groups in particular were typically hostile to, or incapable of, collaboration at *local* levels (Fung and Wright, 2003a, pp280–282), leaving local groups as the most plausible prospective participants. However, even these groups only participated in a limited number of the cases and when they did engage they were commonly ineffective in offsetting the dominance of industry and government. Moreover, their vision was often parochial and they struggled to combine collaboration with environmental advocacy. In consequence, environmental groups rarely fulfilled their potential either as guardians of the environmental interest or as overseers of accountability (see e.g. McCloskey, 1996; Leach, 2006).

To date, the relative failure to engage environmental groups has been largely overlooked by policymakers, notwithstanding the extent to which these groups might potentially enrich NEG processes and outcomes. This suggests the need to develop innovative ways to engage environmental groups in NEG. Our research revealed two particular innovations in this regard that may have wider application. First, operating at multiple scales (as discussed under design principle 5) also provides opportunities to engage 'peak' environmental groups in NEG processes. For example, in the RNRM case the Regional Groups Collective, which operated at the same 'level' and scale as state-based environmental groups, successfully offered an 'easier' and readily accessible avenue for state-based environmental groups to enter into NEG. They did so largely in order to harness government funding to fill gaps in environmental engagement by coordinating and mobilizing other environmental groups at lower collaborative levels (Margerum, 2007, p145).

Second, given the difficulty many environmental interest groups encounter in balancing cooperation and advocacy, there would be considerable value in coordinating the contributions of environmental groups who choose to engage in NEG collaborations with those who do not. The potential benefits of this approach (under which the former engage in cooperation and the latter in advocacy) were illustrated in Chapter 4 in the case of both EIP and CCM. While the division of roles we identified there occurred more by chance than design, such countervailing roles could be nurtured more consciously by cultivating mutually supportive links (e.g., actively establish networks of communication between environmental groups, or actively funding environmental interests groups to carry out such tasks) (Craig et al, 2004).

Design principle 7 – incorporate effective horizontal, as well as vertical, information-exchange mechanisms into NEG structures

The importance of this design principle was also evident by its neglect. As we saw in Chapter 5, because our Australian programmes failed to share information and experience between collaborative groups (horizontally) and/or between collaborative groups and agencies (vertically) they missed considerable opportunities to diffuse innovations, enhance capacities and improve the accountability roles of governments.

Enhancing the flow of information and experience between collaborators both horizontally and vertically would substantially mitigate these weaknesses. Horizontal information-sharing and benchmarking processes, in particular, may foster horizontal forms of accountability that encourage peer review between collaborators and lessen the need for anti-deliberative and anti-collaborative government vetoes of collaborative decisions (as we saw in both NEIP and RNRM) (Sabel and Simon, 2006, pp396–403).

Experimentalist theories have identified these and other benefits of information pooling and diffusion (Dorf and Sabel, 1998). Not least, their work suggests that widespread information sharing can enhance the overall accountability of governance systems, particularly by government bodies utilizing locally reported data to periodically reformulate and progressively refine minimum performance standards, desirable targets and preferred means to achieve them (see Karkkainen et al, 2000, p690; Scheuerman, 2004, p115).

However, obstacles to realizing such benefits are cultural resistance and a lack of capacity in some agencies to adopt information-pooling mechanisms. As we argued, it may accordingly be necessary to look beyond agency action and to nurture other mechanisms to achieve such pooling and diffusion. For example, a state- or national-level collaborative forum might be funded (as in the RNRM case) composed of representatives of localized collaborations. Such representatives appear to have a considerable appreciation of the benefits of information sharing. As we saw, regional groups recognized the lessons they could learn from each other in confronting their new responsibilities under RNRM. They accordingly had the necessary propensity to diffuse innovation, by sharing what they were doing in practice, so as to learn and build capacities to face their many similar challenges.

Design principle 8 – design new implementation mechanisms tailored to delivering the aspirations of NEG

Probably the most profound failing identified in our case studies was one of implementation. For all their focus on adaptive learning, new forms of accountability and participatory democracy, it was the more mundane failure to work out how best to deliver on their aspirations that most seriously undermined each of our Australian programmes. Government agencies often struggled to oversee and facilitate representative participation, to facilitate systemic learning, to deliver accountability in performance regimes, and to engage in genuine deliberation. In each case, these failures undermined their capacity to deliver intended policy outcomes.

Most of these shortfalls can be attributed to inadequate institutional design – be it empowering governments with ultimate vetoes over collaborative decisions, imparting inadequate legislative guidance or allowing agencies to overlook deficits in representation, accountability and learning (Freeman and Farber, 2005, pp900–901; Sturm, 2006, pp331–334; Camacho, 2007, p349). These experiences collectively suggest that as NEG continues its transition from experimentation to consolidation, it will be fundamentally important to develop new legal designs and institutional mechanisms to ensure that agencies become effective overseers and facilitators of NEG. Our findings in the preceding chapters (and our other design principles) offer a number of directions in this regard.

In terms of learning and accountability, our findings suggest that agencies are better equipped to deliver new governance when there is clarity as to what is required of them. Accordingly, there is a need for legislation and guidelines to include more specific requirements regarding the structuring of NEG experiments. There is particular value in specifying with greater precision matters such as: which interests should be represented in NEG experiments; how and in what form learning is to be pursued; and how and what type of performance objectives are to be established and implemented.

The challenge is to provide necessary structures and targets (e.g., performance-based outcomes) without seeking to micromanage the precise means by which these outcomes will be achieved. An over-prescriptive approach would inhibit the very 'learning by doing' that is at the heart of successful NEG experimentation. It may, however, be possible to identify some general 'rules of thumb' regarding the specific categories of participation, learning or outcomes expected (provided sufficient mechanisms are designed to support requirements). For example, consistent with design principle 7, mechanisms might be designed that require collaborators to share information and facilitate benchmarking of their process and performance (Freeman, 1997, p93; Karkkainen et al, 2000). Properly designed and supported, such an approach will likely assist collaborative groups and government overseers to develop a better understanding of when and how particular goals and actions can best be achieved on the ground. Such information would also enable agencies to better identify collaborative groups that are underperforming and bring them into line with others (Bonnell and Koontz, 2007; Cohen and Sabel, 1997).

In many circumstances non-government actors can also be better harnessed to facilitate the achievement of intended outcomes. For example, we described in design principles 6 and 7, one novel form of non-government information diffusion and stakeholder engagement. Another, so the international experience suggests, would be to rely on a professional who has expertise in working with stakeholders (but typically does not have a direct stake in the issue at hand). This will often be a more successful approach than relying solely on public agencies (Susskind et al, 2010, pp31–32; John, 2004, p234).

Theoretical Insights: NEG and the Roles of the State

We began this book with Hobbes' powerful image of a Leviathan, and the notion of 'good governance' as rule by a single sovereign who represents 'the people'. By the time the environment became an issue of social and political concern, a contemporary version of this notion – state power through hierarchy – had become dominant in the Western world. It was taken for granted that command and control regulation (the quintessential hierarchical tool), administered by a government agency, was the way of addressing environmental protection. This form of state power relied heavily on centralized, top-down institutional arrangements and was underpinned by prescriptive controls and instruments capable of directing particular forms of behaviour. This approach, as we have seen, was predictable but rigid and most suited to addressing simple, one-dimensional problems. But, as the environmental crisis deepened, and as the complexity of the environmental challenges increased (and indeed the complexity of the political, social and economic systems within which they are embedded) so the limitations of hierarchy became ever more apparent.

The 1980s and 1990s saw a resurgence of free-market ideology and with it came a shift in the preferred form of governance (although many remnants of hierarchy remained). Market-based governance, as propounded by neo-liberal economists, implied that, insofar as intervention to protect the environment was justified, the best approach was to change behaviour by changing price signals – to which rational and economically driven actors would respond in their own self-interest. From this view, the decentralized power of individual decision-makers could be used as the coordinating mechanism of governance. But markets too have their limitations. In some circumstances it is not practicable to create a market, and even where it is, individuals may not behave as the 'rational persons' that economic models assume. As with hierarchy, the extent to which markets make a positive contribution to environmental protection depends on the contexts in which they are created, the threats to which they are addressed and their particular design and implementation.

It was in this context that new governance has become ascendant, with its promise to 'bridge the gap between the public, the for-profit, and the non-profit sectors and integrate human and financial resources to find solutions to multifaceted problems' (Streck, 2002, p11). Its particular strength is to recognize that complex political, economic and social systems cannot be readily governed either by a single actor (the state alone), or by markets, and that a polycentric and adaptive approach (and one that is therefore experimental and iterative in its approach) may fare better in engaging with such problems. Certainly its proponents would argue that collaborative groups, acting towards commonly agreed (or mutually negotiated) goals, can achieve far more collectively, than individually. This new form of environmental governance is of course, still in its experimental stage, making any final judgement concerning its strengths and weaknesses, premature (although this does not preclude us from proposing a number of design principles with a view to advancing good NEG).

In this section, based primarily on an analysis of our Australian programmes, we return to a central question raised in our opening chapter: what is the relationship between collaboration and the role of the state? More particularly, what is the relationship between these initiatives and state law/guidelines and to what extent is it essential for the state to fulfil certain functions if the new governance is to succeed? Can the state be effectively 'decentred', becoming simply one of a number of actors involved in governance, but no longer privileged in terms of power and influence (see generally Mol, 2007)? Or do states retain crucial and distinctive roles, and if so what are they? These questions will be explored below, while cautioning that the answers are necessarily provisional, given the limitations of our case-study approach.

It is important to recognize that the three programmes vary considerably in their degree of environmental complexity, their scale and the number of stakeholders engaged in them and these factors in themselves may have important implications for the role of the state. EIPs involve a single large enterprise whose activities are relatively easily monitored, a single regulator, a few individuals representing (or acting as advocates for) the local community, and possibly a representative from local government. NEIPs, in contrast, involve a much larger group both of enterprises, individuals, community representatives and state and local governments. They are, however, spatially contained (to the 'neighbourhood') and usually examine only a limited number of issues. Regional bodies addressing NRM problems involve an even broader range of stakeholders, multiple levels of government, a broader geographical scale and a wide range of complex (some would say intractable) environmental challenges.

Unsurprisingly, relatively simple problems involving a small number of actors at a single location are easier to address via direct state intervention than more diffuse problems involving multiple actors and on a broad scale. It may be no coincidence that while the state retains considerable direct involvement and a substantial degree of command and control regulation as regards the first programme, it has not attempted to do so with regard to the second or third. That is, the need for and extent of any shift from hierarchy to polycentric governance may be directly related to the nature and complexity of the environmental challenge.

The fact that the state played very different roles in the three programmes, and that they have had varying degrees of success, is suggestive of a number of other lessons concerning state intervention.

In the case of the EIPs, the VEPA was an active participant in three ways. First, it defined the mechanism through which collaborative governance could take place (that is, the structural and functional definition of a Community Liaison Committee, and the size and nature of participating companies). Second, it provided a strong incentive for many industry enterprises to participate in the programme, either compelling them to do so, engaging in a form of 'arm-twisting' that gave them very little choice, or directly applying the law. Third, it provided a regulatory underpinning that could be invoked in the event of failure (which was assessed on a regular basis by VEPA officials). These roles, particularly the second and third, were also prominent in LSP, where interventions by the state evidently induced farmer engagement and ensured implementation.

Like LSP, the EIP programme has been a considerable success (although primarily in dealing with local issues). Not least, both programmes have on the whole empowered local communities directly, increased pressure on companies to improve their environmental performance and, through structured dialogue, greatly improved relationships between communities, enterprises and the VEPA. In so doing, they have improved environmental outcomes on issues of community concern. While the success of this approach in dealing with environmental laggards has been more qualified than in dealing with leaders (our research suggests that the changes were less deeply embedded) even here the evidence indicates a substantial improvement on the status quo.

However, none of these goals would likely have been achieved without the continuing role of the state as direct regulator, willing to invoke command and control mechanisms to the extent that companies failed to engage directly with community representatives, to develop negotiated environmental improvement plans and to meet the targets they had committed themselves to. That is, an underpinning of conventional regulation was an essential component of the EIP, and communities would have been neither consulted nor empowered in the absence of VEPA oversight and statutory support. Indeed, so important was direct VEPA oversight that there is very little evidence that EIPs have provided any of the regulatory resource savings that the VEPA had initially hoped for.

In stark contrast, state intervention in the NEIP programme was largely confined to the initial definitional phase – assisting in the development of a NEIP agreement, providing some initial seed funding for a series of pilot NEIP projects and setting overarching frameworks, albeit with little specificity, that defined the nature of participation and negotiation and established expectations of performance and processes to be followed. Further, the state retained a veto over the initial decisions and decision-making process. However, participation in the NEIP programme was intended to be purely voluntary and neither sanctions nor incentives were provided to encourage such participation or to ensure implementation. Certainly, NEIP plans are gazetted as legal documents, with the associated legally binding nature that this implies, and those who elected to sign them would be in breach of contract if they failed to honour their undertakings. However, to date the effectiveness of this mechanism remains in serious doubt.

Was it too optimistic to imagine that multiple actors with widely differing interests and aspirations and no single focus, whose activities caused multiple environmental problems, would come together and agree to be bound by common goals? The substantial failure of the Degraded Creek and the Sustainable Township

NEIPs (neither of which appear likely to achieve significant environmental improvements) – suggests it was, and that the primary reason for this failure is NEIP's reliance upon voluntary collaboration. However, this conclusion must be qualified to the extent that the NEIP Water Supply case, involving a small community, powerful drivers for reform and exceptional access to resources, was able to substantially overcome the difficulties to which the other NEIPs succumbed. But even in this case the state played a key resourcing role, funding as it did significant commitments from partners and providing incentives to engage farmers.

Certainly, NEIP has been successful in facilitating government and non-government stakeholders to come together for the first time to take action to address a significant environmental issue at neighbourhood level. Similarly, the negotiation inherent in the collaborative process has made it easier for partners to better understand the interests of others, and to develop an integrated vision and a shared agenda to an extent that would not otherwise have been possible.

However, because the NEIP programme lacked the sanctions, leverage or incentives to successfully engage a range of key stakeholders to collaborate in the process, the Degraded Creek and Sustainable Township NEIPs fell far short of their environmental objectives. Although some informal arm twisting or shaming could be used to get buy-in from some reluctant partners, by and large this proved insufficient to persuade key polluters, like small- and medium-sized enterprises, to engage in the process in any meaningful way, far less reduce their pollution. Moreover, even where industry, businesses and other parties had agreed to collaborate, NEIP has apparently had insufficient 'clout' (even with legally backed plans) to persuade them to take positive follow-up action to date. As we have pointed out, a similar experience arose in CCM, where the programme also relied on voluntary collaboration and lacked design features that harnessed incentives as a means to engage reluctant actors or leverage outcome delivery.

Overcoming these weaknesses would require substantial changes to CCM's and NEIP's basic architecture. While it is conceivable that this could come from third parties (for example, social licence pressures and shaming might be sufficient to persuade large reputation-sensitive industries to participate), for the most part it would seem that the state is either the best or the most likely player to provide intervention, be it in the form of regulatory or economic incentives. However, we cannot state our conclusions in stronger terms than this, given that Elinor Ostrom's extensive research on common pool resources (Ostrom, 1990) suggests that, under the right circumstances, significant success in achieving social and environmental goals can be achieved even in the absence of the above forms of state intervention.

In the case of RNRM, the federal and state government has played three key roles. First, it established criteria that regional bodies must abide by in their formation and operation. In the language of regulatory standards, these are more performance- and process-based than prescriptive in that they describe what is to be achieved but leave individual regional bodies with substantial latitude as to how they structure their particular operations, or they set out various procedures that must be followed (for example in terms of consultation). Second, they provide a powerful motivator for the formation of, and therefore participation in, regional bodies through the offer of substantial sums of money. Third, as with our other programmes, the state provided a level of accountability and compliance, using new accountability mechanisms (such as an administrative 'destabilization right' in the event that NRM performance was deemed to be unsatisfactory) and having 'the final say' over decisions.

An evaluation of regional NRM is difficult, given that many of the RNRM goals extend some 20 to 50 years into the future. From our study, it is clear that RNRM is much more pluralistic and deliberative than previous forms of NRM governance, but there is a notable lack of autonomy and ultimately power for regional bodies such as the one we studied. RNRM has, however, taken significant steps towards success, in no small part because the state continues to play major roles. These include that of kick-starting the regional initiatives, which often involve substantial start-up costs and other initial barriers to their adoption, as well as being the main provider of resources (both in kind and monetary) for the ongoing organization of NEG and its implementation. With regard to the latter state role, it is notable that even though NEIP relied on the resources of collaborators or external sources, such money was typically provided by government grants or agencies collaborators. Where no specific funding was provided (as in the EIP case) the strength of the state still remained vital and evident, although here it was 'command' powers used to encourage or directly compel partners to bring necessary resources to the table. Further, although sources of funding outside of the state were identified in RNRM as means for groups to 'self support', it appeared unlikely to replace government funds as the primary source of support over the longer term.

So too, state funding appeared vital in CWMS, which similarly dealt with a larger regional-scale governance endeavour. Whether funding will continue over the longer term to support the roll-out and implementation of this New Zealand initiative is yet to be seen. Certainly as we saw in the RNRM programme, there are substantial risks that shortcomings in the state's role, including insufficient funding to support such large, regional-scale endeavours, will readily reduce the potential extent and scope of environmental improvements (Head, 2009, pp18–19).

From the above it would seem that where the state does devolve decision-making to the local level, such devolution has a greater degree of success if the state retains particular roles, but this begs the questions: which roles and in which circumstances? Based on the experiences of the three programmes, there are, at a minimum, three clear roles for the state: definitional guidance, participatory incentives and enforcement capability.

Definitional guidance: this refers to the state describing and defining the nature of the collaborative governance arrangement. These might include, for example:

- what issues are to be addressed
- who is able to participate
- what are the geographical boundaries

- what is its legal nature
- what performance outcomes are expected
- what funding arrangements are to be established
- what is the operational relationship to other existing institutional structures.

As we can see from the three programmes, this definitional guidance role can be interpreted widely. Irrespective of the particular form it takes, however, it is difficult to imagine NEG or new governance more generally operating in the complete absence of a government providing some level of definitional guidance.

Participatory incentives: this refers to the state providing incentives, which may be positive (in the form of various inducements) or negative (in the form of punitive sanctions), for targeted actors, be they companies, communities, individuals or NGOs, to participate in the particular form of NEG being established. As seen from the three programmes, these can take many forms, for example, in the case of EIP, the state legally mandated some companies to participate (that is, compulsion) and offered others a voluntary route through the incentive of greater regulatory flexibility and less inspections. In the case of RNRM, there is a powerful incentive to participate in the form of access to substantial funds and resources. Even in the NEIP Water Supply case, government funding played a vital role in bringing farmers to the table. In the programme where there was not a clear and obvious state role in providing participatory incentives (as in the Degraded Creek and Sustainable Township NEIPs), this may have been one of the key factors undermining its eventual success.

Enforcement capability: this refers to the state fulfilling an enforcement role in ensuring that NEG arrangements deliver on their obligations. Such a role may apply to individual participants in NEG arrangements, or to a collaborative governing entity as a whole. In either case, this entails the presence of performance indicators or criteria against which success or otherwise can be judged. In the case of a collaborative governing entity as a whole, such criteria will likely be predetermined by the state itself as part of its oversight role. In the case of individual participants, such obligations, targets or performance objectives as are necessarily built into collaborative agreements would be subsequently referred to the state for performance evaluation.

Beyond the above, a number of other insights may be gleaned with regard to the close and complex connections between NEG and traditional legal regulation (conceived as top-down control using prescriptive legislation, detailed rules and judicial enforcement) (Trubek and Trubek, 2006/2007, p543; Alexander, 2009, pp178–84; Bingham, 2010, p297; Wilkinson, 2010). Of these, perhaps the most important concerns the so-called 'default hybridity' relationship between law and new governance. Based on the optimistic and constructive co-existence of law and new governance, default hybridity sees law playing an 'action forcing' role that is used to induce people to 'contract' out of standard regulatory frameworks and into new governance approaches. The idea is that standard regulatory frameworks may act as a default regime (applicable only in the case of failure to conform to new governance demands), and should be set precisely for the purposes of inducing otherwise reluctant people to embrace NEG (De Burca and Scott, 2006, p9).

At a descriptive level, the EIP programme approximated the conditions contemplated by 'default hybridity', relying heavily as it did on the standard regulatory framework to induce reluctant industry actors to engage and take action. Although we are less confident in our findings, the same could also be said for our LSP example.

Comparisons between the EIP and NEIP programme suggest that NEG approaches that fail to develop 'default hybrid' relationships with the law are likely to be unsuccessful. Not least, such NEG approaches may lack the capacity to coerce polluting stakeholders who have no desire to enter into NEG, fail to curb free riding and thus significantly reduce the likelihood of environmental improvements. One could also make a similar comparison between LSP and CCM, the latter failing to induce affirmative action from key stakeholders because of its failure to incorporate regulatory or other incentives.

A further normative lesson as regards the role of 'default hybridity' can also be taken from the EIP programme. As we saw, while the regulatory 'default position' was sufficiently harsh to compel actors to engage in this new governance experiment, it was insufficiently menacing to ensure compliance (although this weakness can be sidestepped in some situations by the direct application of law). By implication, where existing legal regimes are used as a 'default' for NEG, they will need to be tailored to offer sufficiently 'harsh' default positions as to induce the desired participants not only to contract out and agree to participate in new governance, but also to 'compel' them to take affirmative action that they are otherwise disinclined to pursue (De Burca and Scott, 2006, p9; Karkkainen, 2006b, p298).

Our broader conclusion is that at the same time as the state may be retreating from many of its traditional regulatory functions and from direct hierarchical control, opportunities arise for it to forge new roles, using its influence and resources to coordinate private institutions and to harness actors and resources in furtherance of public policy, while retaining both positive and negative incentives to induce otherwise reluctant actors to participate in collaboration and deliver on its objectives.

All this suggests that the shift to new governance is not a matter of substituting 'new' mechanisms for the state but rather for a hybrid approach, which involves a shift from a situation where the state takes broad governance responsibilities for both steering and rowing (in the terminology of Osborne and Gaebler, 1992) to one where the state still plays important but different roles. Thus, while NEG does involve some of the state's traditional governance functions being adopted by other groups (e.g., civil society and business), and non-state actors taking on a much larger 'hands on' role in environmental governance, nevertheless the state continues to play important roles: direct intervention (at least when things go wrong) as well as coordination, incentivizing, facilitating and steering. As we have seen, many of these roles are absolutely central to the success of new governance initiatives and it seems doubtful, at least from these programmes, whether the state can now be regarded as simply one among a number of other actors, all of whom might be analysed 'in more or less similar ways in terms of power, interests, responsibilities, accountabilities and resources' (Mol, 2007, p230).

This understanding of the state is consistent with the implicit or explicit claims in most NEG theories, namely that the state remains 'active' in new governance (Lobel, 2004b, p502). However, a key insight from our research for NEG theory – particularly the more normative and idealized treatments, such as strands of democratic experimentalism (e.g., Fung and Wright, 2003b) and collaborative governance (e.g., Freeman, 1997) – is that an 'active' state can very often be a 'controlling' state. In broad terms, the above theories often assume that the state will work to support NEG and achieve a more participatory approach to problem-solving by devolving both decision-making power and responsibility for implementation. Yet, as we found, the state can often dominate decisions when it has its own funding or its own programmes at stake in NEG, effectively undermining NEG's deliberative and participatory aspirations. The tendency of the state to 'shed its load' by utilizing inadequately supported volunteers was a related example of the negative role sometimes played by the state – treating groups more as their own 'private' delivery mechanisms rather than as empowered publics. Further, where continued investment is ongoing, as in RNRM, the state commonly maintains and extends its control through rigid accountability controls (Lawrence and Cheshire, 2004, p8), potentially morphing collaborations into bureaucracies.

In the light of the above, NEG theories may be better served if they were able to merge an understanding of the importance of not 'de-responsibilizing' the state (Garland, 1996), with an understanding of the *threat* of 'state' power (Defilippis et al, 2006, pp684–685), particularly given that wider trends in governance have often been revealed to involve participatory, deliberative and community empowerment in name only.

Our broader conclusion, nevertheless, is that it is nation states (at least in advanced Western democracies such as those explored through our programmes) that are best placed to act as a fulcrum point in NEG by taking on the core roles in collaborative governance identified above. In reaching this conclusion we caution against, as the adage goes, throwing out the baby with the bathwater, as governance shifts from more monocentric to more polycentric forms.

Concluding Comments

NEG represents an important innovation in legal and governance processes that goes substantially beyond both command and control regulation and market-based incentives by invoking a range of unique principles – collaboration, participation, deliberation, new forms of accountability and learning frameworks.

This book has focused primarily on the *processes* of NEG collaborations, largely because at this stage in the evolution of NEG it would be premature to make substantial claims with regard to outcomes (Koontz and Thomas, 2006). Nevertheless, it is difficult to write a book of this nature without drawing at least tentative and provisional conclusions about the latter. We have done so at a number of points in the substantive chapters and in this final section it may be helpful to distil our findings as to whether or to what extent NEG 'works', while emphasizing that our answers are necessarily contextual and qualified.

Our analysis of EIP revealed (see Gunningham and Sinclair, 2002) that this programme had achieved significant improvements in the governance of *local* environmental issues. Indeed, it was so successful in reaching some of its objectives that collaborators began to question the desirability of maintaining their involvement. However, the programme was considerably less successful in addressing broader environmental objectives – with only the leading and good industries being able to demonstrate other than parochial achievements. This was due to a range of issues, not least asymmetries in knowledge and skills between industry and local residents (Fung and Wright, 2003b, p23), the latter's lack of interest in broader issues and weaknesses in accountability that failed to address a lack of commitment by poorer performers to improve their environmental performance on broader and more global environmental issues.

In the NEIP case, the likelihood of significant environmental outcomes being delivered was minimal. This was attributable primarily to the fact that in all but quite rare situations, the NEIP failed to engage and obtain commitment from key industry actors, lacked the resources necessary to foster commitments that went substantially beyond 'business as usual' practices, developed weak performance standards, conducted highly ineffective monitoring and implementation, and struggled to maintain a collaborative organization (Bidwell and Ryan, 2006, p840).

The findings regarding the RNRM programme suggest that its regional bodies and strategic planning approach were more likely than NEIP to deliver important environmental improvements, not least because of government investment in monitoring, technical assistance and implementation. At the same time, the potential extent and scope of environmental improvements were constrained by flaws in the programme, including conflict between high levels of government, burdensome accountability arrangements and, most damningly, insufficient funding for achieving desired improvements with regard to complex problems (Head, 2005a, pp145–146).

Although our New Zealand data was more limited, we found similarly mixed results across our demonstration programmes. CWMS (underpinned by substantial government resources) had been able to achieve agreement on a successful water management strategy that obtained a high level of buy-in, and which held out the promise of improved water outcomes down the track (Jenkins, 2009). In CCM, diverse stakeholders had engaged in a sustained and relatively successful collaborative process, in large part because government support and funding had facilitated improved management coordination and research. However, a number of weaknesses, not least a lack of leverage and incentives to persuade or enforce affirmative action, limited CCM's effectiveness and greatly reduced the magnitude of environmental improvements likely to be achieved.

Finally LSP appeared to be the most successful of our demonstration programmes, engaging as it did all relevant stakeholders to deliver demonstrable and significant improvements to local environmental conditions. This success was attributable to a number of key conditions, including ECan's in-kind support, the small scale and small population involved, peer pressure, the ability to harness traditional regulation and short-term grants for new action. However, as we saw, the collaborations in LSP appeared likely to succumb to volunteer fatigue and were unlikely to survive long enough to deliver ongoing environmental management.

In short, our findings across our six programmes suggest that NEG is most certainly not a 'holy grail' for solving environmental problems – but that there are some circumstances in which it may provide, if not an ideal, then at least a more attractive option than available alternatives.

Our main contribution, nevertheless, concerns the processes involved in NEG rather than environmental outcomes directly. In particular we have sought to illuminate the experience of various NEG innovations and provide insights into NEG in practice. We have argued that the processes of NEG can be demonstrably successful, but that they are also likely to face substantial challenges, including collective action problems, accountability shortfalls, undeveloped monitoring and adaption processes, securing representative civil society engagement, and sustaining collaborative action over the longer term.

Drawing on the strengths and weaknesses of the various case studies, we have identified a range of mechanisms and conditions that appear most likely to overcome such impediments and to produce more successful NEG in practice. In particular, we have sought to shed light on a number of key issues in new governance jurisprudence. We have done so not only through reflections and recommendations at the end of each substantive chapter, but also by identifying eight design principles, which we suggest are central to achieving 'good' NEG.

Our analysis also explored the implications of NEG for our understanding of the role of the state, suggesting that while NEG must remain alert to the *risks* of state authority, it is clear that the state has remained an active and pre-eminent player in this new way of governing. We identified three unique roles that define state action within NEG and drew parallels between our conclusions and the default-hybrid relationships that involve interactions between traditional legal regulation and new governance (Trubek and Trubek, 2006/2007, p564; Wiersema, 2008, pp1294–1299).

Finally, it must also be recognized that the conclusions and implications drawn in this book are limited to the cases and programmes from which they were drawn. While the comparative analysis of multiple programmes and cases has allowed us to reflect on a significant variance in NEG designs and contexts, research into other manifestations and experiments in NEG is still vital to test and confirm whether or to what extent the findings and implications drawn here hold for other NEG institutions and contexts.

The above cannot be answered in the absence of appropriate empirical work, which is still relatively thin on the ground. This book cannot resolve these questions, but it may add to the store of knowledge that will assist both policymakers and legal scholars when thinking about, debating and reformulating NEG institutions to ensure that this emerging approach to solving public problems can be a success.

APPENDIX

Methods

Our data was drawn from two broad and interrelated research projects. Project One examined the operation of our Australian programmes and was funded by an Australian Research Council Linkage Grant in partnership with Environment Protection Authority, Victoria (VEPA). Project Two was funded by an ARC Discovery Grant and continued and expanded our research under Project One by assessing new environmental governance (NEG) in New Zealand.

We adopted a single research methodology with regard to both projects, and this is described below. We preferred to rely on a *small-n* sample and qualitative interviewing in preference to *large-n* quantitative research because the former is better able to engage with the complex nature of collaborative efforts and fully capture the context, attitudes and experience of the participants in NEG (Conley and Moote, 2003, p379).

Selecting the Programmes

Mindful of the limitations of the existing research, which has tended to focus on single case studies or limited institutional examples (see, for example, Sabatier et al, 2005a, pp11–12), we selected multiple examples of NEG to study. Initially, a literature review was conducted to identify potential programmes. Approximately 25 Australian and 15 New Zealand environmental governance programmes were identified whose components embraced at least some of the defining characteristics of NEG (see Chapter 1). Some of these examples identified in Australia included: the Murray Darling Basin initiative, Environment Improvement Plans (EIPs), Neighbourhood Environment Improvement Plans (NEIPs), Regional Natural Resource Management (RNRM), 'Share the noise' solution at Sydney airport, Natural Heritage Trust (NHT) phase 1, Regional Forestry Agreements and the National Landcare Programme. Some of these programmes, including Environment

Improvement Plans and Regional Natural Resource Management, took different forms in different Australian state and territory jurisdictions. Examples identified in New Zealand included water user groups in Canterbury, The Mahurangi Action Plan and Hauraki Gulf Forum, Community Pest Control Areas and river schemes of the Bay of Plenty Regional Council.

Consistent with NEG approaches internationally, these programmes exhibited significant variation across a range of variables, including their focus, scale of action, mixes and roles of stakeholders, their age and policy contexts. Given inevitable time and budget constraints, it was not feasible to select examples that specifically reflected the distribution of all given variations across these programmes (Gerring, 2007, pp97–101). However, within budget practicalities, a manageable sample size of six programmes (three in Project One and three in Project Two) were selected with the aim of capturing elements of this variation so as to allow the examination of an extensive range of different NEG approaches, conditions, processes and contexts (Conley and Moote, 2003, p378; Patton, 2002). For example, we selected these programmes to capture differences in:

- problem focus (for example, point source pollution, natural resource management, diffuse urban pollution and developing a water management strategy)
- scale of action (local, catchment and regional)
- different types and ratios of government and non-government stakeholders (for example, some programmes, like EIP, included only one agency and relatively few nongovernment stakeholders; others, like RNRM, involve multiple local, state, regional or national agencies, industry bodies, NGOs, businesses and local citizens)
- different roles of stakeholders (for example, responsibilities such as implementing a plan vary, involving only one industry actor in EIP, the resources of the entire collaborative group in NEIP, or the facilitation and use of government investment in RNRM)
- in the Australian cases, their age (for example, the mature EIP to the more recent RNRM programme) and policy contexts (Queensland, Victoria).

These differences are summarized in Table A.1 below. Two additional considerations should also be noted. First, both the EIP and RNRM programme operated in multiple jurisdictions, so it is worth briefly reflecting on why particular policy contexts were selected for this book. We selected the Victoria EIP programme, as opposed to other manifestations in places such as Western Australia (for further see Holley and Gunningham, 2006), because it was the pioneer and remains the leading exponent of this approach in Australia. This EIP programme had received previous academic attention (see, for example, Wills and Fritschy, 2001; Gunningham and Sinclair, 2002); however, it was considered an apposite case for research in this book because most of the early research was policy-based, lacked a comparative aspect and had not located the EIP initiative within the then embryonic NEG literature.

TABLE A.1 The Programmes

	EIP	*NEIP*	*RNRM*	*LSP*	*CCM*	*CWMS*
Issue	Point source pollution from a single industrial enterprise	Diffuse rural, industrial and urban pollution (e.g., erosion, litter)	Natural resource issues (e.g., salinity, water quality, biodiversity)	Diffuse rural pollution (sediment, phosphorous, nitrogen, E. coli)	Diffuse rural, industrial and urban pollution (e.g., erosion, sewage)	Regional water quantity and quality management
Maturity	1989–ongoing	2001–ongoing	2000/2001–ongoing	2000–ongoing	2000–ongoing	2000–2010
On-ground Collaborations	70	7	14	30	5	1
Scale	Local area near the enterprise	Catchment of urban creeks or small townships	Large regional ecosystem	Sub-catchment of small streams	Catchments of lakes & estuaries	Large regional ecosystem
Intended Stakeholders†	10–20 people, including a single	20–30 people, including industries,	6–20 people, including farmers,	10–15 people, including residents,	15–20 people, including residents,	15 people, including residents, Māori,

	enterprise, residents, NGOs, community groups, local government and the regulator	residents, NGOs, community groups, state and local governments, and the regulator	NGOs, residents, indigenous peoples, catchment groups, industry bodies and local government	NGOs, farmers and the regulator	farmers, Māori, NGOs, community groups, local governments and the regulator	farmers, NGOs, national and local governments and the regulator
Context	Statutory & voluntary programme, Environment Protection Authority, Victoria, Australia	Statutory programme of the Environment Protection Authority, Victoria, Australia	Federal Australian government programme & partnership with the Queensland government	Voluntary programme of Environment Canterbury, New Zealand	Voluntary programme of Environment Canterbury, New Zealand	Voluntary programme of Environment Canterbury and Canterbury District Councils, New Zealand
Interviews	24‡	26	30	15	17	12
Study Date	2005–2008	2005–2008	2005–2009	2008–2009	2008–2009	2008–2009

† Based on agency guidelines, bilateral agreements, legislation and interview evidence.

‡ EIPs were also discussed in three NEIP interviews (two government and one industry).

The choice to study RNRM in Queensland was made on the basis that this state offered a relatively unique approach to the RNRM programme (as opposed to manifestations in other eastern Australian states that fell within our budget range). Indeed, compared to states such as Victoria or New South Wales, the RNRM programme in Queensland is 'community' rather than statutory based (for further, see Robins and Dovers, 2007). This arguably gives RNRM in Queensland a much stronger NEG flavour, with its emphasis on more participatory, collaborative endeavours without formal legal authority.

Second, while we selected six diverse NEG programmes, a notable omission from our research projects was a purely 'bottom up' initiative not specifically developed by government bodies (McCallum et al, 2007). While such examples of NEG are important in their own right, our interest in shifting trends in state-based governance accordingly led us to focus exclusively on examples of NEG that were developed by governmental bodies.

Selecting the Cases

Across the majority of our six programmes there were multiple collaborations (CWMS was the exception, as it was, at the time of research, a 'once off' region-wide collaboration). Accordingly, the second step was to select from within each of the programmes a set of 'on-ground' collaborations to study (the cases). This selection relied on a review of publically available plans and reports, initial 'pilot' case studies and advice from key agency officials to devise a non-random purposive sampling approach that was guided by a number of considerations, including selecting 'information rich' cases (for example, the collaboration had begun to implement their plans of action) and capturing some of the main types of variance between on-ground collaborations (for example, variations in location, focus and maturity of collaborations). Given budgetary constraints, a controllable sample of 18 cases (12 in Project One and six in Project Two) was selected across the six programmes (Gerring, 2007, pp97–101). Table A.2, below, outlines the cases selected from each programme.

Notably only one regional site was examined in RNRM, despite there being 14 regions in Queensland. In an ideal world, with unlimited time and funding, it would also have been beneficial to contrast multiple RNRM cases. However, this was not possible in this, our most complex of programmes, not least because of the extensive data needed to capture fully the conditions under which the RNRM programme operated, both from within and outside of the region, and across an extensive range of local, state and national stakeholders.

Selecting the Interviewees

The research into each of the 18 cases relied primarily on qualitative interviewing. In order to capture a diversity of views and facilitate comparisons between them, the interviewees were primarily selected on the basis that they captured the main

TABLE A.2 The Cases

Case		*Case features*		
	Issue	*Location*	*Start Date*	*Approx. Collaborative Group Size† and Area‡*
EIP 1	Paper production	City suburbs	2000	12 people; area near industry/general environment
EIP 2	Sewage treatment	City suburbs & beach	2003	23 people; area near plant & outfall/general environment
EIP 3	Power station	Rural town	1997	16 people; area near industry/general environment
EIP 4	Power station	Coastal town	2003	17 people; area near industry/general environment
EIP 5	Car production	Industrial city suburbs	2003	9 people; area near industry/general environment
EIP 6	Plastics/resin	Industrial city suburbs	1994	19 people; area near industry/general environment
EIP 7	Wood fibre panel	Rural city	2004	11 people; area near industry/general environment
EIP 8	Rendering plant	Industrial city suburbs	2001	9 people; area near industry/general environment
NEIP 1	Polluted creek & its corridor	Industrial & residential city suburbs	2001	18 people; $20km^2$ catchment
NEIP 2	Sustainable community	Coastal town	2001	23 people; $10km^2$ catchment
NEIP 3	Creek/drinking water	Rural town	2003	35 people; $22km^2$ catchment
RNRM	Land, biodiversity, water coasts and salinity	Rural and coastal region containing cities and towns	2002	11 people; $133,000km^2$ region
LSP 1	Polluted stream	Rural township	2002	14 people; 10–15km long stream in $50km^2$ catchment
LSP 2	Polluted stream	Rural township	2002	13 people; 10–15km long stream in $50km^2$ catchment
LSP 3	Polluted stream	Rural and coastal township	2000/2001	13 people; 10–15km long stream in $50km^2$ catchment
CCM 1	Polluted lake and catchment	Rural and city catchment	2002/2003	15 people; $2,700km^2$ catchment
CCM 2	Polluted estuary and catchment	Urban, residential and industrial catchment	1999/2001	15 people; $200km^2$ catchment
CWMS	Regional water quality and quantity	Region containing rural, urban and coastal landscape	2000	15 people; $42,000km^2$ region

† Group size refers only to the collaborative group that had direct decision-making control in the programme and does not reflect the number of people/organizations who may have indirectly participated in these NEG processes, such as via government oversight or via other forms of public consultation (e.g., notice and comment procedures).

‡ Based on estimates made in interviews and available documents.

stakeholder types involved in or connected to each programme. Again, time and budgetary constrains meant that it was not feasible to select interviewee numbers that specifically reflected the proportion and distribution of stakeholder types in each case. Table A.3 outlines stakeholder type and numbers.

To mitigate the limitation of the interviewee sample consisting largely of active participants who may have a positive bias towards the NEG processes (Coglianese, 2003), the study sought to triangulate opinions of different and diverse respondents,

TABLE A.3 The Interviewees

Case	*Stakeholder Type*	*Stakeholders and interviewees across the six programmes*	
		Total across all cases†	*Interviewees*
EIP	Resident/non-government interest	56	7‡
	Government (EPA & local)	37	8
	Industry	23	9
NEIP	Resident/non-government interest	45	9
	Government (EPA, state & local)	26	14
	Industry	5	3
RNRM	Stakeholders directly connected with regional body (e.g., advisors, community members and staff)	35 (not including individual farmers)	11
	Government (federal, state, local, research bodies)	20	12
	Non-government bodies (e.g., peak agricultural, industry and conservation bodies)	10	7
LSP	Resident/non-government interest	3	2
	Farmers	36	7
	Government (regional and local)	6	6
CCM	Resident/non-government interest	13	7
	Industry/farmers	6	2
	Government (regional and local)	11	8
CWMS	Resident/non-government interest	6	5
	Industry/farmers	3	2
	Government (regional, local and national)	7	5

† These numbers are based on interviewee estimates and offer a snapshot of the composition of the collaborative groups and those connected to the groups at the time of study. Membership in any given case invariably changes over time. Numbers regarding government and industry bodies in the broader national RNRM programme reflect only the number of primary state and federal agencies and representatives of multiple local governments (e.g., regional organization of councils, local government directors of the regional body) involved with the cases at time of research.

‡ One resident was involved in two EIP cases and was interviewed about both.

as well as corroborate the interview data with information from relevant documentary sources (for example, meeting agendas and minutes, annual reports and newspaper articles/newsletters).

The interview questions sometimes varied between interviewees to allow for individual experiences and meanings to emerge (Conley and Moote, 2003). However, all interviews involved in-depth conversations, utilizing a semi-structured interviewing technique that was guided by a standard protocol of largely open-ended questions (see below).

Analysing the Data

Analysis of the interview data was guided by Layder's (1998, p19) Adaptive Theory method, which attempts to 'combine an emphasis on prior theoretical ideas and models, which feed into and guide research while at the same time attending to the generation of concepts and theory from the ongoing generation of data'. Following Adaptive Theory methods, the interviews were coded to capture patterns and themes, as well as discrepancies, and draw conclusions. Not every line or word of text was coded; however, we sought at all times to ensure comprehensive data treatment that coded all pieces of relevant data to the NEG features being examined (Layder, 1998).

Across our six programmes, the validity of our data analysis and its conclusions were also checked through a process of respondent evaluation conducted near the end of the fieldwork (Silverman, 2000). Here, a limited number of key informants were engaged to discuss some preliminary findings from our analysis of the interview data. This involved holding a dialogue/re-interviewing six key government and/or non-government participants (one in EIP, two in NEIP, two in RNRM and one each in LSP, CCM and CWMS) who had significant carriage and/or involvement in each of our six programmes.

Our research was conducted pursuant to the *Australian Code for the Responsible Conduct of Research* (National Health and Medical Research Council, 2007a), the *National Statement on Ethical Conduct in Human Research* (National Health and Medical Research Council, 2007b) and to other relevant legislation and guidelines as required by our university institutions.

Example Interview Protocol

General success and failures of programme

- What would you say you are proudest of in the case process?
- What factors may have contributed to these successes?
- Have there been any frustrations or difficulties faced during the case process?
- What are some of the causes of these frustrations/difficulties?

- In what ways do you think things could have been done differently to avoid such frustrations/difficulties?

Collaboration

- How did the case go about forming the collaborative group?
- Were there any challenges?
- Did any factors assist in the process (for example, trust or funding)?
- Was consensus an important part of the process?
- Do you think the partners are sufficient?
- Is anyone missing?
- Have partners remained active during implementation stages?
- Is the collaboration sustainable over the longer term?
- What factors may assist or detract from it being maintained?

Participation

- How was the membership of the case determined (for example, voting or government selection)?
- How representative is the case?
- What ways or methods were used to achieve representation? What were their advantages/disadvantages?
- Are there any environmental NGOs or community-based groups?
- If so what has their role been? If not, what factors may have contributed to their absence?
- Are there ways that the case or its members seek to interact/communicate with the wider community?

Deliberation

- How did the decision-making process operate (for example, negotiation, voting, mediators)?
- Was there equal influence from partners?
- Can you describe some examples of this influence? What are some of the reasons for this?

Accountability, learning and adaptation

- How were targets and objectives set?
- Are the targets adequate in your opinion? For example, will they lead to positive outcomes for the environment and community?
- What implementation has occurred?

- Has progress been 'on target' or behind? What factors contributed to this?
- How has monitoring of targets, actions and evaluation been going?
- How effective are the accountability arrangements?
- Do partners check each other's behaviour?
- What role does government play?
- Has the case been able to learn from monitoring data and adapted its management process?
- What factors contributed to this?
- Has there been any sharing of learning or experiences between cases?

REFERENCES

Abel, T. and Stephan, M. (2000) 'The Limits of Civic Environmentalism', *American Behavioral Scientist*, vol 4, pp614–628

Abers, R. (2003) 'Reflections on What Makes Empowered Participatory Governance Happen', in A. Fung and E. Wright (eds) *Deepening Democracy: Institutional Innovations in Empowered Participatory Governance*, Verso Press, London

Acar, M. and Robertson, P. (2004) 'Accountability Challenges in Networks and Partnerships: Evidence from Educational Partnerships in the United States', *International Review of Administrative Sciences*, vol 70, no 2, pp331–344

Access Economics (2005) *Measuring the Economic and Financial Value of the Great Barrier Reef Marine Park Authority*, Access Economics, Canberra

Ackerman, B. and Stewart, R. (1985) 'Reforming Environmental Law', *Stanford Law Review*, vol 37, pp1333–1366

Alexander, L. (2009) 'Stakeholder Participation in New Governance: Lessons from Chicago's Public Housing Reform Experiment', *Georgetown Journal on Poverty Law and Policy*, vol 16, pp117–185

Allan, C. and Curtis, A. (2005) 'Nipped in the Bud: Why Regional Scale Adaptive Management is Not Blooming', *Environmental Management*, vol 36, no 3, pp414–425

Arnstein, S. (1969) 'A Ladder of Citizen Participation', *American Institute of Planners*, vol 35, no 4, pp216–224

Australian Government (2010) *Caring for our Country Business Plan 2010–11*, Australian Government, Canberra

Australian National Auditing Office (ANAO) (2001) *Performance Information for Commonwealth Financial Assistance under the Natural Heritage Trust*, ANAO, Canberra

Avon-Heathcote Estuary Ihutai Trust (AHEIT) (2004) *Ihutai Management Plan 2004*, AHEIT, Christchurch

Axelrod, R. (1984) *The Evolution of Cooperation*, Basic Books, New York

Ayres, I. (2006) 'Ya-Huh: There Are and Should be Penalty Defaults', *Florida State University Law Review*, vol 33, no 3, pp589–617

Ayres, I. and Braithwaite, J. (1992) *Responsive Regulation Transcending the Deregulation Debate*, Oxford University Press, New York

Ayres, I. and Gertner, I. (1989) 'Filling Gaps in Incomplete Contracts: An Economic Theory of Default Rules', *Yale Law Journal*, vol 99, no 1, pp87–130

Baker, S. and Eckerberg, K. (eds) (2008) *In Pursuit of Sustainable Development: New Governance Practices at the Sub-national Level in Europe*, Routledge, London

Bayley, D. and Shearing, C. (2001) *The New Structure of Policing*, National Institute of Justice, U.S. Department of Justice, Washington DC

Bellamy, J., Metcalfe, D., Weston, N. and Dawson, S. (2005) *Evaluation of Invasive Species (Weeds) Outcomes of Regional Investment Final Report to the Department of Environment and Heritage Department of Agriculture, Fisheries and Forestry*, Commonwealth, Canberra

Bellamy, J., Ross, H., Ewing, S. and Meppem, T. (2002) *Integrated Catchment Management: Learning from the Australian Experience for the Murray-Darling Basin*, CSIRO Publishing, Canberra

Bidwell, R. and Ryan, C. (2006) 'Collaborative Partnership Design: The Implications of Organization Affiliation for Watershed Partnerships', *Society and Natural Resources*, vol 19, no 9, pp827–843

Biermann, F. (2008) 'Earth System Governance. A Research Agenda', in O. R. Young, L. A. King and H. Schroeder (eds) *Institutions and Environmental Change. Principal Findings, Applications, and Research Frontiers*, MIT Press, Cambridge, MA

Bingham, L. (2010) 'The Next Generation of Administrative Law: Building the Legal Infrastructure for Collaborative Governance', *Wisconsin Law Review*, vol 2, pp297–356

Blackman, A. and Harrington, W. (2000) 'The Use of Economic Incentives in Developing Countries: Lessons from International Experience with Industrial Air Pollution', *The Journal of Environment Development*, vol 9, no 1, pp5–44

Bonnell, J. and Koontz, T. (2007) 'Stumbling Forward: The Organizational Challenges of Building and Sustaining Collaborative Watershed Management', *Society and Natural Resources*, vol 20, pp153–167

Bovens, M. (2007) 'Analysing and Assessing Accountability: A Conceptual Framework', *European Law Journal*, vol 13, no 4, pp447–468

Braithwaite, J. (1999) 'Accountability and Governance under the New Regulatory State', *Australasian Journal of Public Administration*, vol 58, no 1, pp90–94

Buchy, M. and Race, D. (2001) 'The Twists and Turns of Community Participation in Natural Resource Management in Australia: What is Missing', *Journal of Environmental Planning and Management*, vol 44, no 3, pp293–308

Burdekin Dry Tropics Natural Resource Management (BDTNRM) (2005a) *Burdekin Dry Tropics Natural Resource Management Plan 2005–2010*, BDTNRM, Townsville

—— (2005b) *Annual Report 2004–2005*, BDTNRM, Townsville

—— (2005c) *Annual Report Financial Statements*, BDTNRM, Townsville

—— (2005d) *Regional Investment Strategy*, BDTNRM, Townsville

—— (2007) *Business Plan 2007–2010*, BDTNRM, Townsville

Burris, S., Drahos, P. and Shearing, C. (2005) 'Nodal Governance', *Australian Journal of Legal Philosophy*, vol 30, pp30–58

Burris, S., Kempa, M. and Shearing, C. (2008) 'Changes in Governance: A Cross-Disciplinary Review of Current Scholarship', *Akron Law Review*, vol 4, no 1, pp1–66

Camacho, A. (2007) 'Can Regulation Evolve? Lessons from a Study in Maladaptive Management', *UCLA Law Review*, vol 55, no 2, pp293–358

Cannon, J. (2000) 'Choices and Institutions in Watershed Management', *William & Mary Environmental Law and Policy Review*, vol 25, no 2, pp379–428

Canterbury Mayoral Forum (2009) *Canterbury Water Management Strategy*, Canterbury Mayoral Forum, Christchurch

Carr, A. (2002) *Grass Roots and Green Tape*, Federation Press, Sydney

Castells, M. (2008) 'The New Public Sphere: Global Civil Society, Communication Networks and Global Governance', *The ANNALS of the American Academy of Political and Social Science,* vol 616, pp78–93

Coglianese, C. (1999) 'The Limits of Consensus', *Environment*, vol 41, pp28–33

—— (2001) 'Is Consensus an Appropriate Basis for Regulatory Policy', in E. Orts and K. Deketelaere (eds) *Environmental Contracts – Comparative Approaches to Regulatory Innovation in the United States and Europe*, Kluwer Law, London

—— (2003) 'Is Satisfaction Success? Evaluating Public Participation in Regulatory Policymaking', in R. O'Leary and L. Bingham (eds) *The Promise and Performance of Environmental Conflict Resolution*, Resources for the Future, Washington DC

—— (2006) 'Citizen Participation in Rulemaking: Past, Present, and Future', *Duke Law Journal*, vol 55, p943

Coglianese, C. and Lazar, D. (2003) 'Management-Based Regulation: Prescribing Private Management to Achieve Public Goals', *Law and Society Review*, vol 37, pp691–730

Cohen, A. (2008) 'Negotiation, Meet New Governance: Interests, Skills and Selves', *Law and Social Inquiry*, vol 33, no 2, pp501–562

Cohen, J. and Fung, A. (2004) 'A Radical Democracy', *Swiss Journal of Political Science*, vol 10, no 4, pp23–34

Cohen, J. and Rogers, J. (2003) 'Power and Reason', in A. Fung and E. Wright (eds) *Deepening Democracy*, Verso Press, London

Cohen, J. and Sabel, C. (1997) 'Directly-Deliberative Polyarchy', *European Law Journal*, vol 3, no 4, pp313–342

Cole, D. and Grossman, P. (1999) 'When Is Command-and-Control Efficient? Institutions, Technology, and the Comparative Efficiency of Alternative Regulatory Regimes for Environmental Protection', *Wisconsin Law Review*, 1999, vol 5, pp887–938

Collaborative Democracy Network (2006) 'A Call to Scholars and Teachers of Public Administration, Public Policy, Planning, Political Science, and Related Fields', *Public Administration Review*, vol 66, pp168

Commonwealth and Queensland (2004a) *Guidelines for Community Engagement by RNRM Bodies*, Commonwealth and Queensland, Canberra/Brisbane

—— (2004b) *Monitoring and Evaluating Implementation Plan for the National (Australian and State) Program*, draft paper, Commonwealth and Queensland, Canberra/Brisbane

Commonwealth of Australia (2008) *Caring for our Country: Regional Delivery*, Australian Government, Canberra

Conley, A. and Moote, M. (2003) 'Evaluating Collaborative Natural Resource Management', *Society and Natural Resources*, vol 16, pp371–386

Cook, K., Hardin, R. and Levi, M. (2005) *Cooperation Without Trust*, Russell Sage Foundation, New York

Council of Australian Governments (COAG) (2000a) *A National Action Plan for Salinity and Water Quality*, COAG, Canberra

—— (2000b) *Our Vital Resources: A National Action Plan for Salinity and Water Quality*, COAG, Canberra

Craig, G., Taylor, M. and Parkes, T. (2004) 'Protest or Partnership? The Voluntary and Community Sectors in the Policy Process', *Social Policy and Administration*, vol 38, no 3, pp221–239

Crawford, A. (1997) *The Local Governance of Crime*, Clarendon Press, Oxford

Curnow, P. and Fitzgerald, L. (2006) 'Biobanking in New South Wales: Legal Issues in the Design and Implementation of a Biodiversity Offsets and Banking Scheme', *Environmental Planning and Law Journal*, vol 23, pp298

Curtis, A. (2003) 'The Landcare Experience', in S. Dovers and S. Wild River (eds) *Managing Australia's Environment*, Federation Press, Sydney

Curtis, A. and Lockwood, M. (2000) 'Landcare and Catchment Management in Australia: Lessons for State-Sponsored Community Participation', *Society and Natural Resources*, vol 13, pp61–73

Cutting, R. and Cahoon, L. (2005) 'Thinking outside the Box: Property Rights as a Key to Environmental Protection', *Pace Environmental Law Review*, vol 22, pp55–90

Dana, D. (2000) 'The New "Contractarian" Paradigm in Environmental Regulation', *University of Illinois Law Review*, vol 2000, no 1, pp35–60

De Burca, G. (2010) 'New Governance and Experimentalism: An Introduction', *Wisconsin Law Review*, vol 2, pp227–238

De Burca, G. and Scott, J. (2006) 'Introduction: New Governance, Law and Constitutionalism', in G. De Burca and J. Scott (eds) *Law and New Governance in the EU and the US*, Hart Publishing, Oxford

Defilippis, J., Fisher, R. and Shrage, E. (2006) 'Neither Romance nor Regulation: Re-evaluating Community', *International Journal of Urban and Regional Research*, vol 30, no 3, pp673–90

Department of Natural Resource Management (DNRM) (2005) *Options for Future Community Engagement in Regional Natural Resource Management*, DNRM, Canberra

Doremus, H. (2001) 'Adaptive Management, the Endangered Species Act, and the Institutional Challenges of "New Age" Environmental Protection', *Washburn Law Journal*, vol 41, no 1, pp50–89

Dorf, M. and Sabel, C. (1998) 'A Constitution of Democratic Experimentalism', *Columbia Law Review*, vol 98, pp267–473

Dovers, S. (2003a) 'Reflecting on Three Decades: A Synthesis', in S. Dovers and S. Wild River (eds) *Managing Australia's Environment*, Federation Press, Sydney

—— (2003b) 'Processes and Institutions for Resource and Environmental Management: Why and How to Analyse?' in S. Dovers and S. Wild River (eds), *Managing Australia's Environment*, Federation Press, Sydney

Dryzek, J. S. (2000) *Deliberative Democracy and Beyond: Liberals, Critics, Contestations*, Oxford University Press, Oxford

—— (2009) 'Democracy and Earth System Governance', unpublished paper presented at *Earth System Governance: People, Places and the Planet: Conference on the Human Dimensions of Global Environmental Change*, Amsterdam, 2–4 December 2009

Duit, A. and Galaz, V. (2008) 'Governance and Complexity – Emerging Issues for Governance Theory' *Governance*, vol 21, no 3, pp311–335

Durant, R., O'Leary, R. and Fiorino, D. (2004a) 'Introduction', in R. Durant, R. O'Leary and D. Fiorino (eds) *Environmental Governance Reconsidered*, MIT Press, Cambridge, MA

Durant, R., Young-Pyoung, C., Byungseob, K. and Seongjong, L. (2004b) 'Toward a New Governance Paradigm for Environmental and Natural Resource Management in the 21st Century?', *Administration & Society*, vol 35, pp643–682

Emerson, K. (2008) 'On Perfect Storms and Sacred Cows of Collaboration, Comments on Bradley Karkkainen, Getting to Let's Talk: Legal and Natural Destabilizations and the Future of Regional Collaboration', *Nevada Law Journal*, vol 8, pp830–834

Environment and Natural Resource Committee (ENRC) (2005) *Inquiry into Sustainable Communities*, Department of Sustainability and Environment, Melbourne

Environment Australia and the Department of Agriculture, Fisheries and Forestry (2000) *Mid-term Review of the Natural Heritage Trust – The Response*, Commonwealth Government, Canberra

Environment Canterbury (ECan) (2005) *Water Quality – What? Info Sheet 13*, ECan, Christchurch

—— (2007) *Natural Resources Regional Plan*, ECan, Christchurch

—— (2009a) *Living Streams Handbook, Publication E09–014*, ECan, Christchurch

—— (2009b) *Living Streams, Publication E09–001*, ECan, Christchurch

Environment Protection Authority Victoria (VEPA) (1989) *State Environment Protection Policy (Control of Noise from Commerce, Industry and Trade), No N-1*, VEPA, Melbourne

—— (1993) *Information Bulletin: Environment Improvement Plans, Publication 394*, VEPA, Melbourne

—— (1996) *Ten Steps to Successful Community/Industry Consultation, Publication 520*, VEPA, Melbourne

—— (2001a) *Guidelines for Running Community Liaison Committees, Publication 740*, VEPA, Melbourne

—— (2001b) *State Environment Protection Policy (Air Quality Management)*, VEPA, Melbourne

—— (2002a) *Guidelines for the Preparation of Environment Improvement Plans, Publication 739*, VEPA, Melbourne

—— (2002b) *State Environment Protection Policy (Prevention and Management of Contamination of Land)*, VEPA, Melbourne

—— (2002c) *A Guideline for Submitting a Voluntary Neighbourhood Environmental Improvement Plan Proposal, Publication 847*, VEPA, Melbourne

—— (2002d) *Neighbourhood Environment Improvement Plans – Developing a Voluntary Proposal, Publication 846*, VEPA, Melbourne

—— (2002e) *Corporate Plans 2002–2003, Publication 848*, VEPA, Melbourne

—— (2003a) *Annual Report 2002–2003 Compliance Report, Publication 919*, VEPA, Melbourne

—— (2003b) *Corporate Plan 2004–2005, Publication 913*, VEPA, Melbourne

—— (2004a) *Environment Improvement Plans – An Overview, Publication 938*, EPA, Melbourne

—— (2004b) *Annual Report 2003–2004 Community and Environment Report, Publication 962*, VEPA, Melbourne

—— (2006) *Accredited Licensee System Guidelines for Applicants, Publication 424.1*, VEPA, Melbourne

—— (2010) *Things you Need to Know about EPA's Licensing Reform Program, Publication 1324*, VEPA, Melbourne

Ewing, S. (2003) 'Catchment Management Arrangements', in S. Dovers and S. Wild River (eds) *Managing Australia's Environment*, Federation Press, Sydney

Fadeeva, Z. (2005) 'Promise of Sustainability Collaboration – Potential Fulfilled?', *Journal of Cleaner Production*, vol 13, pp165–174

Farber, D. (1992) 'Politics and Procedure in Environmental Law', *Journal of Law, Economics & Organization*, vol 8, pp59–81

—— (1999) 'Models of Reinvention', *Boston Review*, vol Oct/Nov, p24

—— (2000) 'Triangulating the Future of Reinvention: Three Emerging Models of Environmental Protection', *University of Illinois Law Review*, vol 1, pp61–82

Farrelly, M. (2005) 'Regionalisation of Environmental Management: A Case study of the Natural Heritage Trust, South Australia', *Geographical Research*, vol 43, no 4, pp393–405

—— (2009) 'Community Engagement in Natural Resource Management: Experience from the Natural Heritage Trust Phase 2', in M. Lane, C. Robinson and B. Taylor (eds) *Contested Country: Local and Regional Natural Resources Management in Australia*, CSIRO Publishing, Collingwood, Australia

Farrier, D. (1995) 'Conserving Biodiversity on Private Land: Incentives for Management or Compensation for Lost Expectations?', *Harvard Environmental Law Review*, vol 19, pp303–408

Farrier, D. and Whelan, R. (2004) 'Why Do We Need Threatened Species Legislation?', in P. Hutchings, D. Lunney and C. Dickman (eds) *Threatened Species Legislation – Is It Just An Act?*, Royal Zoological Society of NSW, Sydney

Fiorino, D. (2004) 'Flexibility', in R. Durant, R. O'Leary and D. Fiorino (eds) *Environmental Governance Reconsidered*, MIT Press, Cambridge, MA

Fisher, E. (2004) 'The European Union in the Age of Accountability', *Oxford Journal of Legal Studies*, vol 24, pp495–515

Floress, K., Mangun, J., Davenport, M. and Williard, K. (2009) 'Constraints to Watershed Planning: Group Structure and Process', *Journal of the American Water Resources Association*, vol 45, no 6, pp1352–1360

Freeman, J. (1997) 'Collaborative Governance in the Administrative State', *UCLA Law Review*, vol 45, no 1, pp1–98

—— (2000a) 'The Private Role in Public Governance', *New York University Law Review*, vol 75, pp543–675

—— (2000b) 'The Contracting State', *Florida State University Law Review*, vol 28, pp155–214

—— (2005) 'Remarks by Professor Jody Freeman to Japanese American Law Society', *Washington University Law Quarterly*, vol 83, no 6, pp1854–1874

Freeman, J. and Farber, D. (2005) 'Modular Environmental Regulation', *Duke Law Journal*, vol 54, no 4, pp795–912

Frieder, J. (1997) *Approaching Sustainability*, Ian Axford NZ Fellowship in Public Policy, Wellington, New Zealand

Fung, A. (2003) 'Survey Article: Recipes for Public Spheres: Eight Institutional Design Choices and Their Consequences', *Journal of Political Philosophy*, vol 11, no 3, pp338–367

—— (2004) *Empowered Participation: Reinventing Urban Democracy*, Princeton University Press, Princeton, NJ

—— (2006) 'Varieties of Participation in Complex Governance', *Public Administration Review*, vol 66, pp66–75

Fung, A. and O'Rourke, D. (2000) 'Reinventing Environmental Regulation from the Grassroots Up: Explaining and Expanding the Success of the Toxics Release Inventory', *Environmental Management*, vol 25, no 2, pp115–127

Fung, A. and Wright, E. (2003a) 'Countervailing Power in Empowered Participatory Governance', in A. Fung and E. Wright (eds) *Deepening Democracy: Institutional Innovations in Empowered Participatory Governance*, Verso Press, London

—— (2003b) 'Thinking about Empowered Participatory Governance', in A. Fung and E. Wright (eds) *Deepening Democracy: Institutional Innovations in Empowered Participatory Governance*, Verso Press, London

—— (eds) (2003c) *Deepening Democracy: Institutional Innovations in Empowered Participatory Governance*, Verso Press, London

Gaines, S. (2002/2003) 'Reflexive Law as a Legal Paradigm for Sustainable Development', *Buffalo Environmental Law Journal*, vol 10, nos 1&2, pp1–24

Galanter, M. (1981) 'Justice in Many Rooms: Courts, Private Ordering and Indigenous Law', *Journal of Legal Pluralism*, vol 19, no 1, pp1–47

Garbutt, S. (2000) *Environment Protection (Liveable Neighbourhoods) Bill 2000 (Victoria) 2nd Reading*, Hansard Extract, Legislative Assembly, 2 November 2000, www.epa.vic.gov.au/projects/NEIP/docs/protec.pdf, accessed 30 May 2008

Garland, D. (1996) 'The Limits of the Sovereign State: Strategies of Crime Control in Contemporary Society', *British Journal of Criminology*, vol 36, no 4, pp445–471

Gerring, J. (2007) *Case Study Research: Principles and Practices*, Cambridge University Press, Cambridge

Giddens, A. (2000) *The Third Way*, Polity Press, Malden, MA

Gilbey, P. (2002) *Rights and Duty of Care: A Queensland Perspective*, www.clw.csiro.au/lbi/publications/ANCID2002paper-Gilbey.pdf, accessed 30 May 2008

Gormley, W. (1981) 'Public Advocacy in Public Utility Commission Proceedings', *Journal of Applied Behavioral Science*, vol 17, pp446–462

Government of Australia (2007) *National Land and Water Resource Audit 2002–2007*, www.nlwra.gov.au, accessed 30 May 2008

Government of Victoria (2002) *Growing Victoria Together*, Government of Victoria, Melbourne

Gray, B. (1985) 'Conditions Facilitating Interorganizational Collaboration', *Human Relations*, vol 38, no 10, pp911–936

—— (1989) *Collaborating: Finding Common Ground for Multiparty Problems*, Jossey-Bass, San Francisco

Gray, J. (1998) *Hayek on Liberty*, Routledge, London

Groundwork Trust (1998) *Small Firms and the Environment: A Groundwork Status Report*, Groundwork Trust Foundation, San Francisco, CA

Gunderson, L. and Holling, C. S. (eds) (2001) *Panarchy: Understanding Transformations in Human and Natural Systems*, Island Press, Washington, DC

Gunningham, N. (2009) 'The New Collaborative Environmental Governance: The Localization of Regulation', *Journal of Law and Society*, vol 36, no 1, pp145–166

Gunningham, N. and Rees, J. (1997) 'Industry Self Regulation: An Institutional Perspective', *Law and Policy*, vol 19, no 4, pp363–414

Gunningham, N. and Sinclair, D. (2002) *Leaders and Laggards: Next-generation Environmental Regulation*, Greenleaf Publishing, Sheffield

Gunningham, N., Grabosky, P. and Sinclair, D. (1998) *Smart Regulation: Designing Environmental Policy*, Clarendon Press, Oxford

Gunningham, N., Holley, C. and Shearing, C. (2007) 'Neighbourhood Environment Improvement Plans: Community Empowerment, Voluntary Collaboration and Legislative Design', *Environmental and Planning Law Journal*, vol 24, no 2, pp125–151

Gunningham, N., Kagan, R. and Thornton, D. (2003) *Shades of Green: Business, Regulation and Environment*, Stanford University Press, Palo Alto, CA

Habermas, J. (1996) *Between Facts and Norms. Contributions to a Discourse Theory of Law and Democracy*, trans. W. Rehg, MIT Press, Cambridge, MA

Hardin, G. (1968) 'Tragedy of the Commons', *Science*, vol 162, pp1243–1248

Harlow, C. and Rawlings, R. (2007) 'Promoting Accountability in Multilevel Governance: A Network Approach', *European Law Journal*, vol 13, pp542–562

Hatzopoulos, V. (2007) 'Why the Open Method of Coordination is Bad for You: A Letter to the EU', *European Law Journal*, vol 13, no 3, pp309–342

Head, B. (1997) 'Corporatism', in D. Woodward, A. Parkin and J. Summers (eds) *Government, Politics, Power and Policy in Australia*, 6th edn, Longman, Melbourne

—— (2004) 'Letting the Locals Lead', *ECOS magazine*, vol 122, pp30–31

—— (2005a) 'Participation or Co-Governance? Challenges for Regional Natural Resource Management', in R. Eversole and J. Martin (eds) *Participation and Governance in Regional Development*, Ashgate, Hampshire

—— (2005b) 'Governance', in P. Saunders and H. Walter (eds) *Ideas and Influence: Social Science and Public Policy in Australia*, UNSW Press, Sydney

—— (2008) 'Assessing Network-based Collaborations', *Public Management Review*, vol 10, no 6, 733–749

—— (2009) 'From Government to Governance: Explaining and Assessing New Approaches to NRM', in M. Lane, C. Robinson and B. Taylor (eds) *Contested Country: Local and Regional Natural Resources Management in Australia*, CSIRO Publishing, Collingwood, Australia

Head, B. and Ryan, N. (2004) 'Can Co-Governance Work? Regional Natural Resource Management in Queensland, Australia', paper presented at *International Symposium on Public Sector Management VIII*, Budapest, 31 March–2 April 2004, Akademiai Kiado, Budapest

Heikkila, T. and Gerlak, A. (2005) 'The Formation of Large-scale Collaborative Resource Management Institutions: Clarifying the Roles of Stakeholders, Science and Institutions', *Policy Studies Journal*, vol 33, no 4, pp583–612

Hirsch, D. (ed) (2001) 'National Symposium on Second Generation Environmental Policy and the Law', *Capital University Law Review*, vol 29, no 1, pp1–318

Hobbes, T. (1651) *Leviathan*, edited and with an introduction by C. B. Macpherson, 1985, Penguin, London

Holley, C. (2010) 'Facilitating Monitoring, Subverting Self-Interest and Limiting Discretion: Learning from "New" Forms of Accountability in Practice', *Columbia Journal of Environmental Law*, vol 35, no 1, pp127–212

Holley, C. and Gunningham, N. (2006) 'Environment Improvement Plans: Facilitative Regulation in Practice', *Environmental Planning and Law Journal*, vol 23, no 4, pp448–465

Holling, C. S. (ed) (1978) *Adaptive Environmental Assessment and Management*, Wiley, Chichester

Holzinger, K., Knill, C. and Schafer, A. (2006) 'Rhetoric or Reality? The "New Governance" in EU Environmental Policy', *European Law Journal*, vol 12, no 3, pp403–420

Hooghe, L. and Marks, G. (2001) 'Types of Multi-Level Governance', *European Integration online Papers (EIoP)*, vol 5, no 11, http://eiop.or.at/eiop/texte/2001-011a.htm, accessed 10 February 2011

Hornstein, D. (2005) 'Complexity Theory, Adaptation and Administrative Law', *Duke Law Journal*, vol 54, pp913–960

House of Representatives Standing Committee on Environment and Heritage (2000) *Coordinating Catchment Management: Report of the Inquiry into Catchment Management*, Commonwealth Government, Canberra

Howard, J. (2000) 'Transcript of the Prime Minister the Honourable John Howard MP Press Conference on Natural Resource Management', given at Parliament House, Canberra, 10 October 2000

Howes, R., Skea, J. and Whelan, B. (1997) *Clean and Competitive? Motivating Environmental Performance in Industry*, Earthscan Publications, London

Innes, J. (2004) 'Consensus Building: Clarifications for the Critics', *Planning Theory*, vol 3, no 1, pp5–20

Isaac, T. and Heller, P. (2003) 'Democracy and Development: Decentralizing Planning in Kerala', in A. Fung and E. Wright (eds) *Deepening Democracy: Institutional Innovations in Empowered Participatory Governance*, Verso, London

Jenkins, B. (2007a) *Canterbury Strategic Water Study: Briefing Document to Canterbury Mayoral Forum*, ECan, Christchurch

—— (2007b) 'Water allocation in Canterbury', keynote address to the *New Zealand Planning Institute National Conference*, March, Palmerston North, New Zealand

—— (2008) 'ECan's Approach to Water Management', *Canterbury Public Issues Forum*, http://forums.e-democracy.org/groups/canterburyissues/messages/topic/38FfjtgMQfNP17F3kcl8Ou, accessed 6 May 2010

—— (2009) 'Are Regional Councils Past Their Use-by Date?', paper presented to *Environmental Defence Society National Conference*, Auckland, June 2009

Jenkins, B., Russell, S., Sadler, B. and Ward, M. (2010) 'Application of Sustainability Appraisal to the Canterbury Water Management Strategy', *Sustainability Assessment Symposium 2010: Towards Strategic Assessment for Sustainability*, 25–26 May, Fremantle, Western Australia

John, D. (1994) *Civic Environmentalism: Alternatives to Regulation in States and Communities*, Congressional Quarterly Press, Washington, DC

—— (2004) 'Civic Environmentalism', in R. Durant, D. Fiorino and R. O'Leary (eds) *Environmental Governance Reconsidered*, MIT Press, Cambridge, MA

John, D. and Mlay, M. (1999) 'Community-Based Environmental Protection: Encouraging Civic Environmentalism', in K. Sexton, A. Marcus, K. Easter and T. Burkhardt (eds) *Better Environmental Decisions*, Island Press, Washington, DC

Johnston, L. and Shearing, C. (2003) *Governing Security Explorations in Policing and Justice*, Routledge, London

Kahan, D. (2003) 'The Logic of Reciprocity: Trust, Collective Action, and Law', *Michigan Law Review*, vol 102, pp71–103

Karkkainen, B. (2002/2003) 'Collaborative Ecosystem Governance: Scale, Complexity and Dynamism', *Virginia Environmental Law Journal*, vol 21, no 2, pp189–244

—— (2003a) 'Toward Ecologically Sustainable Democracy?', in A. Fung and E. Wright (eds) *Deepening Democracy: Institutional Innovations in Empowered Participatory Governance*, Verso Press, London

—— (2003b) 'Adaptive Ecosystem Management and Regulatory Penalty Defaults: Toward a Bounded Pragmatism', *Minnesota Law Review*, vol 87, pp943–998

—— (2004a) Reply, '"New Governance" in Legal Thought and in the World: Some Splitting as Antidote to Overzealous Lumping', *Minnesota Law Review*, vol 89, pp471–497

—— (2004b) 'Post-Sovereign Environmental Governance', *Global Environmental Politics*, vol 4, no 1, p72

—— (2005) 'Panarchy and Adaptive Change: Around the Loop and Back Again', *Minnesota Journal of Law, Science and Technology*, vol 7, no 1, pp59–78

—— (2006a) 'Managing Transboundary Aquatic Ecosystems: Lessons from the Great Lakes', *Pacific McGeorge Global Business and Development Law Journal*, vol 19, pp209–240

—— (2006b) 'Information Forcing Regulation and Environmental Governance', in G. De Burca and J. Scott (eds) *Law and New Governance in the EU and the US*, Hart Publishing, Oxford

Karkkainen, B., Fung, A. and Sabel, C. (2000) 'After Backyard Environmentalism Toward a Performance Based Regime of Environmental Protection', *American Behavioural Scientist*, vol 44, no 4, pp692–711

Keogh, K., Chant, D. and Frazer, B. (2006) *Review of Arrangements for Regional Delivery of Natural Resource Management Programmes*, Ministerial Reference Group for Future NRM Programme Delivery, Canberra

Koehler, B. and Koontz, T. (2008) 'Citizenship Participation in Collaborative Watershed Partnerships', *Environmental Management*, vol 41, no 2, pp143–154

Koontz, T. and Thomas, C. (2006) 'What Do We Know and Need to Know about the Environmental Outcomes of Collaborative Management', *Public Administration Review*, vol 66, special issue, pp111–121

Koontz, T., Steelmand, T., Carmin, J., Kormacher, K., Moseley, C. and Thomas, C. (2004) *Collaborative Environmental Management: What Roles for Government?* Resources for the Future (RFF), Washington DC

Lane, M. (2006) *Critical Issues in Regional Natural Resource Management*, paper prepared for the Australian State of the Environment Committee, DEH, Canberra, www.enviroment.gov.au/soe/au/soe/2006/publications/integrative/nrm-issues/pubs/nrm-issues.pdf, accessed 20 May 2008

Lane, M., Robinson, C. and Taylor, B. (eds) (2009) *Contested Country: Local and Regional Natural Resources Management in Australia*, CSIRO Publishing, Collingwood, Australia

Latour, B. (2004) *The Politics of Nature: How to Bring the Sciences into Democracy*, trans. C. Porter, Harvard University Press, Cambridge, MA

Lawrence, G. (2004) 'Promoting Sustainable Development: The Question of Governance', paper presented at the *Plenary Address XI World Congress of Rural Sociology*, Trondheim, Norway, 25–30 July

—— (2005) 'Promoting Sustainable Development: The Question of Governance', in F. Buttel and P. McMichael (eds) *Research in Rurual Sociology and Development: New Directions in the Sociology of Global Development*, Elsevier BV, Amsterdam

Lawrence, G. and Cheshire, L. (2004) 'Managing Nature: The Promises and Problems of Regional Environmental Governance in Australia', plenary address at *The Ecopolitics XV Conference Environmental Governance: Transforming Regions and Localities*, Sydney, 12–14 November

Layder, D. (1998) *Sociological Practice: Linking Theory and Social Research*, Sage Publications, London

Lazarus, R. (2004) *The Making of Environmental Law*, University of Chicago Press, Chicago, IL

Leach, W. (2006) 'Collaborative Public Management and Democracy: Evidence from Western Watershed Partnerships', *Public Administration Review*, vol 66, pp100–110

Leach, W. and Sabatier, P. (2005) 'Are Trust and Social Capital the Keys to Success? Watershed Partnerships in California and Washington', in P. Sabatier, W. Focht, M. Lubell, Z. Trachtenberg, A. Vedlitz and M. Matlock (eds) *Swimming Upstream: Collaborative Approaches to Watershed Management*, MIT Press, Cambridge, MA

Lee, K. (1993) *Compass and Gyroscope*, Island Press, Washington DC

Libecap, G. (1989) *Contracting for Property Rights*, Cambridge University Press, New York

Loader, I. (2000) 'Plural Policing and Democratic Governance', *Social and Legal Studies*, vol 9, no 3, pp323–345

Lobel, O. (2004a) 'The Renew Deal: The Fall of Regulation and the Rise of Governance in Contemporary Legal Thought', *Minnesota Law Review*, vol 89, pp342–470

—— (2004b) 'Setting the Agenda for New Governance Research', *Minnesota Law Review*, vol 89, pp498–509

Lockie, S. (2004) 'Collective Agency, Non-human Causality and Environmental Social Movements: A Case Study of the Australian "Landcare Movement"', *Journal of Sociology*, vol 40, no 1, pp41–57

Lockwood, M., Davidson, J., Curtis, A., Stratford, E. and Griffith, R. (2009) 'Multilevel Environmental Governance: Lessons from Australian Natural Resource Management', *Australian Geographer*, vol 40, no 2, pp169–186

—— (2010) 'Governance Principles for Natural Resource Management', *Society & Natural Resources*, vol 23, no 10, pp986–1001

Lubell, M. (2004) 'Collaborative Environmental Institutions: All Talk and No Action?', *Journal of Policy Analysis and Management*, vol 23, no 3, pp549–573

Lubell, M., Sabatier, O., Vedlitz, A., Focht, W., Trachtenberg, Z. and Matlock, M. (2005) 'Conclusions and Recommendations', in P. Sabatier, W. Focht, M. Lubell, Z. Trachtenberg, A. Vedlitz and M. Matlock (eds) *Swimming Upstream: Collaborative Approaches to Watershed Management*, MIT Press, Cambridge, MA

Lubell, M., Schneider, M., Scholz, J. and Mihriye, M. (2002) 'Watershed Partnerships and the Emergence of Collective Action Institutions', *American Journal of Political Science*, vol 46, no 1, pp146–163

Manring, N. (2005) 'The Politics of Accountability in National Forest Planning', *Administration and Society*, vol 37, no 1, pp57–88

Mansbridge, J. (2003) 'Practice-Thought-Practice', in A. Fung and E. Wright (eds) *Deepening Democracy: Institutional Innovations in Empowered Participatory Governance*, Verso Press, London

Margerum, R. (1999) 'Integrated Environmental Management: The Foundation for Successful Practice', *Environmental Management*, vol 24, no 2, pp151–166

—— (2007) 'Overcoming Locally Based Collaboration Constraints', *Society and Natural Resources,* vol 20, no 2, pp135–152

Maribyrnong City Council and Stony Creek NEIP Partners (2004) *Stony Creek Neighbourhood Environment Improvement Plan,* Maribyrnong City Council, Maribyrnong, Australia

Markell, D. (2005) '"Slack" in the Administrative State and its Implication for Governance: The Issue of Accountability', *Oregon Law Review,* vol 84, no 1, pp1–69

Marshall, B. and Jones, R. (2005) 'Citizen Participation in Natural Resource Management: Does Representativeness Matter?', *Sociological Spectrum,* vol 25, no 6, pp715–737

May, P. (2003) 'Performance-Based Regulation and Regulatory Regimes: The Saga of Leaky Buildings', *Law and Policy,* vol 25, no 4, pp381–401

—— (2007) 'Regulatory Regimes and Accountability', *Regulation and Governance,* vol 1, no 1, pp8–26

McCallum, W., Hughey, K. and Rixecker, S. (2007) 'Community Environmental Management in New Zealand: Exploring the Realities in the Metaphor', *Society & Natural Resources,* vol 20, no 4, pp323–336

McCloskey, M. (1996) 'The Skeptic: Collaboration Has Its Limits', *High Country News,* www.hcn.org/servlets/hcn.Article?article_id=1839, accessed 30 May 2008

—— (2000) 'Problems With Using Collaboration to Shape Environmental Public Policy', *Valparaiso University Law Review,* vol 34, pp423–434

—— (2001) 'Is This the Course You Want To Be On?', *Society and Natural Resources,* vol 14, no 7, pp627–634

McDonald, L. (2004) 'The Rule of Law in the "New Regulatory State"', *Common Law World Review,* vol 33, pp197–221

McGinnis, M. (ed) (1999) *Polycentric Governance and Development,* University of Michigan Press, Ann Arbor, MI

Meek, T. (2004) 'Environment Improvement Plans – Going Beyond Compliance to Achieve Sustainability', paper presented at *13th World Clean Air and Environmental Protection Congress and Exhibition,* London, UK, 22–27 August 2004

Menkel-Meadow, C. (2008) 'Getting to "Let's Talk": Comments on Collaborative Environmental Dispute Resolution Processes', *Nevada Law Journal,* vol 8, pp835–852

Mol, A. (2007) 'Bringing the Environmental State Back In: Partnerships in Perspective', in P. Glasbergen, F. Biermann and A. Mol (eds) *Partnerships, Governance and Sustainable Development,* Edward Elgar Publishing, Cheltenham, UK

Moore, S. (2005) 'Regional Delivery of Natural Resource Management in Australia: Is it Democratic and Does it Matter?', in R. Eversole and J. Martin (eds) *Participation and Governance in Regional Development,* Ashgate, Hampshire

Morçöl, G. (2006) 'Business Improvement Districts: A New Organizational Form in Metropolitan Governance', *International Journal of Public Administration,* vol 29, pp1–4

National Health and Medical Research Council (2007a) *Australian Code for the Responsible Conduct of Research,* Australian Government, Canberra

—— (2007b) *National Statement on Ethical Conduct in Human Research,* Australian Government, Canberra

Natural Heritage Trust (NHT) (2002) *Framework for the Extension of the Natural Heritage Trust,* www.nht.gov.au, accessed 27 March 2009

Natural Resource Management Ministerial Council (NRMMC) (2002a) *National Framework for Natural Resource Management (NRM) Standards and Targets,* www.nrm.gov.au, accessed 10 March 2008

—— (2002b) *National Natural Resource Management Monitoring and Evaluation Framework,* www.nrm.gov.au, accessed 10 March 2008

—— (2006) *Framework for Future NRM Programmes*, www.nrm.gov.au/publications/frameworks/pubs/future-programmes.pdf, accessed 30 May 2008

Natural Resource Management Standing Committee (NRMSC) (2003) *Monitoring and Evaluation Key Documents, Drafts Users' Guide (preamble) Monitoring and Reporting on Natural Resource Management*, NRMSC, Canberra

Natural Resource Management Taskforce (NRMTF) (1999) *Managing Natural Resources in Australia for a Sustainable Future*, Department of Agriculture, Fisheries and Forestry, Canberra

NeJaime, D. (2009) 'When New Governance Fails', *Ohio State Law Journal*, vol 70, no 2, pp323–402

New South Wales Environmental Protection Authority (NSW EPA) [now the Department of Environment, Climate Change and Water] (2001) *Load Based Licensing – A Fairer System that Rewards Cleaner Industry*, NSW EPA, Sydney

Newig, J. and Fritsch, O. (2009) 'Environmental Governance: Participatory, Multi-level – and Effective?', *Environmental Policy and Governance*, vol 19, no 3, pp197–214

Nickelsburg, S. (1998) 'Mere Volunteers? The Promise and the Limits of Community-Based Environmental Protection', *Virginia Law Review*, vol 84, no 7, pp1371–1409

O'Leary, R., Nabatchi, T. and Bingham, L. (2004) 'Environmental Conflict Resolution', in R. Durant, D. Fiorino and R. O'Leary (eds) *Environmental Governance Reconsidered*, MIT Press, Cambridge, MA

Odum, E. (1953) *Fundamentals of Ecology*, Saunders, Philadelphia, PA

Okereke, C., Bulkeley, H. and Schroeder, H. (2009) 'Conceptualizing Climate Governance beyond the International Regime', *Global Environmental Politics*, vol 9, no 1, pp58–78

Olson, M. (1965) *The Logic of Collection: Public Goods and the Theory of Groups*, Harvard University Press, Cambridge, MA

Orts, E. (1995) 'Reflexive Environmental Law', *Northwestern University Law Review*, vol 89, no 4, pp1227–1340

Orts, E. and Coglianese, C. (2007) 'Debate, Collaborative Environmental Law: Pro and Con', *University of Pennsylvania Law Review –PENNumbra*, vol 156, pp289–311

Orts, E. and Deketelaere, K. (2001) 'Introduction: Environmental Contracts and Regulatory Innovation', in E. Orts and K. Deketelaere (eds) *Environmental Contracts – Comparative Approaches to Regulatory Innovation in the United States and Europe*, Kluwer Law, London

Osborne, D. and Gaebler, T. (1992) *Reinventing Government: How the Entrepreneurial Spirit is Transforming the Public Sector*, Addison Wesley, Boston, MA

—— (1993) *Inventing Government: How the Entrepreneurial Spirit is Transforming the Public Sector*, Plume, New York

Ostrom, E. (1990) *Governing the Commons: The Evolution of Institutions for Collective Action*, Cambridge University Press, Cambridge

—— (2000) 'Collective Action and the Evolution of Social Norms', *The Journal of Economic Perspectives*, vol 14, no 3, pp137–158

—— (2010) 'Beyond Markets and States: Polycentric Governance of Complex Economic Systems', *American Economic Review*, vol 100, pp641–672

Ostrom, V., Tiebout, C. and Warren, R. (1961) 'The Organization of Government in Metropolitan Areas: A Theoretical Inquiry', *American Political Science Review*, vol 55, no 4, pp831–842

Palmer, K. (2004) 'Local Government Law and Resource Management', *New Zealand Law Review*, pp751–786

Parker, C. (2002) *The Open Corporation*, Cambridge University Press, Cambridge

Parker, C. and Braithwaite, J. (2003) 'Regulation', in P. Cane and M. Tushnet (eds) *The Oxford Handbook of Legal Studies*, Oxford University Press, Oxford, p119

Parker, K., Margerum, R., Dedrick, D. and Dedrick, J. (2010) 'Sustaining Watershed Collaboratives: The Issue of Coordinator-Board Relationships', *Society and Natural Resources*, vol 23, no 5, pp469–484

Parkinson, J. (2006) *Deliberating in the Real World*, Oxford University Press, Oxford

Paton, S., Curtis, A., McDonald, G. and Woods, M. (2004) 'Regional Natural Resource Management: Is it Sustainable?', *Australasian Journal of Environmental Management*, vol 11, pp259–267

Patton, M. (2002) *Qualitative Evaluation and Research Methods*, 3rd edn, Sage, London

Porte, C. (2002) 'Is the Open Method of Coordination Appropriate for Organising Activities at European Level in Sensitive Policy Areas', *European Law Journal*, vol 8, no 1, pp38–58

Posner, P. (2002) 'Accountability Challenges of Third-Party Government', in L. Salaman (ed) *The Tools of Government: A Guide to the New Governance*, Oxford University Press, Oxford

President of the United States, Barack Obama (2009) *Transparency and Open Government: Memorandum for the Heads of Executive Departments and Agencies* (21 January 2009, Part IX, 74 Federal Register 4685), US Government Printing Office, Washington DC

Putnam, R., Leonardi, R. and Nanetti, R. (1993) *Making Democracy Work: Civic Traditions in Modern Italy*, Princeton University Press, Princeton, NJ

Rauschmayer, F., Paavola, J. and Wittmer, H. (2009) 'European Governance of Natural Resources and Participation in a Multi-Level Context: An Editorial', *Environmental Policy and Governance*, vol 19, pp141–147

Raymond, L. (2006) 'Cooperation without Trust: Overcoming Collective Action Barriers to Endangered Species Protection', *The Policy Studies Journal*, vol 34, no 1, p37

Reddel, T. (2004) 'Third Way Social Governance: Where is the State?', *Australian Journal of Social Issues*, vol 29, no 2, pp129–142

Renn, O. and Schweizer, P. (2009) 'Inclusive Risk Governance: Concepts and Application to Environmental Policy Making', *Environmental Policy and Governance*, vol 19, pp174–185

Rhodes, R.A.W. (1997) *Understanding Governance: Policy Networks, Governance, Reflexivity and Accountability*, Open University Press, Buckingham, UK and Philadelphia, PA

Ribot, J. (2002) *Democratic Decentralization of Natural Resources: Institutionalizing Popular Participation*, World Resources Institute, Washington DC

RM Consulting Group with URS, Rural Directions, Griffin NRM and Mark Gardner and Associates (RM Consulting Group) (2006) *Evaluation of Sustainable Agriculture Outcomes from Regional Investment (NAP and NHT)*, Commonwealth, Canberra

Robins, L. and Dovers, S. (2007) 'Community-based NRM Boards of Management: Are They Up to the Task?', *Australasian Journal of Environmental Management*, vol 14, issue 2, pp111–122

Robinson, B. (1999) 'Cleaner Production – Pathways for the Future', paper presented at *2nd Asia Pacific Cleaner Production Roundtable*, Brisbane, Australia, 21–23 April 1999

Robinson, C., Lane, M. and Taylor, B. (2009) 'The Changing and Contested Governance of Australia's Environmental Heritage', in M. Lane, C. Robinson and B. Taylor (eds) *Contested Country: Local and Regional Natural Resources Management in Australia*, CSIRO Publishing, Collingwood, Australia

Roma, A. (2006) 'Energy, Money, and Pollution', *Ecological Economics*, vol 56, pp534–545

Ruhl, J. (2005) 'Regulation by Adaptive Management – Is It Possible?', *Minnesota Journal of Law, Science and Technology*, vol 7, no 1, pp21–57

Rural and Regional Affairs and Transport (RRAT) References Committee, the Senate (2009) *Natural Resource Management and Conservation Challenges*, Senate Printing Unit, Canberra

Ruru, J. (ed) (2010) 'Contemporary Indigenous Peoples' Legal Rights To Water in the Americas and Australasia', *Journal of Water Law*, vol 20, nos 5/6, pp221–292

Sabatier, P., Focht, W., Lubell, M., Trachtenberg, Z., Vedlitz, A. and Matlock, M. (2005a) 'Collaborative Approaches to Watershed Management', in P. Sabatier, W. Focht, M. Lubell, Z. Trachtenberg, A. Vedlitz and M. Matlock (eds) *Swimming Upstream: Collaborative Approaches to Watershed Management*, MIT Press, Cambridge, MA

Sabatier, P., Leach, W., Lubell, M. and Pelkey, N. (2005b) 'Theoretical Frameworks Explaining Partnership Success', in P. Sabatier, W. Focht, M. Lubell, Z. Trachtenberg, A. Vedlitz and M. Matlock (eds) *Swimming Upstream: Collaborative Approaches to Watershed Management*, MIT Press, Cambridge, MA

Sabel, C., Fung, A. and Karkkainen, B. (1999) 'Beyond Backyard Environmentalism', *Boston Review*, October/November, p1

Sabel, C. and Simon, W. (2006) 'Epilogue: Accountability without Sovereignty', in G. De Burca and J. Scott (eds) *Law and New Governance in the EU and the US*, Hart Publishing, Oxford

Sabel, C. and Zeitlin, J. (2008) 'Learning from Difference: The New Architecture of Experimentalist Governance in the EU', *European Law Journal*, vol 14, no 3, pp271–327

Salamon, L. (2002) *A Guide to the New Governance*, Oxford University Press, Oxford

Samuelson, C., Vedlitz, A., Whitten, G., Matlock, M., Alston, L., Peterson, T. and Gilbertz, S. (2005) 'Citizen Participation and Representation in Collaborative Engagement Processes', in P. Sabatier, W. Focht, M. Lubell, Z. Trachtenberg, A. Vedlitz and M. Matlock (eds) *Swimming Upstream: Collaborative Approaches to Watershed Management*, MIT Press, Cambridge, MA

Scheuerman, W. (2004) 'Democratic Experimentalism or Capitalist Synchronization? Critical Reflections of Directly-Deliberative Polyarchy', *Canadian Journal of Law and Jurisprudence*, vol 17, no 1, pp101–127

Schlager, E. (2004) 'Common Pool Resource Theory', in R. Durant, D. Fiorino and R. O'Leary (eds) *Environmental Governance Reconsidered*, MIT Press, Cambridge, MA

Schramm, D. and Fishman, A. (2010) 'Legal Frameworks for Adaptive Natural Resource Management in a Changing Climate', *Georgetown International Environmental Law Review*, vol 22, pp491–520

Scott, C. (2000) 'Accountability in the Regulatory State' *Journal of Law and Society*, vol 27, no 1, pp38–60

Scott, J. (ed) (2009) *Environmental Protection: European Law and Governance*, Oxford University Press, Oxford

Scott, J. and Holder, J. (2006) 'Law and New Environmental Governance in the European Union', in G. De Burca and J. Scott (eds) *Law and New Governance in the EU and the US*, Hart Publishing, Oxford

Segerson, K. and Dawson, N. (2001) 'Environmental Voluntary Agreements: Participation and Free Riding', in E. Orts and K. Deketelaere (eds) *Environmental Contracts – Comparative Approaches to Regulatory Innovation in United States and Europe*, Kluwer Law International, London

Seidenfeld, M. (2000) 'Empowering Stakeholders: Limits on Collaboration as the Basis for Flexible Regulation', *William and Mary Law Review*, vol 41, pp411–501

Selin, S. and Chavez, D. (1995) 'Developing a Collaborative Model for Environmental Planning and Management', *Environmental Management*, vol 19, no 2, pp189–195

Silverman, D. (2000) *Doing Qualitative Research: A Practical Handbook*, Sage Publications, London

Sirianni, C. and Friedland, L. (2001) 'Civic Environmentalism', in C. Sirianni and L. Friedland (eds) *Civic Innovation in America: Community Empowerment, Public Policy and the Movement for Civic Renewal*, University of California Press, Berkeley, CA

Smismans, S. (2008) 'New Modes of Governance and the Participatory Myth', *West European Politics*, vol 31, no 5, pp874–895

Smith, A. (1776) *An Inquiry into the Nature and Causes of the Wealth of Nations*, reprint 2007, Cosimo, New York

Solomon, J. (2008) 'Law and Governance in the 21st Century Regulatory State', *Texas Law Review*, vol 86, pp819–856

Stavins, R. (1998) 'What Can We Learn from the Grand Policy Experiment? Lessons from SO2 Allowance Trading', *Journal of Economic Perspectives*, vol 12, no 3, pp69–88

Stavins, R. and Whitehead, W. (1997) 'Market Based Environmental Policy', in M. Chertow and D. Esty (eds) *Thinking Ecologically: The Next Generation of Environmental Policy*, Yale University Press, Cambridge, MA

Steinzor, R. (1998a) 'Reinventing Environmental Regulation: The Dangerous Journey from Command to Self-Control', *Harvard Environmental Law Review*, vol 22, pp103–202

—— (1998b) 'Reinventing Environmental Regulation: Back to the Past by way of the Future', *European Law Review*, vol 28, pp10,361–10,372

—— (2000) 'The Corruption of Civic Environmentalism', *Environmental Law Reporter*, vol 30, pp10,909–10,921

Stewart, J. and Jones, G. (2003) *Renegotiating the Environment*, Federation Press, Sydney

Stewart, R. (2001) 'A New Generation of Environmental Regulation?', *Capital University Law Review*, vol 29, pp21–182

Stiglitz, J. (2002) *Globalization and Its Discontents*, Norton, New York

Streck, C. (2002) 'Global Public Policy Networks as Coalitions for Change', in D. Esty and M. Ivanova (eds) *Global Environmental Governance: Options and Opportunities*, Yale School of Forestry, New Haven, CT

Sturm, S. (2006) 'Gender Equity Regimes and the Architecture of Learning', in G. De Burca and J. Scott (eds) *Law and New Governance in the EU and the US*, Hart Publishing, Oxford

Surf Coast Shire Council and Anglesea NEIP Partners (Surf Coast Shire Council) (2002) *Proposal to Develop a Neighbourhood Environment Improvement Plan*, Surf Coast Shire Council, Torquay, UK

—— (2004) *Anglesea Neighbourhood Environment Improvement Plan*, Surf Coast Shire Council, Torquay, UK

Susskind, L., Camacho, A. and Schenk, T. (2010) 'Collaborative Planning and Adaptive Management in Glen Canyon: A Cautionary Tale', *Columbia Journal of Environmental Law*, vol 35, no 1, pp1–54

Taylor, M. (2003) *Public Policy in the Community: Public Policy and Politics*, Palgrave Macmillan, London

—— (2007) 'Community Participation in the Real World: Opportunities and Pitfalls in New Governance Spaces', *Urban Studies*, vol 44, no 2, pp297–317

Taylor, M. and Warburton, D. (2003) 'Legitimacy and the Role of UK Third Sector Organizations in the Policy Process', *International Journal of Voluntary and Non-profit Organizations*, vol 14, no 3, pp321–338

Taylor, M., Wilson, M., Purdue, D. and Wilde, P. (2007) *Changing Neighbourhoods: Lessons from the JRF Neighbourhood Programs*, The Policy Press, Bristol

Thomas, C. (2003) 'Habitat Conservation Planning', in A. Fung and E. Wright (eds) *Deepening Democracy: Institutional Innovations in Empowered Participatory Governance*, Verso Press, London

Thomson, A. and Perry, J. (2006) 'Collaboration Processes: Inside the Black Box', *Public Administration*, December, pp20–32

Towong Shire Council and Partners of Little Snowy Creek NEIP (Towong Shire Council) (2006) *Little Snowy Creek Neighbourhood Environment Improvement Plan*, Towong Shire Council, Tallangatta, Australia

Trachtenberg, Z. and Focht, W. (2005) 'Legitimacy and Watershed Collaborations: The Role of Public Participation', in P. Sabatier, W. Focht, M. Lubell, Z. Trachtenberg, A. Vedlitz and M. Matlock (eds) *Swimming Upstream: Collaborative Approaches to Watershed Management*, MIT Press, Cambridge, MA

Traditional Custodians of Country in the Burdekin Dry Tropics Region (2005) *A Caring for Country Plan*, BDTNRM, Townsville

Trubek, D. and Trubek, L. (2005) 'The Coexistence of New Governance and Legal Regulation: Complementary or Rivalry?' unpublished paper presented at the *Annual Meeting of the Research Committee on Sociology of Law*, Paris, July 2005

—— (2006/2007) 'New Governance and Legal Regulation', *Columbia Journal of European Law*, vol 13, no 3, pp540–564

—— (2010) 'Part I: The World Turned Upside Down: Reflections on New Governance and The Transformation Of Law', *Wisconsin Law Review*, vol 2, pp719–726

Tushnet, M. (2003) *The New Constitutional Order*, Princeton University Press, Princeton, NJ

United Nations Development Programme (UNDP) (1997) *Reconceptualising Governance: Discussion Paper 2*, UNDP, New York

United States Environmental Protection Agency (US EPA) (1994) *The New Generation of Environmental Protection: A Summary of EPA's Five-year Strategic Plan*, US EPA, Washington, DC

—— (1997) *EPA Strategic Plan 83–85*, US EPA, Washington, DC

—— (1999) *EPA's Framework for Community-Based Environmental Protection*, US EPA, Washington, DC

Varughese, G. and Ostrom, E. (2001) 'The Contested Role of Heterogeneity in Collective Action: Some Evidence from Community Forestry in Nepal', *World Development*, vol 29, no 5, pp747–765

Vindevogel, F. (2005) 'Private Security and Urban Crime Mitigation: A Bid for BIDs', *Criminal Justice*, vol 5, no 3, pp233–255.

Waihora Ellesmere Trust (WET) (2004) *A Community Strategy for the Future Management of Lake Ellesmere/Te Waihora and its Tributaries*, WET, Christchurch

Walker, N. (2006) 'EU Constitutionalism and New Governance' in G. De Burca and J. Scott (eds) *Law and New Governance in the EU and the US*, Hart Publishing, Oxford

Walters, C. (1986) *Adaptive Management of Renewable Resources*, Macmillan, New York

Watts, M. (2004) *Getting on Track?* Australian Conservation Foundation, Carlton, Victoria

Weber, E. (1999) 'The Question of Accountability in Historical Perspective: From Jackson to Contemporary Grassroots Ecosystem Management', *Administration and Society*, vol 31, no 4, pp451–494

Weil, D., Fung, A., Graham, M. and Fagotto, E. (2006) 'The Effectiveness of Regulatory Disclosure Policies', *Journal of Policy Analysis and Management*, vol 25, no 1, pp155–181

Weiland, P. and Vos, R. (2002) 'Reforming EPA's Organizational Structure: Establishing an Adaptable Agency Through Eco-Regions', *Natural Resources Journal*, vol 42, pp91–132

Western Australia Department of Environment and Conservation (WA DEC) (2006) *Halt the Haze 2006 Wood Heater Replacement Program*, WA DEC, Perth

Whelan, J. and Oliver, P. (2005) 'Regional Community-Based Planning: The Challenge of Participatory Environmental Governance', *Australasian Journal of Environmental Management*, vol 12, pp126–135

—— (2006) 'The Place, Limit and Practice of Collaboration: Lessons from Case Studies in Community Participation in Natural Resource Management', in N. Lazarow, R. Souter, R. Fearon and S. Dovers (eds) *Coastal Management in Australia: Key institutional and Governance Issues for Coastal Natural Resource Management and Planning*, Coastal CRC, Brisbane, Australia

Wiersema, A. (2008) 'A Train without Tracks: Rethinking the Place of Law and Goals in Environmental and Natural Resources Law', *Environmental Law*, vol 38, pp1239–1300

Wilkinson, M. (2010) 'Three Conceptions of Law: Towards a Jurisprudence of Democratic Experimentalism', *Wisconsin Law Review*, vol 2, pp673–718

Wills, I. and Fritschy, S. (2001) 'Industry-Community-Regulatory Consultation in Improving Environmental Performance in Victoria', *Australian Journal of Environmental Management*, vol 8, no3, pp158–168

Wilson, M. and Weltman, E. (1999) 'Government's Job', *Boston Review*, October/November, p13

Wiseman, J. (2006) 'Local Heroes? Learning from Recent Community Strengthening Initiatives in Victoria', *Australian Journal of Public Administration*, vol 65, no 2, pp95–107

Wolf, J. F. (2006) 'Urban Governance and Business Improvement Districts: The Washington, DC BIDs', *International Journal of Public Administration*, vol 29, pp53–75

Wondolleck, J. and Yaffee, S. (2000) *Making Collaboration Work: Lessons from Innovation in Natural Resource Management*, Island Press, Washington DC

Young, O., Schroeder, H. and King, L. (2008) *Institutions and Environmental Change: Principal Findings, Applications, and Research Frontiers*, MIT Press, Cambridge, MA

Zammit, C., Head, B., Miles, R. and McDonald, G. (2004) *A Review of the NRM Arrangements in Queensland*, Department of Natural Resources and Mining, Brisbane, Australia

INDEX

Page numbers in *italics* indicate boxes and tables.